The Flag Was Still There

A History of the American Experiment in Five Anniversaries

David McKean

and

M. Todd Bennett

PublicAffairs

New York

Cover design by Daniel Valadéz
Cover images: Library of Congress, Prints & Photographs Division, LC-DIG-pga-04849; © Daboost / Shutterstock.com

PublicAffairs
Hachette Book Group
1290 Avenue of the Americas, New York, NY 10104
www.publicaffairsbooks.com

Printed in the United States of America

First Edition: May 2026

Published by PublicAffairs, an imprint of Hachette Book Group, Inc. The PublicAffairs name and logo is a registered trademark of the Hachette Book Group.

The Hachette Speakers Bureau provides a wide range of authors for speaking events. To find out more, go to hachettespeakersbureau.com or email HachetteSpeakers@hbgusa.com.

PublicAffairs books may be purchased in bulk for business, educational, or promotional use. For more information, please contact your local bookseller or the Hachette Book Group Special Markets Department at special.markets@hbgusa.com.

The publisher is not responsible for websites (or their content) that are not owned by the publisher.

Library of Congress Cataloging-in-Publication Data has been applied for.

ISBNs: 9781541704169 (hardcover), 9781541704183 (ebook)

LSC-C

Printing 1, 2026

To my grandchildren:
Welles Winthrop McKean, Katherine Buckley McKean, and
future Kaye McKeans of their generation

—D.M.

To my daughter, her generation, and the next:
May they know the freedoms we have known up until now.

—M.T.B.

CONTENTS

Prologue

On Friday, July 9, 1858, US Senator Stephen Douglas checked into the newly renovated five-story Tremont Hotel in Chicago, reputed to be the best hotel in the western United States. That evening at 8 p.m., as twilight descended on the city, Douglas delivered a well-publicized speech on the portico of the hotel to a crowd that his campaign estimated at 30,000. One of the city's leading newspapers pointed out that such an enormous gathering would have been "more than the whole male adult population of the city." Nevertheless, the crowd was sizable: Perhaps as many as 12,000 had assembled to hear Douglas in his first major speech since announcing his campaign for reelection.[1]

Abraham Lincoln, a lawyer by trade, was also in Chicago to attend an opening session of the United States District Court; he came to hear Douglas's speech. Lincoln, a former one-term congressman, had received the nomination of the Republican Party in Illinois in June to challenge Douglas. The major issue in the race was the future of slavery: Lincoln maintained that it should be abolished, while Douglas argued that the decision should be left to the states.

Lincoln sat on the portico, behind his opponent, "furnished with a seat very convenient for hearing him." Lincoln showed little emotion as the senator railed against his "House Divided Speech," delivered nearly a month earlier when Lincoln accepted his party's nomination for the Senate seat. In that speech Lincoln had asserted, "A house divided against itself cannot stand." He then said, "I believe this government cannot endure, permanently half slave and half free." He also made a prediction: "I do not expect the Union to be dissolved—I do not expect the house to fall—but I do expect it will cease to be divided. It will become all one thing, or all the other."[2]

Now standing on the balcony of the Tremont Hotel, Senator Douglas took command of the stage and, in a fast-paced and vigorous voice, defended the institution of slavery while characterizing his opponent as well-meaning but naive and reckless. Douglas gave an impassioned defense of states' rights, but he anchored his reasoning in pure racism, declaring, "In my opinion this government of ours is founded on the white basis. It was made by the white man, for the benefit of the white man, to be administered by white men."[3]

The next evening was Lincoln's turn. Whereas Douglas had spoken the night before of racial nationalism—that is, of American national identity being defined by race and limited exclusively to Whites—Lincoln offered a very different vision of Americanism in his rebuttal. He embraced civic nationalism, a vision of Americans united not by blood but by belief in the ideals inscribed in America's founding documents.

Although Douglas did not attend, Lincoln spoke on the same balcony to deliver his rebuttal. The crowd was about three-fourths as large as that of the previous evening, but according to one newspaperman, "in point of enthusiasm" Lincoln's reception by the crowd was "about four times as great." For some moments, Lincoln, at six feet, four inches tall, stood awkwardly as the cheering continued unabated, until at last he stilled the crowd with a wave of his hand.[4]

Lincoln then addressed a number of issues ranging from the meaning of popular sovereignty to the impact of the decision in *Dred Scott v. Sandford*, the 1857 Supreme Court ruling that declared enslaved people, and by extension people of African descent, were not American citizens and therefore could not sue in federal court. He spoke, too, of the Declaration of Independence—the "old Declaration," as he called it—which, he reminded his listeners, held "these truths to be self-evident," namely, "that all men are created equal; that they are endowed by their Creator with certain inalienable rights; that among these are life, liberty, and the pursuit of happiness." To secure these rights, he continued, "governments are instituted among men, deriving their Just powers from the consent of the governed."[5]

In many respects, the United States of 1858 was quite different from the United States of 1776, when those words were written. "We are now a mighty nation," Lincoln said, with a population of some thirty million people inhabiting thirty-two states, including Texas and California. Yet eighty-two years later, the principles inscribed in the Declaration continued to act as an "electric cord" that linked "the hearts of patriotic and liberty-loving men together, that [would] link those patriotic hearts as long as the love of freedom exists in the minds of men throughout the world." And every year Americans gathered on July Fourth, as Chicagoans had done days earlier, to celebrate the American journey and "to remind [them]selves of all the good done in this process of time, of how it was done and who did it, and how we are historically connected with it." Lincoln continued, "We go from these meetings in better humor with ourselves—we feel more attached the one to the other, and more firmly bound to the country we inhabit. In every way we are better men, in the age, and race, and country in which we live, for these celebrations." Even so, he cautioned that these celebrations of progress must always be tempered with the knowledge that the Declaration's ideals were not yet realized. As Lincoln said, "We have not yet reached the whole." America remained a work in progress.[6]

As the United States approaches its 250th anniversary, millions of Americans are deeply concerned about our nation's future, perhaps as deeply as they have been since Lincoln's day. After all, recent presidential elections have revealed that we are a country divided by politics, by race, by class, by culture, and by algorithms. What, if anything, do we have in common? What does it actually mean to be an American? While definitive answers may be elusive, perhaps clues can be gleaned from two ten-foot-high marble statues that stand guard outside the imposing limestone and granite National Archives Building on Constitution Avenue in Washington, DC. One statue, titled *Heritage*, depicts a robed man clutching a book and bears an inscription imploring passersby to "Study the Past"; the other, *Guardianship*, of a young woman peering into the future, explains why: "What Is Past Is Prologue." These statues greet visitors as they enter the archives—home of the Declaration of Independence, which, together with the US Constitution and the Bill of Rights, has inspired the American people to pursue a more perfect union since 1776.

Looking to the nation's past, there is nothing more American than July Fourth, the date in 1776 when thirteen North American colonies declared their independence from Great Britain to form a nation. Ever since, neither war, nor depression, nor partisan difference has prevented Americans from gathering every year on the Fourth to commemorate the nation's founding principles. Though some rituals have changed over the years, on Independence Day Americans of all races, religions, political stripes, and incomes celebrate with parades, picnics, public readings, and, of course, brilliantly colored, ear-splitting fireworks.

In 1826, only weeks before his death on July Fourth, Thomas Jefferson wrote about the importance of celebrating Independence Day and the unalienable rights expressed in the Declaration: "Let the annual return of this day forever refresh our recollections of these rights, and undiminished devotion to them." Jefferson did not live long enough to fully appreciate that with the 1826 celebration, the first Jubilee, Americans would begin another tradition of holding dedicated celebrations every fifty years. Jubilees—"timekeepers of progress," as President William McKinley once called such events—are understudied by historians. The very term *jubilee* is seldom used today, occurring less than once per million words in modern written English. Yet jubilees have occupied a special place in the American experience since the early republic even though they were a British import: English monarchs began celebrating fiftieth anniversaries in the fourteenth century, a tradition that traces back to the Catholic Church, ancient Rome, and even the Hebrew Bible. In fact, this rich tradition of associating jubilees with not only respite from toil but deliverance from bondage, heralded by trumpets, voices uplifted in song, and general public rejoicing, may well explain why golden anniversaries gained such a purchase in the United States—where the idea of freedom, however imperfect, has worked to define and redefine an exuberant national identity for 250 years and counting.[7]

President John Quincy Adams, son of founder John Adams, spoke to this emerging tradition on the eve of America's diamond anniversary in 1826. "The year of Jubilee," he said, marked the end of the initial phase of US history, the period dedicated to "the first formation of Our Union," and the beginning of a new chapter that would see the realization of the American Revolution's democratic principles. The fulfillment, he said, "of the Declaration of our Independence is at hand." The republic is dead; long live the republic.[8]

In years ending in twenty-six or seventy-six, the fifty-year celebrations of independence usually span months, generally reaching a crescendo on July Fourth. More significantly, the fifty-year celebrations have increasingly become a means to affirm the success of American democracy. That has broadly been interpreted to mean that Americans have a representative government elected by its citizens and undergirded by the rule of law, from which they enjoy expansive rights. *The Flag Was Still There* tracks the evolution of these fundamental principles as well as others embedded in the Declaration.

Of course, the jubilees don't necessarily coincide precisely with seminal events in American history. Certainly, most of what Americans regard as the country's important historic events began and ended on days other than July Fourth and in years that didn't end in twenty-six or seventy-six. Lincoln debated Douglas in 1858, for example. Nevertheless, the 1826 Jubilee, the 1876 Centennial, the 1926 Sesquicentennial, and the 1976 Bicentennial—together with the impending 2026 Semiquincentennial—offer valuable opportunities for taking stock of the nation's journey, for measuring change over time. They show growth. They show advances. They show traditions made and unmade, turmoil and triumph, progress and retreat. Each jubilee has found the United States at an inflection point: political, economic, or cultural. Mostly, though, they show the union persevering, even as the very same rights, ideals, and beliefs that Americans hold dear have threatened on occasion to tear the country apart. In other words, they show the "electric cord" of which Lincoln spoke, linking generations of Americans of all races, ethnicities, and religions in an ongoing effort to realize the Declaration's lofty ideals—often in the face of fierce and at times violent opposition. Perfecting the Union, despite its faults: this is the idea of America, the vision that has defined Americans since 1776.[9]

THE FLAG WAS STILL THERE IS NEITHER a detailed examination of our democracy nor a comprehensive survey of US history. Nor is it an uncritical celebration of American greatness—though we do believe in the American experiment and its capacity to inspire. Rather, *The Flag Was Still There* is an attempt to reach across the aisle and the algorithms and everything else that divides Americans today to find common cause in our shared experience as told through the stories of people and events and voices—some well-known, others less so—that have shaped the nation's journey at fifty-year intervals. Stopping history at these points, though it may halt the flow of time, has the advantage of showing clearly how, over the course of their country's 250 years, Americans have periodically attempted a form of self-reflection, with the goal of taking stock of the nation's journey and setting the tone, if not a course, for the future. Each jubilee is unique, though they all share similarities. Each jubilee reveals glorious strengths and glaring imperfections of our democracy at a particular moment in time. Each jubilee is punctuated by events that are disdained by the next generation, but likewise, each anniversary provides a message of hope, of deliverance from repression, however defined, that has sustained Americans through troubled times.[10]

The Declaration of Independence, the cornerstone of each jubilee, was a truly revolutionary idea; it breached uncharted territory, and there was no reason to believe that it would work, much less endure. Yet, for 250 years, citizens of the United States have sustained, though often imperfectly, the founding idea of self-government as an example (and sometimes a lesson) to the world.

How the United States celebrates its Semiquincentennial in 2026, as in each previous jubilee, will reveal much about our country at this particular time and about the nation's progress over the centuries in realizing the evolving idea that is America. And, more fundamentally, how the nation conducts itself during this anniversary year will shine a light on us as a people. Perhaps in better understanding that the past is prologue, we may take care to chart a course for the future that all Americans can be proud of.

1

First Fourths

> I am apt to believe that it will be celebrated, by succeeding Generations, as the great anniversary Festival. It ought to be commemorated, as the Day of Deliverance . . . with Pomp and Parade, with Shews, Games, Sports, Guns, Bells, Bonfires and Illuminations from one End of this Continent to the other from this Time forward forever more.
>
> —JOHN ADAMS (1776)[1]

"REMEMBER THE LADIES," ABIGAIL ADAMS IMPLORED HER husband, John. It was March 31, 1776. He was away in Philadelphia, where he and his fellow members of the Continental Congress were preparing to declare "independency" from Great Britain. She remained at home in Braintree, Massachusetts, managing the family farm and caring for the couple's four children, ages three through ten.[2]

Though a trusted advisor to John, Abigail Adams could not vote. Nor could she hold political office because political rights were generally tied to property ownership at the time, and as a married woman she could not legally own property. Whatever property a bride brought to a marriage—and Abigail, a descendant of the prominent Massachusetts Quincy family, brought at least a modest dowry to her 1764 union with John—became her husband's for the duration of the marriage, under the legal doctrine of *femme coverture*. A European import, *femme coverture* held that a married woman, "a woman covered" (*feme covert*), had no legal, political, or economic authority or identity separate from her husband. Exceptions existed, and single women enjoyed some latitude. But coverture generally prevented married women such as Abigail from writing or signing contracts, suing in a court of law, filing for divorce, serving on juries, or doing any number of other things that citizens do in republics. Patriarchal norms largely defined the roles of eighteenth-century women as daughters and wives and mothers.[3]

Times were changing, though. The first shots of the Revolutionary War had been fired eleven months earlier, in April 1775, at Lexington and Concord—only about twenty miles from Braintree, as the crow flies. As the conflict expanded, it had an indelible effect on women, in many instances expanding their roles, responsibilities, and aspirations.

That was certainly the case with Abigail Adams, who in her husband's absence took on greater responsibility for managing not only the family farm but the family's finances. Indeed, she proved to be a shrewd businessperson, profiting handsomely from investments in government securities that raised the fortunes of the Adams family—and her place within it.[4]

Anything seemed possible in late March 1776. Only days earlier, General George Washington's Continental army had forced 11,000 British soldiers and hundreds of Loyalists to evacuate Boston. So Abigail wrote her husband a letter—one of approximately 1,160 she and John would exchange during their lifetime together, a testament to the intellectual and emotional depth of their relationship. She pressed him to "Remember the Ladies" when he and his colleagues in Philadelphia wrote "the new Code of Laws" she assumed the newly independent republic would need. She urged, "I desire you would . . . be more generous and favourable to [women] than your ancestors. Do not put such unlimited power into the hands of the Husbands." Paraphrasing one of John's own political maxims, she reminded him that "all Men would be tyrants if they could."[5]

Though Abigail's wording was vague—was she demanding the vote or equal rights under the law?—she was clearly declaring citizenship for women on a full and equal basis with men. She was equally clear that congressional inaction would have consequences. "If particular care and attention is not paid to the Ladies," she warned, "we are determined to foment a Rebellion, and will not hold ourselves bound by any Laws in which we have no voice, or Representation."[6]

John was dismissive of Abigail's plea in his reply, dated April 14. "I cannot but laugh" at your proposal, he wrote. Breaking from Great Britain was the main issue before Congress; domestic questions such as who should vote would have to take a backseat. Besides, neither he nor any of the other congressmen who convened in Philadelphia in 1776 had any intention of extending full citizenship rights to women, free Blacks, enslaved persons, Native Americans, or poor White men. For those without property were considered "dependent" and therefore unable to render independent judgment at the ballot box, in the jury room, or anywhere else citizenship responsibilities are exercised in a free republic. "We know better than to repeal our Masculine systems," he wrote Abigail. Were he and his fellow lawmakers to give up their male prerogatives, they would soon find themselves subject "to the Despotism of the Peticoat."[7]

Two months later, John Adams would serve on a five-man committee appointed by Congress to draft a declaration of independence from Britain. The final text, as adopted on July 4 by three dozen members of

Congress—all men, some of them slaveholders—who were present in Pennsylvania's State House, did not "remember the Ladies," as Abigail Adams had hoped it might. In fact, it did not say a word as to what rights some 1.25 million women, roughly half the population, would enjoy in the newly independent states. Neither did the document specify what effect independence might have on the roughly 500,000 persons—one-fifth of the nation—who were enslaved in those thirteen states or on the millions of Native Americans who inhabited North America in 1776. Whatever lofty rhetoric emerged from Philadelphia didn't erase the ugly reality of captivity and inequality and dispossession.

Drafted principally by Thomas Jefferson, the Declaration of Independence did, however, announce the existence of a new nation dedicated to the proposition that all are created equal, endowed with "certain unalienable rights," including the rights to "Life, Liberty and the pursuit of Happiness." Furthermore, to secure these rights, the Declaration asserted that governments were "instituted among Men, deriving their just powers from the consent of the governed." These were radical ideas in 1776, a time when monarchs and authoritarians and emperors ruled, and it would take decades, centuries even, for the democratic ideals unleashed by the American Revolution to address inequalities of race, of class, and of gender—and even now that work remains woefully unfinished in many respects. Yet the fact that a group of colonial rebels in 1776 had the audacity and the courage to confront the most powerful empire in the world, and to do so by asserting that no one was better than another by virtue of their economic, geographic, or familial position, launched Americans on a continuing 250-year journey to secure a more perfect union.

The day after the Continental Congress adopted the Declaration, Thomas Jefferson awoke at 6 a.m. in his rented room on

Philadelphia's Market Street. He likely breakfasted on cornbread and his favorite drink, high sun tea. Jefferson liked to record the weather two times a day. He had recently purchased a new thermometer, and he noted in his journal that the morning temperature outside was already seventy-one degrees.

After breakfasting on a cup of hard cider and boiled vegetables in his rented room at 190 High Street, John Adams, who dreaded "the heats of a Philadelphia summer," retired to his desk. He wrote to his niece Mary Palmer, "I will inclose to you a Declaration, in which all America is remarkably united. . . . It compleats a Revolution."[8]

Contrary to Adams's assertion of colonist unity, expressed in his letter to his niece, a large percentage of the population of 2.5 million people remained uncertain about the idea of separating from Great Britain. Though generally aware of what was happening in Philadelphia, colonists held differing views depending on where they lived. British and American troops had been fighting one another for more than a year in Boston, where colonists overwhelmingly favored independence. Redcoats and Bluecoats had been skirmishing in New York as well, but there the population was divided over the issue of separation from Britain. Tories opposed breaking from the mother country altogether.[9]

As the delegates poured into the Pennsylvania State House for the morning session on July 5, John Hancock, president of the Continental Congress, gaveled the meeting to order. The delegates authorized the printing of the Declaration of Independence and proclaimed that it should be distributed far and wide. A handwritten version of the Declaration was then carried down the street to the shop of John Dunlap, the official printer of the Congress. The printers in Dunlap's shop likely spent the better part of the day setting the type, then printed a proof copy, made a few minor edits, and ultimately published approximately 200 copies of the Declaration.[10]

After the Declaration was adopted and published, Congress ordered that copies be sent to governmental authorities and military commanders, as well as the British Crown in London. They agreed it should be posted in businesses, in town halls, and in taverns. Most Americans would learn about the Declaration of Independence via newspapers and printed broadsides. The July 6, 1776, issue of *The Pennsylvania Evening Post* published the first newspaper printing of the newly adopted Declaration.[11]

Two days later, General George Washington, whose army was then fighting the British on Staten Island, received a copy of the Declaration at Number One Broadway in New York City; his headquarters happened to be located less than a mile from a larger-than-life equestrian statue of King George III in Bowling Green. Washington issued an order for his troops to assemble on the "common" the following evening at 6 p.m. for a public reading of the Declaration.

The next evening, July 9, thousands of colonial volunteers filled the common to hear their brigade commanders read aloud the Declaration. According to one senior commander, it was "received with three huzzahs by the troops." Indeed, the soldiers became so animated by the news that they marched up Broadway to Bowling Green and tore down the statue of George III. Washington disapproved of the vandalism, but the soldiers made good use of the statue by melting down its 4,000 pounds of gilded lead to manufacture more than 40,000 musket balls.[12]

That a likeness of the king should be treated with such disrespect isn't surprising. After all, opposition to monarchy had played a significant role in inspiring the American Revolution in the first place. Hundreds of thousands of copies of Thomas Paine's *Common Sense* were in circulation in the American colonies by July 1776. Published in January, Paine's incendiary pamphlet, read widely not only in the halls of Congress but also in the taverns and inns where mechanics and farmers and soldiers congregated, made a compelling case for independence in part

An artist's view of the first reading of the Declaration of Independence in New York. (Credit: A. R. Waud / Miriam and Ira D. Wallach Division of Art, Prints and Photographs: Print Collection, New York Public Library)

by directly attacking the institution of monarchy—which Paine, the son of an English tenant farmer and corset maker, claimed ran afoul of man's natural state of freedom and equality. "One of the strongest natural proofs of the folly of hereditary right in kings, is, that nature disapproves it, otherwise she would not so frequently turn it into ridicule by giving mankind an ass for a lion," he wrote. Far from being a protector of the people, as many believed, George III was an oppressive tyrant, as all monarchs were, Paine argued. Therefore, it only made common sense to break away from a system of government that was so inimical to the interests of everyday Americans: "O ye that love mankind! Ye that dare oppose, not only the tyranny, but the tyrant, stand forth! Every spot of the old world is overrun with oppression. Freedom hath been hunted round the globe. . . . O! receive the fugitive, and prepare in time an asylum for mankind."[13]

Aided by the king's own actions, *Common Sense* captured the imagination of Americans like no other pamphlet: An estimated 500,000 copies were published in 1776 alone, and according to Paine, the work sold some 120,000 copies in its first three months. Dr. Benjamin Rush, the Philadelphia physician who had encouraged Paine to write *Common Sense*, recalled, "It burst from the press with an effect which has rarely been produced by types and papers in any age or country." Benjamin Franklin described its effect in turning public opinion in favor of independence as "prodigious."[14]

The Declaration of Independence itself included a lengthy list of grievances against the king. These grievances recounted the "long train of abuses and usurpations" by which George III and his minions had attempted, in the view of Congress, to establish "absolute Tyranny" over the North American colonies. For example, the Declaration accused the "present king" of obstructing the "Administration of Justice," of making "Judges dependent on his Will alone," and of rendering "the Military independent of and superior to the Civil power." It accused him, as well, of "cutting off our Trade with all parts of the world," of "imposing Taxes on us without our Consent," and of "transporting us beyond Seas to be tried for pretended offences." He even stood accused of exciting "domestic insurrections amongst us." These were among the facts "submitted to a candid world," the reasons why representatives of the thirteen states, in Congress duly assembled, felt compelled to sever connections with Great Britain.

Although he never visited America, George III met an unhappy fate in many of his former colonies. He was hanged in effigy on Long Island, buried in absentia in Savannah, Georgia, and paraded in jest through the streets of Baltimore, Maryland. With the city illuminated at night in honor of the Declaration, Baltimoreans saw "the Effigy of our Late King . . . carted through the town, and committed to the flames amidst the acclamations of many hundreds.—The just reward of a tyrant." George's symbolic death represented the end of monarchical authority, and his mock funerals upended the tradition, imported from Britain, of celebrating royal birthdays and accession days with public proclamations, bonfires, bells, and promenades. Vestiges of British rule—Union Jacks, portraits of British nobility, and, of course, British goods such as tea—were removed or destroyed.[15]

At the same time, the Declaration heralded the birth of a new country, with new traditions. On July 8, in accordance with the wishes of Congress, the Declaration was read aloud before a great crowd of people assembled outside Philadelphia's State House. "Three Cheers" greeted the news, wrote John Adams. Battalions of soldiers paraded on the commons and fired a *feux de joie*, a rifle salute—"notwithstanding the Scarcity of Powder," Adams noted with some distaste. Bells rang all day and much of the night. Even some who had been lukewarm about independence now rallied around the American cause. "We never can again be happy, under a single Particle of British Power," Adams wrote. This sentiment was widespread.[16]

Word of the events in Philadelphia soon spread throughout the colonies. One by one, American communities became aware that they were now bound together, not just with other communities in their colony but with other colonies in a fledgling nation. At Easton, Pennsylvania, on July 8, a "great number of spectators" who heard the Declaration "gave their hearty assent with three loud huzzahs, and cried out, 'May God long preserve and unite the Free and Independant [*sic*] States of

America.'" Residents of Trenton, New Jersey, responded to the news "with loud acclamations." In Providence, Rhode Island, "The Declaration was received with joy and applause by all ranks." Some 1,000 people attended a celebration in Richmond, Virginia, where "the satisfaction visible in every countenance," a newspaper said, evinced "their determination to support [independence] with their lives and fortunes." From Georgia to Massachusetts, and everywhere in between, soldiers paraded, cannons sounded, and toasts were drunk, often thirteen at a time, in shows of unity.[17]

As word spread, the Declaration worked to define a new American identity. Americans, even in 1776, were a diverse mix of people of Dutch, German, French, and African descent, as well as Englishmen, Scotsmen, and Irish, spread across thirteen semiautonomous entities stretching from north to south, with varying attitudes about breaking from Britain. Yet the Declaration spoke of Americans as "one people," comprising, as Abraham Lincoln would later put it, "a new nation, conceived in Liberty, and dedicated to the proposition that all men are created equal." The Declaration was the first public document to use the name "the united States of America."

To be sure, American statehood was still a plural construct, a lowercase collection of roughly coequal states operating with limited direction from the Continental Congress. The United States of America would not assume a singular, uppercase identity in the minds of many for almost a century yet—when the Union's victory in the Civil War empowered the federal government over the individual states.

Yet the primary purpose of the Declaration was to establish the international legal sovereignty of the United States, "to dissolve the political bands" that once connected the former colonies with Great Britain and to assume the new nation's rightful place "among the powers of the earth." And in that regard the Declaration succeeded in announcing the birth of a new nation. When the document was read in August 1776 to Continental army troops stationed at Fort Ticonderoga, in northern New York, they responded, "Now we are a people! We have a name among the states of this world!" The first loyalty oath issued by the new United States similarly asked officials to "acknowledge the UNITED STATES of AMERICA to be Free and Sovereign States, and declare that the people thereof owe no allegiance or obedience to George the Third, King of Great Britain."[18]

The tradition that began in 1776 of reading aloud the Declaration in town halls, in public parks, and in state capitols across the country has continued for 250 years. That tradition endures in part because, as historian Peter de Bolla has argued, the performative act of reciting the Declaration's self-evident truths expresses "a commonly held architecture of belief" that unites Americans. But it has endured, too, because the realization of those truths remains as elusive and open to interpretation today as two-plus centuries ago.[19]

Word of American independence quickly spread overseas, thanks in part to friendly ship captains. August 5, 1776, already found residents of the Caribbean Island of Saint Kitts toasting "WASHINGTON, LEE, and INDEPENDENCY to America."[20]

London periodicals published the news about a week later. The *Gentleman's Magazine*, a popular news monthly, printed the text of the Declaration along with a commentary written by the editor under a pseudonym, "Sylvanus Urban." "Whether those grievances were real or imaginary, we will not presume to decide," the editor remarked, adding, "The ball is now struck, and time only can shew it where it will rest."[21]

Some Britons expressed support for the American cause. John Wilkes, a radical member of Parliament, hailed the "spirit and courage" behind the Declaration of Independence and predicted that "posterity" would do it justice. "I hope, and believe, you never will conquer the free spirit of the descendants of Englishmen, exerted in an honest cause."[22]

Predictably, however, most British officials denounced the "insolence" of the American rebels, in part because their talk of rights, of independence, and of much else besides risked stirring up opposition to British rule in other parts of the empire. The British were especially worried about the "sugar" islands in the Caribbean where they had substantial trade, but holdings closer to home were also a concern: Irish journals noted the Declaration in August. "When America manifests to the world her independence and power," Irish patriot Henry Grattan asked rhetorically, "do you imagine you will persuade Ireland to be satisfied with an English Parliament making laws for her?" America's war was Ireland's harvest, he said.[23]

The exiled former governor of Massachusetts, Thomas Hutchinson, was in London just as news of the Declaration arrived: "The Congress has issued a most infamous Paper reciting a great number of Pretended and tyrannical deeds of the King and declaring their Independence." As for George III himself, he waited until October 1776 to respond. In a speech to Parliament drafted by his prime minister, Lord North, he condemned the "daring and desperate" spirit displayed by the leaders of his American colonies, traitors who had "presumed to set up their rebellious confederacies for independent states."[24]

Critics mocked the hypocrisy of those colonists who held slaves even as they spoke about individual rights. Hutchinson wished "to ask the Delegates of Maryland, Virginia, and the Carolinas, how their Constituents justify the depriving more than a hundred thousand Africans of their rights to liberty, and *the pursuit of happiness*, and in some degree, to their lives, if their rights are so absolutely unalienable." The English abolitionist Thomas Day went even further: "If there be an object truly ridiculous in nature, it is an American patriot, signing resolutions of independency with the one hand, and with the other brandishing a whip over his affrighted slaves."[25]

If London greeted the Declaration with hostility, Paris responded with silence, and that was worrisome because the Continental Congress realized that American independence could not be won without French diplomatic recognition—and the military and economic assistance that might well come with it. That was one of the main reasons why Thomas Jefferson, John Adams, Benjamin Franklin, and the other members of the committee that drafted the Declaration submitted the facts, as they saw them, "to a candid world"—to mobilize international opinion behind the colonists' cause. Accordingly, Congress instructed its commissioners in Paris—Silas Deane, Benjamin Franklin, and Arthur Lee—"to obtain as early as possible a publick acknowledgement of this Independency of these States of the Crown and Parliament of Great Britain by the Court of France."[26]

Delays hampered this effort, however. Deane, the first American representative in Paris, did not receive a copy of the Declaration that was sent to him on July 8, 1776, along with instructions to "immediately communicate the piece to the Court of France, and send copies of it to the other Courts of Europe." A second copy arrived only in November 1776, by which time news of American independence had been circulating in Europe for months.[27]

Upon receiving the copy, Deane promptly handed it to the Comte de Vergennes, Louis XVI's foreign minister, informing Vergennes that France was the first foreign power to be formally notified of American independence. Deane also renewed his request for French recognition. Vergennes was favorably disposed to Deane's request. He already had pointed out to the king the advantages France might derive from America's push for independence. But he remained noncommittal, and as long as France stayed neutral, the American cause risked failure.[28]

THE DECLARATION'S FINE WORDS ABOUT EQUALITY AND rights and liberty rang hollow for the half million persons who toiled in bondage in the thirteen states—all of which still permitted slavery when independence was declared on July 4, 1776. In Virginia, the largest slaveholding state, some 130 persons were enslaved on the Monticello plantation owned by the Declaration's principal author, Thomas Jefferson. They included three-year-old Sally Hemings, one of eleven enslaved men, women, and children Jefferson had recently inherited from his father-in-law—along with 4,819 acres of land, a riding horse named Allycroker, and her foal, Caractacus.

Treated not as human beings but property that could be bought, sold, mortgaged, and given as gifts, enslaved persons had no legal rights whatsoever. They could not legally marry. They had no claim to their children, who could be traded away on auction blocks alongside furniture, livestock, and other possessions. They had no legal recourse if they were raped or beaten or tortured, including by those working for Jefferson himself. They could be worked to death, and sometimes were, to produce profits for the White people who owned them. In fact, notes journalist Nikole Hannah-Jones, creator of the 1619 Project, the wealth and prominence that enabled Jefferson and many of the other founding fathers to break from the mighty British Empire was generated by chattel slavery. Enslaved persons helped build and maintain Jefferson's home at Monticello. They laid its floors. They crafted its furniture. They tended its gardens and performed other essential tasks throughout the plantation. An enslaved man, Robert Hemings—Sally Hemings's half-sibling—accompanied Jefferson to Philadelphia to ensure his every comfort as he drafted the announcement of a new nation dedicated to the proposition of human equality.[29]

Thousands of enslaved men fought for their freedom during the Revolutionary War. Many supported the patriot side once General Washington—a slaveowner, like Jefferson—lifted a 1775 order he himself had given barring Blacks from serving in the Continental army. Many more joined the British side in response to a November 1775 proclamation issued by Lord Dunmore, the royal governor of Virginia, promising freedom to "all indentured Servants, Negroes, or others" who joined the British army—which is why the Crown stood accused, in the Declaration of Independence, of exciting "domestic insurrections amongst us." Indeed, for some White colonists, protecting Black slavery from such meddling was a motivating factor in breaking from the British. Some Southern patriots even took up arms in the War for Independence "to preserve slavery for blacks as well as the liberty of whites," according to historian Alan Taylor, for slave labor was regarded as an essential economic foundation for sustaining the freedom of White men.[30]

Other African Americans fought for freedom using the power of words. Take Prince Hall, for instance, a free Black tradesman living in Boston at the time of the Revolution. Many details of Hall's story remain unknown today, even to scholars of African American history: It is not clear when he was born or how he gained his freedom. But Hall emerged in the 1770s to become a pivotal figure in the long struggle for Black liberation.[31]

In January 1777, just six months after the promulgation of the Declaration, Hall joined seven other Black men in petitioning the Massachusetts legislature for emancipation—with language that invoked the Declaration itself. "A Great Number of Blackes detained in a State of Slavery in the Bowels of a free & christian Country," the petition began,

> have in Common with all other men a Natural and Unaliable Right to that freedom which the [Great]—Parent of the

> [Universe] hath Bestowed equalley on all menkind and which they have Never [forfeited] by Any Compact or Agreement whatever—but thay [were] Unjustly Dragged by the hand of cruel Power from their Derest [friends] and sum of them Even torn from the Embraces of their tender Parents—from A [populous] [Pleasant] And plentiful country And in Violation of Laws of Nature and off Nations And in defiance of all the tender feelings of humanity [Brought] hear Either to Be sold Like Beast of Burthen & Like them Condemnd to Slavery for Life—among A People Professing [the spirit of human equality].[32]

Attributed to Hall, the petition was not the first effort by African Americans to abolish enslavement in Massachusetts. In 1773, at least six known petitions had been put forth by African Americans from Bristol and Worcester counties as well as Boston and its neighboring towns. But Hall may well have been the first American, Black or non-Black, to publicly use the language of the Declaration of Independence for a political purpose other than justifying war against Britain. In invoking the core concepts of social-contract theory, which grounded the American Revolution, to argue for an extension of the claim to equal rights to those who were enslaved, Hall adopted the intellectual framework articulated by the founders to make a case against slavery.[33]

Though the legislature took no immediate action on Hall's petition, the document advanced the cause of abolition in Massachusetts. The state constitution, adopted in 1780 and drafted by John Adams, expanded upon the Declaration of Independence in proclaiming that "all men are born free and equal." In 1783, on the basis of that "free and equal" clause, the Massachusetts state court ruled enslavement unconstitutional in a case brought by Quock Walker, an enslaved man who sued for his freedom. The first judicial abolition of slavery in the United States, the Massachusetts court's decision ended slavery in the state and contributed to abolitionist movements elsewhere. By 1784, six Northern states or territories had passed laws or court rulings limiting or abolishing slavery.

Southern states did not follow suit. Slavery would continue to exert its dehumanizing force for decades, as it had done since a ship had arrived in Virginia in 1619 bearing a cargo of more than twenty enslaved people from Africa. They were among the 12.5 million Africans who were kidnapped from their homes and brought in chains across the Atlantic Ocean in the largest forced migration in human history. Hundreds of thousands of enslaved Africans were sold in America, where for centuries the institution of slavery wreaked terrible damage on virtually everything and everybody it touched. Slavery's "poisonous breath," in the evocative words of the pioneering nineteenth-century historian George Washington Williams, sickened American society, "destroyed" the country's best statesmen, fouled public opinion, "strangled the voice of the press," cowed the pulpit, and eventually dragged the nation "by the fore-hair through the stormy sea of civil war."[34]

Yet 1619 also marked the moment when persons of African descent began building America, both with their backbreaking contributions to the country's economic growth and with their determined pursuit of the nation's founding creed. The long struggle for Black liberation to which Prince Hall and Quock Walker had contributed would continue well beyond the late eighteenth century. Led by persons of color, both free and enslaved, who insisted on their humanity, on their citizenship as a gateway to the rights to life, liberty, and property enumerated in the Declaration, that struggle would profoundly alter the direction and character of the country, impacting everything from politics to culture—all to realize the nation's principles, as stated in 1776. That, too, is an indispensable part of the American story, even though the goal of realizing those principles was far, far away. "Around us the history of the land has centered for thrice a hundred years," W. E. B. Du Bois wrote in 1903.[35]

A year after the Continental Congress adopted the Declaration of Independence, John Adams and the other representatives were back in Philadelphia during the summer months after having decamped to Baltimore during the winter to avoid a potential British incursion. Victory in the war was far from certain. Indeed, a series of humiliating defeats suffered by General Washington's troops led Thomas Paine to write of "times that try men's souls." Nevertheless, Washington demonstrated remarkable ingenuity and resilience in late December 1776 and early January 1777 with his crossing of the Delaware and defeat of the British and their Hessian forces at Trenton and Princeton, New Jersey. Patriot morale soared even though the Continental army was tired and poorly equipped. Adding to Washington's worries, a new British general, Henry Clinton, had taken over command of British forces from General Sir William Howe. The British, in a plan that came to be known as the Saratoga campaign, intended to march a strong, well-armed force of 8,000 soldiers under the command of General John Burgoyne down from Canada to take Fort Ticonderoga at the southern end of Lake Champlain. Continuing down the Hudson Valley to Albany, Burgoyne's army would join with other British forces coming north from New York City and cut the newly independent United States in two.[36]

Notwithstanding General Washington's successes at the turn of the year, by July 4, 1777, many in Congress questioned his leadership as well as the long-term viability of the Revolution itself. Recognition from France had not yet come, and some voiced doubts about whether foreign aid would ever arrive or questioned the wisdom of having sought it in the first place. John Adams, for one, was skeptical of consorting with wily European diplomats, warning that the "French intend to make Use of Us." However, Thomas Jefferson viewed foreign assistance as a matter of survival. Jefferson joined others, such as fellow Virginian Richard Henry Lee, who had first proposed an alliance with France.[37]

There was also debate over what a future government should look like. While the trappings and symbols of royalty had disappeared from America, and republicanism had filled the void in towns, cities, and the newly christened states, there was no ready and immediate answer as to what unified the states beyond separation from the Crown. Would Americans simply exist as thirteen separate entities, or would there be a national government? And if there was a central government, how would it be formed, how much control would it have over the people, and where would it be located? Historian John Ferling has suggested that the two most debated models were Thomas Paine's vision outlined in his forty-seven-page *Common Sense* and John Adams's *Thoughts on Government*, published three months later in April 1776. Paine argued for a unicameral assembly elected annually by "the whole body" of the people, while Adams, suspicious of direct elections, envisioned a more complex arrangement of checks and balances among legislative, executive, and judicial power.[38]

Arming and supplying General Washington's army as well as debating a future governance structure were priorities, but the Continental Congress also took time to plan a one-year anniversary of the Declaration of Independence. As part of its effort to celebrate both the sacrifices and promise of the Revolution, in mid-June 1777 Congress passed a resolution "that the flag of the United States be thirteen stripes, alternate red and white; that the Union be thirteen stars, white in a blue field representing a new constellation."

Just as plans for future governance remained somewhat amorphous, the founding fathers left much about the flag undefined, including its size, the number of points on each star, and their arrangement on a blue field. Nevertheless, Francis Hopkinson, a signer of the Declaration and a commissioner on the Continental Congress's Navy Board, claimed credit for the conceptual design of the flag and billed the Continental Congress for $24. Congress refused payment on the grounds that he "had not been the only one to work on the project" and because "individuals already receiving a salary from Congress should not try to charge the public more for 'these little assistances.'"[39]

Otherwise, first-anniversary planning took a backseat. Congressional preparations began only on July 2—"too late to have a sermon," John Adams complained to his daughter Abigail, who was nicknamed "Nabby," "so this must be deferred another year."[40]

In a way, it was fitting that commemorative planning began on July 2. After all, John Adams had initially predicted that July 2 would be remembered as Independence Day because it was the day in 1776 when the Continental Congress had formally adopted the Lee Resolution, introduced by Virginia's Richard Henry Lee, declaring that the colonies were "free and independent States" and no longer subject to British rule. It was July 2, John Adams had written his wife, Abigail, in 1776, that would go down in history as "the most memorable Epocha," the "Day of Deliverance" that would be commemorated "with Pomp and Parade, with Shews, Games, Sports, Guns, Bells, Bonfires and Illuminations from one End of this Continent to the other from this Time forward forever more."[41]

Adams was wrong, of course. July 4, the day Congress adopted a text, the Declaration of Independence, justifying its actions before the eyes of the world, went down in history as Independence Day. And first-anniversary plans came together at the last minute to include parades, troop reviews, and a formal dinner for the Congress. By all accounts, the 1777 celebration in Philadelphia was a great success. "Considering the lateness of the design and suddenness of the execution," Adams wrote his daughter, "I was amazed at the universal joy and alacrity that was discovered, and at the brilliancy and splendour of every part of this joyful exhibition." The festivity and ceremony befitted the occasion.[42]

Notably, there was a grand display of fireworks. This was something new for Americans. Europeans had imported fireworks from the Chinese, who invented them as an offshoot of military technology. For centuries the British had set off fireworks to entertain royalty. Now, to mark America's first Fourth of July commemoration, brilliant orange explosions lit up the night sky over the Schuylkill River in Philadelphia. Adams went for a walk that evening for exercise and a little fresh air, and he was surprised to discover that it was easier than usual to navigate the city's streets at night due to the light from the fireworks overhead and from the windows of the houses illuminated with candles in celebration. "I think it was the most splendid illumination I ever saw," he wrote Nabby. Another eyewitness corroborated Adams's account: "In the evening the whole City were Illuminated with Lights at every window . . . til 12 O clock at which time the Lights were Ordered to be extinguished." Impromptu bonfires burned in some neighborhoods.[43]

General Washington traveled from New Jersey for the occasion and, accompanied by Adams, visited the frigate *Delaware*, which fired a thirteen-gun salute that was answered "by thirteen others from each armed vessel in the river." The firing of cannons and artillery was a symbolic representation of the new and unified nation, and it became a staple of future July Fourth celebrations. Adams recalled how when they returned in a barge to the shore, they were "saluted with three cheers, from every ship, galley, and boat on the river."[44]

According to newspaper accounts, Adams and Washington later attended an "elegant" dinner with members of Congress during which a Hessian band, captured in Trenton, performed, while "a corps of British deserters taken into the service of the continent by the state of Georgia . . . filled up the intervals with a feux de joie." Philadelphia's wharves and shores were lined, Adams reported in his letter to his daughter, "with a vast concourse of people, all shouting and huzzahing, in a manner which gave great joy to every friend to this country, and the utmost terror and dismay to every lurking tory."[45]

In many respects, the Declaration of Independence might have seemed destined to become a historical relic by July 1777. Overtaken by events, its flowery assertion of rights was of limited use to a young nation on the move, grappling with practical questions of military and political necessity. Few of the state constitutions that emerged in the months after July 4, 1776—in Delaware, Pennsylvania, Maryland, North Carolina, Georgia, and New York—made much reference to it. Virginia's Declaration of Rights, drafted by George Mason in 1776, served as a far more common model.

Yet the fact that thousands of Americans, not only in Philadelphia but in every one of the thirteen states, paid homage to a document adopted by a handful of congressional representatives in a second-floor room in the Pennsylvania State House only twelve months earlier attested to its enduring rhetorical power and lasting appeal.

In Boston, the Massachusetts General Court invited the Reverend William Gordon to preach a Fourth of July sermon to its members. Afterward, from the balcony of the State House, John Hancock proposed thirteen toasts, one for each of the states. In Boston Harbor, ships fired volleys to celebrate the occasion, while the Sons of Liberty, a political group that opposed British rule, exploded fireworks over Boston Common. A correspondent noted, "The cheerful Appearances of the gentleman and Ladies in the Park, and the Pleasantness of the Evening, closed with universal Satisfaction the Joys of the Day."[46]

Sixty miles north of Boston, in Portsmouth, New Hampshire, Captain Thomas Thompson, commander of the Continental frigate *Raleigh*, invited "all true friends to American Independency" to witness a thirteen-gun salute, which, to the delight of onlookers gathered on the wharves, was answered by a French ship and a Portsmouth privateer. And in Charleston, South Carolina, the Charleston Artillery Company, dressed in full regalia, assembled on parade grounds where they were received by the governor of the state and the privy council. At 1 p.m., Charleston's harbor forts discharged a total of seventy-six cannons. The day's celebration concluded with an evening candlelight illumination of the city.[47]

Not everyone was enthusiastic. The windows of Philadelphia's "Torrey Houses," as a Continental army officer called them, remained dark. They made inviting targets for reprisals, especially as the evening wore on and more and more patriotic toasts were drunk. Darkened "Windows Paid for their Obstinancy," the officer reported. "I conclude much Tory unilluminated glass will want replacing," confirmed Continental Congress member William Williams of Connecticut, who disapproved of the excessive revelry. "Yesterday was in my opinion poorly spent in celebrating the Anniversary of the Declaration of Independence." A "great expenditure of liquor, powder etc., took up the Day and of candles thro the City good part of the night."[48]

Most, though, considered the young nation's first anniversary cause for celebration. *The Pennsylvania Evening Post* captured the spirit: "Thus may the fourth of July, that glorious and ever memorable day, be celebrated though America, by the sons of freedom, from age to age till timc shall bc no morc."[49]

Joseph Brant arrived in America on July 29, 1776. A Mohawk leader also known as Thayendanegea, Brant had been away for months on a diplomatic mission to London, seeking British help in protecting his nation's dwindling lands from ever-encroaching American colonists. When he had sailed for London in November 1775, Anglo-American affairs were still in a state of flux, teetering on (but not yet past) the breaking point. Now he returned to North America—on a British ship, at British-controlled Long Island—just weeks after American independence had been declared. "It was a vastly different country and vastly different circumstances to which [Brant and his fellow] travelers returned," a biographer has written.[50]

Native Americans haven't featured prominently in accounts of America's founding. As historian Ned Blackhawk has noted, American Indians often "remain absent or appear as hostile or passive objects awaiting discovery and domination." Indeed, the Declaration of Independence referred to Indigenous peoples only to characterize them, stereotypically, as "merciless Indian savages"—a people beyond the pale of civilization, an enemy to conquer.[51]

As recent research has shown, however, Native nations were anything but peripheral to the American experience. Euro-American advancement was predicated on the exploitation of Native peoples, the expropriation of their land, and the extraction of their resources. These realities not only render Native American history as essential as African American history to a full understanding of US history; they also call into question the nation's founding premise. "American democracy arose from the dispossession of American Indians," Blackhawk asserts.[52]

Horizons, rapidly expanding for Euro-Americans in 1776, were shrinking just as quickly for Native North Americans. Though estimates vary, their numbers were down to some four million—almost half of the seven million to eight million they had been in 1492, according to one measure, due mainly to epidemics caused by contact with Europeans. Moreover, Indigenous Americans residing at the leading edge of settler colonialism in eastern North America, in or near the thirteen states, faced growing pressure from American settlers, who increasingly intruded on their hunting and fishing lands. The outbreak of the Revolutionary War and the dislocations it caused only accelerated outmigration of Europeans from cities and towns, deepening the challenges many Indigenous peoples already faced in procuring food, maintaining shelter, and providing for their families. By one account,

Native nations lost tens of millions of acres of land in the quarter century after the first shots of the war were fired.[53]

Mohawk were not immune from these pressures. One of six nations of the Iroquois Confederacy, an influential political union of Iroquoian-speaking peoples, based primarily in New York, the Mohawk were relatively prosperous in the late eighteenth century. Situated in the Mohawk Valley, they occupied a strategically important position in northeastern North America, along a waterway, the Mohawk River, that controlled the flow of trade and people into the colonial trading center of Albany and beyond.

However, as Brant explained in a 1776 letter to Lord George Germain, the British secretary of state for the American colonies, the Mohawk had "been very badly treated by [the] people in that country, the City of Albany laying an unjust claim to the lands on which our Lower Castle is built." The Crown's local superintendent for Indian affairs (who also happened to be Brant's brother-in-law) had always treated the Mohawk fairly, Brant hastened to say. American colonists were the problem. They continued to press on Mohawk lands, located on the easternmost edge of the Iroquois region—that is, the area nearest American settlements—from almost every direction. Surrounded by Whites, the size of the Mohawk footprint seemed to be decreasing each day. "Indeed," he concluded, "it is very hard when we have let the King's subjects have so much land for so little value, they should want to cheat us in the manner of the small spots we have left for our women and children to live on. We are tired out in making complaints & getting no redress."[54]

In November 1775, Brant sailed across the Atlantic Ocean in hopes of gaining the Crown's support for the preservation of Mohawk lands. His pleas for assistance were well received in London, where British officials were looking to organize Indian resistance against the American rebels. In February 1776, Brant received an audience with George

III himself. Although Brant, when presented to the king, reportedly refused to kiss the monarch's hand, as was customary—"I bow to no man for I am considered a prince among my own people," Brant is supposed to have said—British high society feted him nevertheless. Welcomed into the homes of noblemen and aristocrats, he met with important officials, attended masquerade balls, and toured the great and historic sites of London. He received an array of gifts, including silk shirts, an engraved rifle and pistol, and a silver watch. He even sat for a portrait by the fashionable English painter George Romney. Brant came away from the whole experience greatly impressed. He recalled years later, "I have had the honour to be introduced to the King of England—a finer man than whom I think it would be a truly difficult task to find."[55]

Assured of British support, Brant returned to America, arriving in late July. He soon rallied four of the six Iroquois nations—Seneca, Onondaga, and Cayuga, in addition to Mohawk—to ally with the British against the American rebels. Those four Iroquois nations, like most Native nations, allied with Britain in the Revolutionary War not because they necessarily agreed with the British politically but because the British represented a lesser threat to their lands than the land-hungry American settlers, who were widely distrusted. In August 1777, Brant led a volunteer force composed of Iroquois and Loyalist Whites who inflicted heavy casualties on their patriot opponents in the Battle of Oriskany, an engagement of the Saratoga campaign, in which the British attempted to gain control of the strategically important Hudson River valley.[56]

Despite their victory at Oriskany, the Saratoga campaign ended poorly for the British in October 1777, turning the war in the patriots' favor. Joseph Brant and his followers eventually headed to Canada for safety. And American victory in the war would open Native lands west of the Appalachian Mountains to further dispossession.

The outcome at Saratoga and, more broadly, of the Revolutionary War itself underscores the common denominator of loss that characterized the Native experience at the beginning of the United States. Although Joseph Brant may have picked the losing side, his courage exemplified something else that has distinguished the 250-year Indigenous history of these United States: resistance, struggle, and survival.[57]

DECLARING INDEPENDENCE HAD CHANGED AMERICANS, DR. DAVID Ramsay said in an oration given on July 4, 1778, in Charleston. Spirits were high in the port city that day, the second anniversary of the Declaration of Independence, buoyed by reports of French recognition of American independence, which had appeared in local newspapers only weeks earlier. The American experiment seemed assured, and Dr. Ramsay, a physician who had become active in state politics since moving to South Carolina from New Jersey in 1773, exuded confidence in his oration—only the second July Fourth oration on record and by all accounts the most memorable of the two.[58]

In colonial times, said Ramsay, Americans had lived in a world where "favour is the source of preferment" and where "he that can best please his superiors, by the low arts of fawning and adulation, is most likely to obtain favour." That is, they had lived in a monarchical society of the kind against which Thomas Paine had railed in *Common Sense*. In dissolving their allegiance to the Crown, Americans, said Dr. Ramsay, had created a new society, a world in which "all offices lie open to men of merit, of whatever rank or condition." Even the reins of state "may be held by the son of the poorest man, if possessed of abilities equal to the important station." In other words, Americans had established the basis of republicanism, rooted in political principles such as popular sovereignty, the rule of law, and civic virtue—the sacrifice of individual interest to the pursuit of the common good—but also social principles such as general equality and economic justice. In a republic, Ramsay said, persons of low or middling birth were no longer subjects, forced to "look up for the blessings of government to hungry courtiers, or the needy dependents of British nobility." They were citizens able to look their fellow countrymen in the eye.[59]

In truth, the American Revolution was not very revolutionary in terms of leveling the playing field for the majority of working Americans. The Revolution did not dismantle preexisting class structures; nor did it redistribute wealth or land. With the exception of Loyalists who fled the country, colonial elites generally remained in positions of authority, leaving working people very much in their same situations as before. Property qualifications continued to prevent many laborers, tenant farmers, apprentices, and urban workers from voting and holding office in all but one state, Pennsylvania, whose state constitution eliminated such requirements in 1776. In 1786 and 1787, Daniel Shays would lead an armed rebellion of 4,000 Massachusetts farmers and war veterans to demand debt relief and economic assistance.[60]

But the American Revolution had been motivated in part by a desire to make individuals free and independent of the social hierarchies and hereditary privileges that characterized traditional monarchical society. And the Revolution gave expression to a powerful meritocratic belief that talented, hardworking people could lift themselves up by their bootstraps. Republican competition, predicted David Ramsay, who would go on to write one of the first major histories of the American Revolution, was sure to "fan the spark of genius in every breast," kindle it into flame, and draw "from obscurity many illustrious characters, which will dazzle the world with the splendor of their names." Led by the spirit of public service, they would enter "the bench, the army, the navy, the learned professions, and all the departments of civil government."[61]

A bright future lay ahead for the republic, Ramsay predicted. With the encouragement of the "free governments of America," there would be "poets, orators, criticks, and historians, equal to the most celebrated of the ancient commonwealths of Greece and Italy." American arts and sciences would "spread far and wide, till they [had] reached the remotest parts of this untutored continent." Trade and commerce would travel on great ships "to ride triumphant on the ocean, and to carry American thunder around the world."[62]

The journey would not be untroubled. Charleston, for example, would fall to British forces in 1780 in one of the worst American defeats of the war. But Ramsay's July Fourth oration received "the warmest marks of approbation," according to a local newspaper, which praised Ramsay for pointing out "the many advantages resulting from Independence, the superiority the citizens of a free republick enjoy over the subjects of a despotick monarchy, and the prospects of the arts and sciences being soon cultivated with unexampled ardour in this western world." A military parade, the firing of musketry, and a dinner followed Ramsay's remarks, after which thirteen toasts were drunk, each accompanied by thirteen discharges from artillery commanded by a Charleston militia regiment. In the evening, candles illuminated the town.[63]

Real or not, the American Dream had begun.

After eight long years, the American Revolutionary War officially ended in 1783 with the Treaty of Paris, though most of the fighting had concluded two years earlier with the surrender of Lord Cornwallis to General Washington at Yorktown. Even during the bleakest moments of the conflict, Americans celebrated July Fourth with cannon salutes, fireworks, ringing of bells, parties and toasts, patriotic songs, and displays of the American flag. These traditions, many of which originated in England, seemed to have been widely adopted by the first anniversary of the signing in 1777, though the celebrations varied from town to town, city to city, and depended almost entirely on the initiative and energy of local everyday citizens. As author Diana Appelbaum has pointed out, "The Fourth of July was an important holiday in a society that had relatively few holidays." The traditions have continued, with varying levels of commitment and intensity from Americans depending on their race, their gender, where they live, and at times, such as in the early 1800s, their political views. The way in which Americans have celebrated—or not celebrated—the Fourth has often reflected parochial concerns. In territorial Wisconsin, for instance, descendants of French settlers refused to celebrate the holiday in 1818. For Black slaves and Native Americans, July Fourth's celebrations of freedom and democracy had little meaning.[64]

Even though the Declaration of Independence remains an imperfect document, it has guided Americans for 250 years with a clear vision for the natural rights of man. John Adams had been prescient in 1776 when he wrote to his wife, "I am well aware of the Toil and Blood and Treasure, that it will cost Us to maintain this Declaration, and support and defend these States. Yet through all the Gloom I can see the Rays of ravishing Light and Glory. I can see that the End is more than worth all the Means." Abigail Adams might not have seen things quite the same way as her husband. After all, the Declaration had not remembered the ladies—nor would American law do so for quite some time yet. But every fifty years, Americans collectively work to give meaning to his vision.[65]

2

Jubilee

> For ourselves let the annual return of this day, forever refresh our recollections of these rights and an undiminished devotion to them.
>
> —THOMAS JEFFERSON (1826)[1]

ON JUNE 30, 1826, THE MAYOR JOSIAH Quincy III of Boston paid a visit to his neighbor, John Adams, at Peacefield, the former president's bucolic farm in Braintree. Though the men were of different generations, their families had been intertwined for decades. Prior to the War for Independence, John Adams had worked closely with the mayor's father, Josiah Quincy II, as legal cocounsel defending Captain Thomas Preston, whose British troops, fearing they might be overcome by a mob of angry protesters that had approached them, killed five colonists and wounded six others outside the Boston Customs House on March 5, 1770. The "Boston Massacre," as it was known, led to a dramatic escalation in the tensions between the occupying British troops and the colonists.

There were other connections as well between Quincy and Adams: They were distantly related through Adams's wife, Abigail Smith

Adams. Indeed, the former president's son, John Quincy Adams—who in 1826 happened to be the current president of the United States—was named after his mother's maternal grandfather, Colonel John Quincy, a former Speaker of the Massachusetts House of Representatives and the grandfather of Mayor Quincy.

As the former president sat on the porch with his younger friend, he gazed over the fields he had once tilled. He missed his beloved wife, Abigail, who had died in 1818; two of his four children, Charles and Nabby, were deceased as well. Now ninety years old, he was in failing health; his eyesight was poor, and his joints ached, but on this day his spirits were nevertheless high. He and Quincy reminisced about past events and spoke about the upcoming Jubilee, the fifty-year anniversary of the signing of the Declaration of Independence, just four days away.

John Adams was proud of his role as a member of the Continental Congress during the tumultuous events of 1776. He had served as a member of the five-man committee charged with drafting the Declaration, though Thomas Jefferson, largely at Adams's urging, wrote most of the document's language.

More importantly, Adams tenaciously defended the Declaration from congressional detractors and helped marshal its passage through the Congress. Now, in 1826, he was one of only three surviving signers of the Declaration: Charles Carroll of Maryland and Thomas Jefferson of Virginia were the other two.

Adams and Jefferson had been allies and collaborators in 1776, but had fallen out in 1796 when Adams was elected president, a rift that only deepened when Jefferson—his vice president—defeated him in the election of 1800. Despite his bitter resentment toward Jefferson, who he felt had both encouraged and abetted the press and anonymous pamphleteers in a deeply personal and unfair campaign against him, Adams accepted defeat. He did not attend the swearing in of Thomas Jefferson but instead left Washington early in the morning and returned with Abigail to Peacefield. Leaving office after two terms, President George Washington had set the precedent for the peaceful transfer of power, and Adams understood it to be a cornerstone of America's fledgling nation.

During his postpresidency, Adams tended to his farm and wrote prolifically—from his autobiography to wide-ranging commentary and voluminous correspondence with friends and acquaintances. However, he and Jefferson had no communication whatsoever. Then, after a twelve-year hiatus, Adams wrote a conciliatory letter to the third president that rekindled their friendship. What followed was a remarkable series of deeply personal letters and reminiscences about the Revolutionary War period. In recognition of their immense contributions to the founding of the nation, in 1824 John Quincy Adams, then the secretary of state, sent two copies of an engraving of the Declaration to each of its three living signers. The cover letters sent to Jefferson and Carroll were nearly identical to the one Adams sent to his father:

> Of this Document, unparalleled in the Annals of Mankind, the original deposited in this Department exhibits your name as one of the Subscribers. . . . While performing the duty thus assigned to me, permit me to felicitate you and the Country which is reaping the reward of your labours, as well that your hand was affixed to this record of glory, as that after the lapse of near half a century, you survive to receive this tribute of reverence and gratitude from your children, the present fathers of the Land.[2]

Fifty years after the signing of the Declaration of Independence, the United States prepared to celebrate its Jubilee. While there was no formal, organized, "national" celebration per se, Americans across the country and from all walks of life wanted to recognize the great service that men like Adams and Jefferson had done their country, as well as the enormous strides the nation had taken since declaring its independence fifty years earlier.

By 1826 America had a nascent democracy and not a monarchy. When Adams and Jefferson signed the Declaration of Independence, America had consisted of thirteen British colonies located along the Eastern Seaboard with a population of approximately 2.5 million. Yet fifty years later, the United States was a sovereign nation with more than 11 million people living in twenty-four states; nearly 1.5 million were enslaved persons living mostly in the South. There were also several hundred thousand Indigenous people living in various regions of the country.[3]

After the Declaration of Independence, people had initially looked to their state assemblies for governance, but in 1787, delegates to the Constitutional Convention created a federal governance document, the US Constitution, which the states subsequently ratified in 1787 and 1788. The National Archives, the repository for the American government's documentary history, states the Constitution can best be described as a "colossal merger, uniting a group of states with different interests, laws, and cultures."[4]

Although urban centers like New York, Philadelphia, and Boston existed, most people lived either in small towns or in rural areas. In order to appease pro-slavery states, Congress decided the new federal government should be located in Washington, DC—not Philadelphia, where the Declaration of Independence had been signed and where the Constitutional Convention had taken place. Congress also authorized the construction of a capitol building to house the legislature and an executive residence for the president. John Adams was the first president to reside in the mansion. During the War of 1812, prompted by US grievances over British violations of sovereignty, impressment of American sailors, and support for Indigenous resistance to American westward expansion, the British burned the Capitol to the ground and heavily damaged the executive residence. However, both buildings had been rebuilt by 1818. Eight years later, as the United States prepared to celebrate its Jubilee, the nation was at peace, and though hardly an international power, it increasingly engaged European nations and their governments in trade and foreign affairs.

The Jubilee would be celebrated in different ways and for different reasons around the country. In lieu of coordinating with a central organizing body, cities and towns held their own celebrations. In Washington, DC, Congress worked with the city's mayor to organize a day of activities on July Fourth, but it did not even issue a national proclamation. Still, for many, especially those of an older generation, the Jubilee represented America's newfound standing as a sovereign nation; for others it highlighted America's economic opportunity and prowess, and if you were White and male, the Jubilee meant virtually unlimited freedom to live and work as you pleased. One thing is certain, the nation was changing: Its borders were expanding; cities were being built; innovation was underway; and the social order, while still almost as rigid as it had been in 1776, was being questioned in ways that were likely not apparent to the vast majority of Americans.

John Adams was surely pleased that his son, the president, was presiding over such a monumental event as the nation's Jubilee. Yet his view was likely not shared by many in the country, who believed that President John Quincy Adams only became the sixth president of the United States because of a "corrupt bargain."

Two years earlier, the younger Adams had faced off against Senator Andrew Jackson and two other candidates in the presidential election of 1824. The election marked the first time that a congressional caucus had not selected a major party's presidential nominee. Secretary of State

Adams simply declared his candidacy, but Senator Jackson, seeking a popular mandate, was nominated by the Tennessee legislature, whose members had been elected by voters. While not pure democracy, this change signaled a trend among new states to constitutionally provide for a more democratic process than had existed in 1789. Then, electors in the original thirteen states—some of whom had been popularly elected but most of whom had been appointed—chose George Washington as the nation's first president. Moreover, in a move that would have been considered radical during the Revolutionary War period, most states had abolished property requirements for voting and now provided for the popular election of delegates to the Electoral College.[5]

Adams and Jackson, the leading contenders in 1824, traded barbs in a hard-fought and often ugly campaign, waged not by the candidates themselves but rather by their supporters in the press and by surrogates in towns and cities across the country. Adams's backers hailed him as the candidate whose entire professional life had led him to this moment: Besides being the son of a former president, he had been a US senator, spoke seven languages, and had served as minister to Russia as well as secretary of state.

Jackson had gained recognition for his military exploits as the hero of the Battle of New Orleans in 1815, when he led his troops to a resounding victory against the British. Significantly outnumbered, he lost only a handful of men while the enemy suffered hundreds of fatalities in a brief but decisive battle for the strategic port. This stunning military triumph rekindled the sense of patriotism that had swept the country after Washington's victory over Charles Cornwallis at Yorktown. The nation celebrated Jackson as a hero, and many viewed him as George Washington's rightful successor.[6]

Three years later, in 1818, Jackson was again lauded for his leadership when he commanded a 3,000-man army against the Seminole Indians in Spanish-held Florida, ultimately leading to the transfer of huge swaths of

Native American territory to the United States. However, during the presidential campaign of 1824, Adams's supporters portrayed General Jackson as a mercurial and volatile personality: a military dictator-in-waiting. His past exploits were revisited and turned against him.

During the Seminole campaign, Jackson had executed two British agents, leading to a congressional investigation. In 1819, a number of prominent politicians, including Henry Clay, the powerful Speaker of the House, accused him of insubordination. After a lengthy inquiry, House investigators castigated Jackson as having engaged in "an unnecessary act of severity . . . and a departure from that mild and humane system . . . honorable to the national character." Clay, also a candidate for president in 1824, characterized Jackson's behavior as representing "a triumph of the military over civil authority—a triumph over the powers of this house—a triumph over the constitution of this land." Though the House ultimately refused to reprimand Jackson, as Clay had suggested, the two men were bitterly opposed to one another from that point forward.[7]

In response to the personal attacks against their candidate, Jackson's supporters criticized John Quincy Adams as an ineffectual and effete leader who had cozied up to America's perennial enemy, England. Rumors spread that Adams's father, the second president, had broken with him politically. This was false but difficult to refute, given the number of disparate news sources spread across the country and the time it took to correct misinformation in those days. John Quincy bristled at his opponents' hypocrisy, writing that his complaint was not "that attempts were made to tear my reputation to pieces" but that such slanders were "accompanied by professions of great respect and esteem."[8]

There was no single election day in 1824. Instead, votes accumulated through the autumn as citizens cast ballots for individuals or slates of electors who typically pledged to support a certain candidate in the Electoral College. In six states—Delaware, Georgia, Louisiana, New

York, South Carolina, and Vermont—legislatures chose the electors just as they had done in the first nine elections. But elsewhere—in eighteen of the twenty-four states—for the first time the popular vote determined the number of electoral votes allotted to each candidate. Some electors were not pledged to a specific candidate, while others were pledged but subsequently changed their minds.[9]

While the advent of the popular vote in the tenth presidential election signaled a democratizing trend, citizen participation was low. In Virginia, for instance, an estimated population of 625,000 cast only 14,955 votes. This was likely due somewhat to the novelty of a direct-vote election, but largely to the fact that only property-owning White males, twenty-one years of age or older, were allowed to vote. Still, in those states that tallied the popular vote, Andrew Jackson received nearly 8 percent more than Adams.

Although Jackson received more electoral votes than Adams, he failed to win an outright majority. Under the Twelfth Amendment—ratified in 1804 after an electoral tie between Thomas Jefferson and Aaron Burr four years earlier—the election reverted to the House of Representatives, where each state would cast a single vote to determine the winner. Henry Clay, who finished last in the electoral vote count but had nevertheless won Ohio, Missouri, and Kentucky, pulled out of the race for president and threw his support to Adams. Using his influence as Speaker of the House, he persuaded a majority of his House colleagues to support Adams's candidacy. Clay argued that a Jackson presidency would "give the strongest guarantee that the republic [would] march in the fatal road which has conducted every other republic to ruin."[10]

Clay's support for Adams proved decisive, as Adams picked up sufficient votes in the House to emerge as the winner of the election. While Jackson had significant policy differences with Adams, the two men had enjoyed a cordial and respectful relationship. Jackson reluctantly accepted the results of the House election and congratulated Adams on his victory. He then promptly resigned his seat in the Senate and returned to Tennessee.

John Quincy Adams was sworn in as the sixth president of the United States in March 1825. He was the first president to wear long pants instead of knee breeches and hose at his inaugural and, more importantly, the first to refer to the nation as a "democracy" in his maiden speech. Although his inaugural address was well received, Adams stumbled early in his presidency. In one of his first official acts, he appointed Henry Clay as his secretary of state, leading to charges that the two men had struck a deceitful deal: The allegation was that Adams had previously promised Clay the job of secretary of state in exchange for his support in the House of Representatives. Whether true or not—and it was almost certainly not true—the appearance of a quid pro quo proved harmful to Adams.[11]

The alleged corrupt bargain foreshadowed a presidency marked by political missteps. Nearly 200 years later, author and former Secretary of Education William J. Bennett captured not only the uneven and uncertain trajectory of the Adams presidency but also the essence of the man himself: "Few American presidents could surpass the towering intellect, the capacity for hard work, the personal integrity, the religious faith, and sincere devotion to his country. . . . But it is also true that few men have reached the presidency without developing at least some skills as a politician. John Quincy Adams was one of them."[12]

Not surprisingly, Andrew Jackson took exception to Adams's appointment of Clay. He deeply resented that Clay had questioned both his character and patriotism with regard to his actions during the Seminole War. When he learned that Adams had rewarded the Speaker with a plum position in his cabinet, Jackson's contempt for Clay intensified, and his scorn for Adams flared. According to historian Robert Remini, Jackson's "well-known temper blazed up in all its fury. He was seized with anger, convinced that he had been cheated of the Presidency by Adams and Clay."[13]

Although no longer in government, Jackson remained on the political stage. In fact, he began a well-orchestrated campaign to discredit the Adams administration. He wrote personal letters to friends and supporters around the country arguing that the Adams victory had been rigged and that the cabal with Clay represented an affront to the Constitution. Jackson's supporters in Congress took up the cudgel and amplified their leader's message at every opportunity. Senator John Randolph of Virginia was an especially loud and vociferous critic of Clay, calling him a "blackleg"—a cheating gambler—and causing the designee for secretary of state to challenge the senator to a duel, which ended with a minor injury to Randolph but did little to end the acrimony between him and Clay.[14]

President Adams, a former diplomat, and Clay, his secretary of state, had ambitious goals for the administration that extended beyond the borders of the United States. They viewed the United States as a beacon of freedom around the world, and during the Jubilee year, they sought to encourage democracy in Latin America. However, many in the country questioned the legitimacy of the Adams presidency—word of the "corrupt bargain" between Adams and Clay had spread—and his administration, now at its midpoint, had the feeling of a lame duck; Adams suffered defeat upon defeat in Congress, which extended to his foreign policy agenda as well.

President Adams was especially interested in building relations among the nations of the Western Hemisphere to act as a bulwark against European adventurism and interference. He endorsed Venezuelan Simon Bolivar's plan to create an inter-American congress for the newly independent nations of Latin America. However, US participation never materialized because the Senate delayed confirmation of Adams's nominees. Although Congress eventually approved delegates, one subsequently died and the other backed out, so that when the inter-American congress assembled in June 1826, just one month before the Jubilee, no US delegate was present. The US Congress then adjourned, neglecting to provide instructions for any potential future delegates, which historian George Herring later called "a fitting epitaph to a comedy of errors."[15]

Notwithstanding the lack of popular support for his administration, as the July Fourth Jubilee celebration drew near, John Quincy Adams prepared to honor the memory of his father and his father's contemporaries. He was fully aware that Andrew Jackson would once again challenge him two years hence and that the volatile Tennessean would likely mount an antiestablishment campaign rife with the kinds of personal character attacks that he had endured during his presidency. The president's father, John Adams, in his final letter to Thomas Jefferson, deplored the state of politics in 1826, observing that there appeared to be "perpetual chicanery and rather more personal abuse than there used to be." In particular, the elder Adams objected to the malevolence directed toward his son by Jackson and his supporters, especially those in Congress such as Senator Randolph. As Adams put it, "Our American Chivalry is the worst in the World. It has no Laws, no bounds, no definitions; it seems to be all a Caprice."[16]

More important than political chivalry in 1826, Jackson's denunciation of the electoral process and the flawed election of 1824 had called into question the institution of the presidency, a cornerstone of America's young democracy. Since the presidency of George Washington, the nation's process for electing the president had undergone significant changes, with the advent of a fledgling Electoral College, the abolition of property requirements for White males to vote, and campaigns that highlighted policy positions. However, the success of the American democratic experiment depended on the trust of the people, and for many that trust had been eroded. It was only the beginning of a more serious disintegration of confidence in government over another more highly charged issue: A little more than a quarter century later, the nation would divide over the issue of slavery.

As they sat on the porch at Peacefield, former President John Adams asked Mayor Quincy about progress on the first American railroad, a short length of track then under construction to carry granite from Boston to Bunker Hill in neighboring Charlestown. Adams hoped to see it completed before he died. The granite was needed for a monument being constructed to commemorate the battle fought on June 17, 1775, when his close friend Joseph Warren was killed during the siege of Boston.

Adams and fellow patriots like Warren had played a pivotal role in the birthing of the new nation. The railroad track to Bunker Hill was only a small reminder of the progress Americans had witnessed in the last fifty years. Nowhere was this more evident than in the increase in population, which had quadrupled since the first Fourth of July. More than 90 percent of the American people were still living on farms, but the spectacular development of industry following the War of 1812 was attracting more and more laborers to the northeastern cities.[17]

By 1826, the territory of the United States had expanded significantly: 1,749,462 square miles of land were under US jurisdiction—more than double the 864,746 square miles recorded in 1790. Growth was due largely to the Louisiana Purchase in 1803, which added more than 800,000 square miles of territory to the United States.[18]

Yet, in some important respects, the America of 1826 still resembled the America of 1776. Just as it had fifty years earlier, news in 1826 traveled by foot, wagon, horse, or sail. Wars were still fought mostly between soldiers on a battlefield. Women still could not vote. African Americans were still enslaved in much of the United States. Although Native Americans had signed a number of treaties with the US government, they were still commonly referred to as "savages" and would soon be subject to forced removals, which led to upheaval and suffering for many tribes.

At the same time, innovation was changing the ways many Americans established community and connected with one another. In his first annual message to Congress, John Quincy Adams had championed the building of a national transportation infrastructure. Canals were being built constantly in this period—no fewer than 102 projects were underway in various parts of the union—enabling commerce by water from cities in the Northeast all the way to New Orleans. One year before the Jubilee, on July 4, 1825, the Chesapeake and Delaware Canal was toasted as "a national work destined to produce incalculable national benefits" by Maryland Governor Samuel Stevens Jr. and other dignitaries at a dinner held in a hotel overlooking the Delaware River.

It had taken eight years, but the Erie Canal in upstate New York had also recently been completed. A revolutionary feat of engineering and labor, the Erie Canal connected the Hudson River to the Great Lakes, allowing goods to be transported by water across vast distances that not long before had required horse-drawn wagons over rugged terrain. The Marquis de Lafayette, who had visited the United States in 1824 on the invitation of President James Monroe, traveled 363 miles down the Erie Canal from Niagara Falls to the Hudson River at Albany. Perhaps the first indication that this feat of American engineering would not only accelerate the pace of industrial progress but also have a social impact came as word spread along the route of the general's voyage; people came out of their houses and farms to pay their respects and cheer the French hero of the American Revolution who fifty years earlier had so ably assisted the army of George Washington.[19]

In addition to changes in migration patterns, American Indians confronted an unsympathetic US Supreme Court and openly hostile state governments, especially in the South, where states' rights proponents abhorred federal treaty making as a violation of their sovereignty. In 1823, the US Supreme Court in *Johnson v. McIntosh* affirmed that Native nations could cede land to the federal government and that only the US government could in turn grant tribal jurisdiction over land. Yet Southern states viewed both the Court's and the federal government's power warily. During the Jubilee year, Savannah's most widely read newspaper, *The Georgian*, declared, "The protections guaranteed by the United States to the Nations of Indians . . . [are] unconstitutional . . . and a trespass of State sovereignty." Even though Cherokee leaders were educated in American schools and the tribe itself was recognized as one of the "Five Civilized Tribes" for embracing American institutions, Georgia's political leaders turned a blind eye when the state-sponsored Georgia Guard committed acts of violence against Cherokee. US Secretary of State John Calhoun warned Cherokee leaders in 1824 that it was impossible for them "to remain . . . as a distinct society or nation, within the limits of Georgia."[20]

Hostility to Indigenous peoples had existed for centuries and was widespread. Though few European Americans had much personal contact with "Indians," as Indigenous peoples were then commonly called, Native Americans were regarded with a mix of fear and fascination. The most celebrated writer of historical fiction was James Fenimore Cooper, whose novel *The Last of the Mohicans* was released during the Jubilee year to great fanfare and distributed widely across the country.

The book, set during the French and Indian War of 1754 to 1763 in colonial upstate New York, touches on a number of issues central to the changing attitudes of Americans in the early nineteenth century, including territorial expansion, the role of women in society, and national identity. But the most controversial themes of the book dealt with racial prejudice and race mixing.

Cooper tells the story of Alice and Cora Munro, daughters of a British colonel, who are making a treacherous voyage to visit their father, the commander of Fort William Henry in northern New York. They are escorted by the frontiersman Natty Bumppo (also known as Hawkeye), British Major Duncan Heyward, and the novel's title characters, Chingachgook and Uncas, who are the only two surviving members of the Mohican tribe.

Though the book is set during the French and Indian War, its principal characters are in many ways a reflection of American society at the Jubilee. Cooper offers stereotypical portraits of some of his characters, such as the helpless female and the noble savage. And the publication of *The Last of the Mohicans* roughly coincided with the forcible removal of Native Americans from their lands. During the administrations of Presidents James Monroe and John Quincy Adams, five Native nations—known in Washington, DC, as the "civilized tribes" and including Cherokee, Choctaw, Chickasaw, Creek, and Seminole—negotiated treaties with the US government concerning their landholdings. The Creek National Council, which had already relinquished twenty-two million acres to the government by the time of the Jubilee celebration, signed the Treaty of Washington in 1826, ceding the remainder of their land in Georgia in exchange for a onetime payment of $217,000, an annuity of $20,000 a year in perpetuity, and the promise of land west of the Mississippi.[21]

Only a few years later, in 1830, the United States, under the leadership of President Andrew Jackson, would begin the forced displacement of approximately 60,000 people of the "civilized tribes," a process that can only be described as ethnic cleansing. Over the next twenty years, thousands of Native Americans were uprooted and displaced.

Known as "The Trail of Tears," this tragedy dealt a devastating blow to Native American languages and cultural practices in the eastern United States. The narrative promoted by the US government at the time—that many Native Americans had either assimilated or disappeared—allowed settlers occupying former Indigenous lands to see themselves as the "original Americans." This perspective reinforced the myth of European ethnic and racial superiority.[22]

In 1826, at age ninety, John Adams was optimistic about the future. That day on his porch at Peacefield, he remarked to Mayor Quincy, "What wonderful improvements those will see in this country who live fifty years hence. But I am thankful I have seen those which have taken place during the last fifty." Adams also expressed a hope that he would be well enough to attend Quincy's oration on July Fourth in Boston.[23]

John Adams had indeed witnessed a number of "improvements" during his lifetime. Twenty years earlier, Robert Fulton, a former landscape painter, had revolutionized river transportation by opening America's rivers and waterways to more efficient commerce and trade with the invention of the steamboat. The *Clermont*, the first steamboat in public service, could travel 150 miles upstream from New York to Albany at an average speed of five miles per hour. That same year, Congress passed legislation enabling the construction of the nation's first multistate, federally funded highway, the Cumberland Road, which would be known as the "National Road." An even more significant development had been Eli Whitney's cotton gin, a machine that not only galvanized agrarian economies in the Southern states but more efficiently provided a steady stream of raw materials to new factories in the North.

Adams was also prescient in believing more sensational improvements were yet to come. Only months earlier Samuel Morey had patented the internal combustion engine (named the "gas or vapor engine"). Steam engines were in use in England, but the first fully functioning steam-powered locomotives wouldn't be brought into service in the United States for another three years, and railroads would not crisscross the country until after the Civil War. Samuel Morse would not invent the Morse Code until 1837 and would not receive a patent until 1840 for his telegraph system, which President Abraham Lincoln would use effectively to connect him to the battlefield operations in real time. Samuel Colt would not patent the revolver until 1839, ushering in the time when repeating rifles would transform the tools of war by permitting a greater number of rounds to be fired before reloading.[24]

Of course, improvements can be measured in many ways beyond technology and innovation. The hopes of the eighteenth-century revolutionaries had been realized on one level: Americans who had emigrated from Europe prior to 1776 were free, and there was growing prosperity. But the picture of general advancement was complicated by some mitigating factors. Many Americans felt abandoned. Since the first Fourth of July, divisions within the country had grown between urban and rural populations, between the economically advantaged and the disadvantaged, and between races.

The United States was experiencing a profound economic transformation, marked by the rise of industrialization and the emergence of a market economy. Factories were being rapidly constructed in cities across the Northeast and along the Great Lakes, transforming these regions into industrial hubs. Meanwhile, the South experienced a dramatic expansion of slavery. The cotton gin revolutionized cotton processing but also led to increased demand for enslaved labor; as a result, the Southern economy became even more deeply dependent on slavery. And while industrialization in the North often opened new opportunities—many young women left rural communities to work in textile mills in towns such as Lowell, Massachusetts, incorporated in 1826—the emerging capitalist economy also reinforced some preexisting inequities. For example, as men left home to work for wages in the "public sphere," unpaid housework performed primarily by women in the "domestic sphere"—cooking, cleaning, caring for children, and generally managing the home—was increasingly devalued, even though such work was economically significant.[25]

Despite the era's "free labor" rhetoric, which insisted that all men could rise from humble beginnings to achieve positions of authority and wealth with hard work, many laborers found the republican ideals of the American Revolution to be unattainable. To be sure, indentured servitude, apprenticeships, and many other vestiges of monarchism were just that by 1826—remnants of a colonial system that were rapidly disappearing as industrialization transformed Northern cities. Freed from the paternalistic obligation of apprenticeship or the legal subjugation of servitude, wage laborers could, in theory, work when and where they wanted. But they entered an impersonal economic world of employers and employees, bosses and workers, and owners and producers, where they worked, without social security or other modern benefits, long hours (sometimes thirteen a day, six days a week) for minimal pay, and where they could be hired and fired as the market dictated. The Panic of 1819, the first major economic depression in US history, had caused widespread unemployment. Many working Americans found themselves trapped in endless cycles of poverty, separated by a growing gap between them and wealthy business owners.[26]

Some workers organized unions to win higher wages and better working conditions. In 1825, a group of journeymen in Boston formed a carpenters' union to protest their inability "to maintain a family at the present time, with the wages which are now usually given." These early unionization attempts, though, often met with stiff opposition from employers, politicians, and prosecutors, who claimed that unions were unlawful combinations in restraint of trade. To workers, such claims, which usually prevailed in court and were based in part on English common law, hardly seemed consistent with the republican values unleashed by the American Revolution—all the more so because, in many cases, their forefathers had been among the tradesmen, mechanics, and farmers who had fought and died for those values while serving in General Washington's Continental army.[27]

The disjuncture between American ideals and the realities of American life was all too apparent to Philadelphia's *Mechanics' Free Press*, the first labor paper published in the United States. In an 1830 editorial titled "Fourth of July," the paper noted that whereas the working-class heroes of 1776 had ended foreign tyranny, an even greater and more insidious domestic foe remained in place: "monied aristocracy," which operated in tandem with crooked politicians and law-and-order jurists to make a mockery of the republican principle of government by and for the people. Working people, not the powerful interests who opposed them, were the true heirs of the spirit of '76, the paper claimed.[28]

The disconnect was also evident to an "Unlettered Mechanic" who in 1827 asked a group of working Philadelphians why "we, who bring wealth into existence, are deprived of the comfort it yields? Why are we reduced to poverty, slighted and despised by those who live at ease upon the products of our labor?" The answer was "easy," said the "Unlettered Mechanic," believed to be William Heighton, a twenty-seven-year-old shoemaker, who proceeded to explain how the mechanics, artisans, and laborers who had fought for liberty and equality had been systematically dispossessed of their gains by "the non-productive and accumulating classes" since laying down their arms in 1783. Working-class "degradation and oppression" had been handed down through the generations, he said, and would continue to grow deeper and more severe until such time as laborers came together to reclaim their rights.[29]

And the gap was clear to George Henry Evans, an editor who had been apprenticed to a printer in Ithaca, New York, after immigrating from England. Evans penned "The Working Men's Declaration of Independence." Inspired by Jefferson's Declaration, Evans's text held certain truths to be self-evident, namely, that all are created equal and endowed with unalienable rights. These rights, however, were threatened by "the undue influence of other classes of society," which produced "a long train of abuses and usurpations" that ended with "the oppression and degradation of one class of society."

"Therefore," Evans concluded, "we, the working class of society . . . do, in the spirit, and by the authority, of that political liberty which has been promised to us equally with our fellow men, solemnly publish and declare . . . 'that we are, & of right ought to be,' entitled to EQUAL MEANS to obtain equal moral happiness, and social enjoyment, and that all lawful and constitutional measures ought to be adopted to the attainment of those objects." Toward that end, the declaration pledged mutual support, forever more.[30]

But the workingmen's declaration did more than repeat the words of the Declaration; it expanded them to make a new statement on behalf of the interests of underserved Americans. In that regard, it marked the first of many alternative declarations of independence that would emerge over the next 200 years. Issued not just by trade unionists and labor groups but by farmers and women's rights advocates and abolitionists, these alternative declarations would hold the nation to account to the words of 1776. For they were more than just words: They arguably comprised America's single most concentrated expression of radical thought. And Americans returned to them, time and again, whenever change seemed necessary.[31]

Such populist critiques grew in response to financial swindles. By the early 1820s, thousands of small business corporations had been created, and a few of these were publicly traded. In July 1826, only days after the celebrations, six of the sixty-seven companies traded on the New York Stock Exchange would go out of business. Most of the companies that failed were new financial companies whose shares had risen dramatically in the previous two years. The founders of these firms disdained the more traditional and conservative mode of operation of many of New York's oldest banks. Instead, they borrowed tremendous sums of money to buy out other companies. Beyond the speculative nature of their business practices, they formed pyramid-like networks of companies—early versions of the Ponzi scheme—and used the money to enrich themselves. In a market downturn that began in 1825—partly as a result of a financial contagion that emanated from England—the value of their assets fell precipitously, and they resorted to fraudulent transactions among the companies they controlled to keep them solvent. Ultimately the investors and creditors of these firms lost millions. More significantly, news of corporate failures led to a run on banks and recession in the national economy.

Populist anger at perceived widespread "swindling" produced calls for criminal investigations to punish the "coldly calculating criminals" and clear out the "feculence of Wall Street." *The Weekly Register*, a national magazine published in Baltimore, opined, "If a negro steals a pair of shoes, away he must go to hard labor and solitary confinement—but if a gentleman violates his honor and oath, and boldly plunges into the vault of a bank or otherwise steals and carries off 50 or 100,000 dollars belonging to widows and orphans—he rides in a coach and eats and drinks of the best, and keeps 'the best' company."[32]

The impending Jubilee prompted some Americans to reflect on the previous fifty years and patriotically declare the United States to be exceptional. Yet one issue loomed larger than all the others, with profound economic and social implications: The generation that celebrated the Jubilee was also decidedly divided over the issue of race. According to historian John Hope Franklin, "Within fifty years after the Declaration of Independence was written, the institution of slavery, which received only a temporary reversal during the Revolutionary era, contributed greatly to the two worlds of race in the United States." The Declaration's expression of human rights appeared to have little effect, he said, on slaveholders and their apologists.[33]

Yet it was also a moment for new voices to reclaim the spirit that had once galvanized a fledgling band of revolutionaries in 1776. Among these new voices were two individuals from strikingly different backgrounds who pursued varied paths toward the goal of equality: Frances "Fanny" Wright and David Walker.

Born in Scotland in 1795, Frances Wright became an American citizen in 1825, a year before the Jubilee. Wright, orphaned at the age of two, and her younger sister lived with their great uncle, a professor at Glasgow College. As a young woman with access to the college library, Wright read Carlo Botta's history of the American Revolution (*Storia della guerra dell' Independenza degli Stati Uniti d'America*, 1809), a work admired by Thomas Jefferson. Against her uncle's wishes, she decided in 1818 to travel to America in order to observe how the ideals of the Declaration of Independence played out in reality. After two years in America, she moved to London, where she continued her education, and in 1821, while visiting Paris, Wright befriended the Marquis de Lafayette. Impressed by her intellect and charm, Lafayette invited Wright to join his upcoming tour of the United States in 1824—a celebrated journey that lasted for thirteen months and covered over 6,000 miles across the twenty-four states. During that time, she met America's leading statesmen, including Presidents James Monroe, Thomas Jefferson, John Adams, and Andrew Jackson.

After Lafayette's departure, Wright stayed on in America and became a citizen. Although Wright greatly admired American democracy,

Frances Wright, circa 1825. (Credit: J. Gorbitz and John Chester Buttre/Prints and Photographs Division, Library of Congress)

she abhorred slavery and was among the first women of note to speak out publicly against the institution. Deciding that she needed to lead by example, she obtained financial support from prominent figures both in the United States and abroad and in 1825 purchased a 2,000-acre tract of land about twenty miles outside Memphis, then a small Mississippi River trading post. Wright established a commune that she named Nashoba after the Chickasaw word for "wolf." Her goal was to create a model community to educate and then gradually free enslaved people.

Although Thomas Jefferson declined to offer financial backing, he expressed his moral support in a letter to Wright: "At the age of 82, with one foot in the grave and the other uplifted to follow it, I do not permit myself to take part in any new enterprises, even for bettering the condition of man. . . . Every plan should be adopted, every experiment tried, which may do something towards the ultimate object. That which you propose is well worthy of trial."[34]

Nashoba employed approximately thirty formerly enslaved people, who cultivated cotton for sale and grew food crops for their own needs. However, Wright's progressive vision quickly met resistance, fueled by her abolitionist views as well as her outspoken opinions on sexual freedom. In an article about Nashoba, she controversially described sexual passion as "the strongest and . . . the noblest of the human passions" and "the best source of human happiness"—a radical sentiment in an era when women were expected to publicly exhibit only innocence and purity. Further scandal enveloped Nashoba when a diary detailing interracial relationships, including one between a White trustee and a woman of color in the commune, became public, leading to widespread outrage and a loss of financial support.[35]

In the end, Wright proved to be more skilled as a social commentator than as a farmer or manager. She underestimated the immense labor involved in establishing and sustaining an agricultural community in an isolated region with a harsh climate. The farm yielded poor profits and ultimately failed. Wright later took the remaining enslaved population to Haiti and granted them their freedom.

During the Jubilee year, 1826, Wright contracted malaria and returned to Europe for medical treatment, but by 1828 she was back in the United States. On July Fourth she delivered a widely publicized speech in New Harmony, Indiana, a utopian community located not far from the banks of the Wabash River. In her remarks she referred to the Declaration of Independence as "one of the most beautiful inventions of the human intellect. It has been in government what the steam engine has been in mechanics, and the printing press in the dissemination of human knowledge." However, Wright referred to "negro slavery and the degradation of our coloured citizens" as an "evil . . . of immense magnitude." She urged Americans to use the Fourth of July as a time for honest reflection and reform: "It would be useful, if on each anniversary we examined the progress made by our species in just knowledge and just practice. Each Fourth of July would then stand as a tide mark in the flood of time, by which to note the rise and fall of each successive error, the discovery of each important truth, the gradual melioration in our public institutions, social arrangements, and, above all, in our moral feelings and mental views."[36] For Wright, the uniqueness of the United States lay in its ability to embrace change, which she argued allowed for the possibility of improvement.

A year later Wright relocated to New York City and became the first woman in America to edit a newspaper and the first to deliver a popular lecture series to audiences of both men and women. She continued to critique the imperfections of American democracy, condemning capital punishment, religious intolerance, and gender inequality. In championing equal education, legal rights for married women, and liberalized divorce laws, Wright cemented her legacy as a pioneering voice for social reform.

BOSTON, DESPITE BEING AN OVERWHELMINGLY WHITE CITY in which less than 5 percent of the population was Black, was in 1826 an emerging hub of the abolitionist movement. As such, the city served as a beacon for free Blacks such as David Walker, who had been born in Wilmington, North Carolina, to a free Black mother and an enslaved father.

As a young man, Walker left Wilmington and moved to Charleston, South Carolina, a major trading center at the time. With a population of approximately 25,000, Charleston boasted a busy harbor where ships arrived and departed daily carrying cargo destined for Boston, New York, and Philadelphia.

Charleston was, paradoxically, a center for upwardly mobile free Black Southerners as well as the South's hub for slave trading. Near the harbor was the Customs House where Blacks were bought and sold.

Behind the Customs House was another building known as the Sugar House, where slaves who had disobeyed or attempted to run away were beaten, tortured—and often killed.

While not a great deal is known about Walker's time in Charleston, he became affiliated with the African Methodist Episcopal (AME) Church. This first Black denomination in the United States counted among its followers a number of political activists. However, in 1822, after an all-White jury convicted Denmark Vesey, a free Black man, of planning a major slave revolt, city and state authorities clamped down on the activities of both enslaved and free persons of color.

At some point after the Vesey trial, Walker moved to Philadelphia, where the AME Church had been founded. At the time Philadelphia had the largest free Black population in the country, but there were nevertheless numerous instances of slave catchers from the South hunting down both escaped and freed slaves and selling them back into bondage. Walker would have undoubtedly been aware of these reports, but whatever the reason, he didn't stay long in Philadelphia and moved north to Boston. There he married Eliza Butler in 1826 and took a job selling used clothing. He also wrote for a Black-owned newspaper, *The Freedman's Journal*, becoming one of the most influential African American voices in the country.

Only three years after the Jubilee, when he was thirty-two years old, Walker published his famous pamphlet *Appeal to the Colored Citizens of the World*. In it, Walker called on African Americans to rise up in revolt against slave owners: "They want us for their slaves, and think nothing of murdering us. . . . [T]herefore, if there is an attempt made by us, kill or be killed . . . and believe this, that it is no more harm for you to kill a man who is trying to kill you, than it is for you to take a drink of water when thirsty." Fellow Bostonian and staunch abolitionist William Lloyd Garrison, in an editorial in his newspaper *The Liberator*, objected to Walker's embrace of violence.[37]

Walker, undoubtedly inspired by his time in Boston during the Jubilee, concluded the *Appeal* by quoting from the Declaration of Independence's list of grievances addressed to the British king and challenging his White readers, "Do you understand your own language? . . . Compare your own language above, extracted from your Declaration of Independence, with your cruelties and murders inflicted by your cruel and unmerciful fathers and yourselves on our fathers and on us. . . . Now, Americans! I ask you candidly, was your suffering under Great Britain, one hundredth part as cruel and tyrannical as you have rendered ours under you?"[38]

White Southerners were especially outraged by Walker's calls for a Black revolution. A number of states enacted laws banning circulation of "seditious publications." North Carolina's governor called the *Appeal* "totally subversive of all subordination in our slaves." The state legislature enacted the most repressive measures ever passed, including the prohibition of any written material considered likely to "incite revolution or resistance among black people." Outrage over the *Appeal* even led the state of Georgia to announce a reward of $10,000 for the capture and delivery of David Walker alive, and $1,000, if dead. Four years after the Jubilee, Walker was found dead in the doorway of the shop he owned on Boston's Beacon Hill. There was speculation that he had been murdered, but more likely he died of tuberculosis.[39]

In the nation's capital, a committee headed by Mayor Roger Weightman drew up plans for the Jubilee celebration. The mayor had invited to the ceremonies all living signers of the Declaration of Independence—Adams, Jefferson, and Carroll—as well as the former presidents James Madison and James Monroe. None was able to attend, but each one wrote a letter praising the American people and exalting the nation's progress over fifty years. Not surprisingly, Thomas Jefferson most eloquently captured both the spirit and importance of the coming anniversary. Jefferson remarked on the "consolatory fact that our fellow citizens, after a half century of experience and prosperity, continue to approve the choice we made." He predicted that the Jubilee would send "the Signal of arousing men to burst the chains, under which Monkish ignorance and superstition had persuaded them to bind themselves, and to assume the blessings and security of self-government," ultimately restoring "the free right to the unbounded exercise of reason and freedom of opinion." Jefferson concluded by expressing his hope for "the annual return of this day forever [to] refresh our recollections of these rights and an undiminished devotion to them."[40]

On the morning of July 4, 1826, volunteer military companies assembled in Lafayette Square, opposite the Executive Mansion, to salute President John Quincy Adams and his wife, Louisa. The volunteers then marched to the Capitol accompanied by the US Marine Band, followed by the president's carriage, cabinet members, and military and naval officers on horseback. Congress had been out of session for over a month, and most representatives had returned to their homes, but the floor of the House chamber and the gallery above were nevertheless overflowing with ordinary citizens, members of the military, and foreign guests. Though ladies had been permitted to take their seats early, gentlemen were obliged to wait until the procession informally entered the hall. The president entered the House chamber with Treasury Comptroller Joseph Anderson. After an opening prayer, Anderson read the text of the Declaration of Independence. Then Walter Jones, a prominent Washington attorney who during his lifetime would argue before the US Supreme Court more cases than any other attorney in American history, delivered a speech lasting nearly an hour. Despite Jones's reputed prowess as a courtroom lawyer, President Adams later described the address as consisting of "loose fragments without much connection."[41]

After the ceremonies at the Capitol, President and Mrs. Adams returned to the Executive Mansion and greeted guests—members of the general public—for several hours. One Washington newspaper praised the president for opening the doors of the mansion to the "citizens and strangers" who had brought up the rear of the Capitol procession that morning. After fulfilling his obligations as host, President Adams oversaw the planting of oak, hickory, and chestnut trees—long-held symbols of life, growth, and prosperity—around Washington.[42]

Elsewhere in America, the Jubilee was celebrated with pageantry, parades, and patriotic speeches. Citizens gathered in public parks, town squares, and meeting houses to listen to bands play patriotic music, watch fireworks, and hear local politicians offer toasts and read aloud the Declaration of Independence. The first performance of "The Star-Spangled Banner," played by the Marine Band, had occurred nine years earlier on July 4, 1817, at Marshall Garden in Philadelphia. The song, written by Francis Scott Key, a slaveholder and avowed racist, one night after witnessing British warships bombard Fort McHenry during the War of 1812, was set to the tune of a popular English drinking song, "To Anacreon in Heaven." The song originally had three verses and referred to Black Americans potentially siding with the British, warning that "no refuge could save the hireling and slave." The song had gained popularity in the South, but now it was sung or played at numerous celebrations in the North as well, including in New York, Annapolis, Pittsburgh, and Philadelphia.[43]

"Hail Columbia" also had become a standard tune performed on Independence Day in celebrations across the nation. First published in 1798 by Joseph Hopkinson, son of Francis Hopkinson, a signer of the Declaration of Independence, it competed with "The Star-Spangled Banner" for the distinction of national anthem throughout the nineteenth century. Music was also used as an accompaniment to fireworks.

One of the earliest events occurred in New York City four years before the Jubilee, when musical interludes were provided during the fireworks spectacle.

The drinking of patriotic toasts was an important celebratory function that occurred at Independence Day dinners. However, the ritual was strictly a male affair in 1826. Toasts were presented in a prescribed order: for example, toasts "to the day" of independence, to the country, and to the "heroes of 76," often followed by a final toast dedicated to females, who were commonly referred to as the "American fair." Although only very rarely did women initiate their own celebrations that included alcoholic toasts, they did play prominent roles in some events. The first published Independence Day address by a woman in the Washington, DC, area had occurred five years earlier, on July 4, 1821, at Market Square in Alexandria, Virginia, when Eletia Hubball spoke on the occasion of a flag presentation to the Alexandria Company of Light Infantry. She spoke about the responsibilities of the "citizen soldier" to uphold freedom and honor and never to be "tarnished with vice or immorality."[44]

At sunrise in Newark, New Jersey, July 4, 1826, began with "a merry peal" of church bells, followed by the thunder of a cannon salute. At 9 a.m. there was a parade of Revolutionary War veterans, only one of whom was reportedly in complete uniform "with a cockaded hat," though many wore "fragments of uniforms" and carried over their shoulders the muskets they had once used in war. The old soldiers led a procession that included ox teams hauling a fifty-foot obelisk to a site where it was erected as a monument to "Independence and Government." That night, residents gathered on the town common where they set ablaze thirteen barrels of tar and watched "a fine display of fireworks."[45]

In Boston, the birthplace of the American Revolution, Mayor Quincy gave a rousing oration punctuated by references to "our fathers' glory" and to their "labors and sacrifices." He termed the Fourth of July assembly "a solemn, and somewhat a religious duty." He painted, too, a vivid picture of fifty years past, though he himself was only a toddler then and unlikely to have remembered when "sentries with fixed bayonets [were] at the State-house doors;—while Boston was but a garrison; its islands and harbors, possessed by a vindictive and indignant foe . . . and the blood of its slaughtered citizens flowed, like water, in the streets." Few orations around the country that day were as unforgiving of the British, with whom Americans now enjoyed a businesslike, if not exactly warm, relationship.[46]

In the state capital of Albany, New York, several balloons emblazoned with patriotic messages were sent aloft just as soon as the ceremonial reading of the Declaration was complete. In New York City, the highlight of the day, according to *The New York American* newspaper, was a huge banquet table set up to entertain 800 citizens. There were "oxen, roasted whole, [which] filled the stomachs of the attendees," along with "an endless quantity of hams and loaves of bread, interspersed with barrels of beer and cider on tap."[47]

If Boston represented the birthplace of American democracy and New York celebrated with greater relish than any other city, Cincinnati was now the epicenter of America's westward expansion. The city's *National Crisis* newspaper had editorialized two weeks earlier that the power of the Jubilee ought to match the growth of the country. The West, having "arrived at a tolerable stage of permanency and security," ought somehow to be woven into the national creation story. In rain-soaked Cincinnati, the Declaration of Independence was read by a Mr. Looker, a survivor of the Revolution. Rain fell in Lexington, Kentucky, too, but this did not prevent the light infantry from parading at daybreak and firing a salute of fifty guns.[48]

One of the most poignant orations on July Fourth, 1826, was delivered by William Maynadier, a nineteen-year-old cadet who had finished third in his class and been selected to give the Jubilee oration at the United States Military Academy at West Point. "The Jubilee has come and found us—how? Does it find us as we were, when the glad tidings of Independence first went forth and through the land . . . ? No! What fifty years have ever witnessed greater improvements in science, literature, and politics?" He marveled that the United States "is advancing with rapid strides in power, wealth, and respectability. . . . The time will come when the world shall behold the blissful reality. The bright star that appeared first in our own horizon, is shining on with increasing effulgence."[49]

Notwithstanding the patriotic speeches, songs, fireworks, and toasts that added pomp and ceremony to the 1826 Jubilee, America's first fifty-year celebration would be remembered chiefly for the deaths of Thomas Jefferson and John Adams.[50]

On July 3, 1826, Daniel Webster, at the time a US congressman from Massachusetts, visited John Adams at Peacefield. The ninety-year-old former president, clad in a cotton dressing gown and cap, spoke so softly that he could barely be heard. But his mind was still sharp. Webster asked Adams how he was feeling, and Adams replied, "Not very well. I inhabit a weak, frail, decayed tenement, battered by the winds and broken in upon by the storms, and, from all I can learn, the landlord does not intend to repair."[51]

Five hundred miles away, in Charlottesville, Virginia, Thomas Jefferson, the eighty-three-year-old third president of the United States, had been confined to his bed at his Monticello estate for several weeks and was near death. On July 3, Jefferson's personal physician offered him opiate laudanum for pain, but the former president refused because the drug had previously made him delirious.[52]

Drifting in and out of consciousness during the night, Jefferson awoke at approximately 7 p.m. "Is it the Fourth?" Jefferson reportedly asked in a "husky and indistinct voice." His doctor replied, "It soon will be." Assured that he had lived to witness the fiftieth anniversary of the signing of his masterpiece, the Declaration of Independence, Jefferson closed his eyes. He awoke several hours later but was unable to speak, and at approximately 11 a.m. on the Fourth, he died in his sleep.[53]

The same morning, John Adams had been awakened by the sound of a bell ringing and a cannon firing. A servant asked the former president if he knew what day it was, and Adams replied, "O yes, it is the glorious Fourth of July—God Bless it—God bless you all." Later that morning, Adams had another visitor, the Reverend John Whitney, who was scheduled to deliver an oration that day in Adams's hometown of Quincy. Whitney asked Adams for a "sentiment" to be read honoring the occasion, and the former president declared, "Independence forever."[54]

At some point just prior to his death at approximately 5 p.m., Adams, unaware that his longtime friend and collaborator had passed away at Monticello, is reputed to have stated, "Jefferson survives!"—though the exact hour is not known, or who was present, or, indeed, if Adams even uttered these precise words. What is certain is that two giants of the American Revolution, who together were more responsible for producing the Declaration of Independence than any of the other founders (save perhaps Benjamin Franklin, who had died years before), passed away on the fiftieth anniversary of the formal adoption of the document in Congress. The deaths of the nation's second and third presidents, only hours apart, together formed undoubtedly the most extraordinary event of the Jubilee—and perhaps of any July Fourth anniversary.[55]

President John Quincy Adams learned of Thomas Jefferson's death on July 6. Three days later, aware that his own father had been gravely ill, President Adams set out to visit him in Massachusetts. After stopping for breakfast in Baltimore, the president learned from an innkeeper that his father had died on the afternoon of July 4. The president did not reach Quincy until July 13. The funeral had already taken place on July 7.[56]

Back in Washington, Secretary of War James Barbour delivered the extraordinary news that Jefferson's demise occurred at the same hour of the day that the Declaration of Independence was read in Congress fifty years earlier.[57]

ON AUGUST 2, 1826, THE CITY OF Boston observed the deaths of Jefferson and Adams: Flags were lowered to half-staff, businesses closed, and the bells of the North Church tolled. Americans were saddened but also stunned by the coincidence. How could two former presidents, two signers of the Declaration of Independence, separated by hundreds of miles, have died within such close temporal proximity to one another? What did it mean? Daniel Webster delivered a two-hour eulogy at Faneuil Hall in which he called their deaths on July 4 an "epic consummation." Webster claimed that the deaths were "proofs that our country, and its benefactors, are objects of His care." Besides Webster's view of divine intervention, there were also conspiracy theories around the deaths of Adams and Jefferson. In a letter to a friend, Senator John Randolph, writing from The Hague, falsely, and inexplicably, labeled Adams's death as "Euthenasia," equally fallaciously adding, "They have killed Mr. Jefferson, too, on the same day, but I don't believe it." Most Americans, however, probably saw the deaths of Adams and Jefferson as neither a sign from God nor some insidious plot but rather as a poignant reminder that a small band of Americans had fought for their freedoms and had persevered.[58]

"No document in American history has shaped the world so decisively as the Declaration of Independence," writes historian David Armitage, who has traced how the text's language of rights has animated movements for independence, autonomy, and liberation across the globe, turning the United States into a widely accepted symbol of freedom. Submitted to a "candid World," the Declaration had inspired more than twenty states or provinces in the Caribbean, the Americas, and Europe to issue declarations of their own by the time Jefferson died in 1826. "We, the representatives of the United Provinces of South America, assembled in General Congress," began Argentina's declaration, issued in July 1816.[59]

Despite its enormous contributions to the nation and, indeed, the world, the work of Adams and Jefferson remained unfinished. In many ways, July 4, 1826, represented nothing more than a way station in the nation's development as a democracy. During the country's first fifty years, Americans had built new machines, created infrastructure, and found new methods of transportation; this spirit of innovation would continue, sometimes at a dizzying pace. However, the challenges that confronted America at the Jubilee would also persist and would bedevil the lofty goals of "Life, Liberty and the pursuit of Happiness" set forth in the Declaration of Independence. The processes for political elections and the conduct of campaigns would evolve—though not always in a positive direction, as the outcome of elections, similar to the one in 1824, would sometimes be contested. The divisive matter of race, which the founding fathers had tried to sidestep, would emerge as the seminal issue during the next fifty years. Women would continue to be treated as second-class citizens, and Native Americans would be cheated, lied to, and deprived of their ancestral lands. Yet Adams and Jefferson, though imperfect, had nobly served their country. The country's failings would not be addressed for several more decades but would reach a watershed moment with the outbreak of the Civil War. Then new heroes would emerge—men such as Abraham Lincoln, Frederick Douglass, and Ulysses S. Grant and women such as Elizabeth Cady Stanton—to help shape the next fifty years of America's journey.[60]

3

Centennial

> The history of our country the past hundred years has been a series of assumptions and usurpations of power over woman, in direct opposition to the principles of just government, acknowledged by the United States as its foundation.
>
> —NATIONAL WOMAN SUFFRAGE ASSOCIATION (1876)[1]

ON APRIL 14, 1876, AS THE NATION prepared to celebrate its Centennial in a little more than two months, President Ulysses S. Grant, members of Congress, and justices of the Supreme Court were among the hundreds of guests who gathered for the dedication of the first public memorial for Abraham Lincoln in Washington, DC.

Frederick Douglass, the prominent leader of the movement for African American civil rights, stepped up to the plain, wooden podium in Lincoln Park, on Capitol Hill, to offer remarks and reminiscences about the president who had been assassinated eleven years earlier. Although he didn't say so at the time, Douglass didn't care much for the life-size bronze sculpture that depicted Lincoln extending one hand over a kneeling African American man while holding the Emancipation Proclamation in the other. Douglass felt the sculpture was patronizing and ignored the role Black Americans had played in abolishing slavery in the United States.[2]

Douglass had first met Lincoln in 1863 when he visited the White House to complain to the president that Black soldiers fighting in the Union army were not receiving equal pay and were being denied promotions. A former slave, he remembered that Lincoln had warmly greeted him: "I know who you are, Mr. Douglass. . . . Sit down. I am glad to see you."[3]

The president was undoubtedly aware of Douglass's abolitionist past, including his much-heralded speech on July 5, 1852, to the Ladies Anti-Slavery Society of Rochester, New York. Douglass had been invited to give a July Fourth speech but opted instead to speak on the following day as a form of protest. Addressing an audience of several hundred, Douglass delivered one of the most iconic speeches of his long career. He famously posed the question, "What to the American slave is your Fourth of July?" Douglass then answered, "A day that reveals to him, more than all other days in the year, the gross injustice and cruelty to which he is the constant victim."[4]

Douglass had previously referred to Lincoln as "emphatically the black man's president," but at the memorial dedication in 1876, he surprised the audience by calling Lincoln "preeminently the white man's President." His sobriquet for the slain president appeared to be a stark revision of his past praise, but he was making a subtler point: Douglass asserted that Lincoln "was ready and willing at any time during the first years of his administration to deny, postpone, and sacrifice the rights of humanity in the colored people to promote the welfare of the white people of this country." However, he also noted that Lincoln "came into the Presidential chair upon one principle alone, namely, opposition to the extension of slavery." Aware that President Grant was in the final months of his presidency, Douglass worried about the possible rollback of Reconstruction, the policy that reintegrated the Confederate states into the Union and, more importantly to Douglass, sought to ensure that former slaves enjoyed the same rights and legal protections as all American citizens. At the memorial for Abraham Lincoln, Douglass undoubtedly wanted the assembled to know that as the nation prepared to celebrate its accomplishments over the past 100 years, the job of making Black Americans free and equal was far from complete.[5]

In 1876 the United States was a very different country from what it had been at its founding: The nation's growth and progress had been nothing short of astronomical. Whereas there had originally been thirteen colonies, by 1876 there were thirty-seven states, with Colorado poised to enter the Union as the thirty-eighth. The nation's land area had grown to almost 3 million square miles, more than three times the 864,746 square miles measured in 1790. Due to the arrival of millions of immigrants, a population of 2.5 million in 1776 had mushroomed to more than 46 million. Even more noteworthy than America's size and population was the country's rapid economic expansion, industrialization, and urban growth. During the colonial era, the US economy had been overwhelmingly agricultural, and Britain traded more with its colonial islands in the Caribbean than with its colonies in North America. However, by 1876 manufactured goods helped push the gross national product to $7.4 billion. Largely due to the expansion of railroads, which brought remote parts of the country into a national market economy, commerce was flourishing. In Chicago, trade amounted to $450 million annually. Eighty thousand miles of telegraph line now crisscrossed the country, and in New York City alone Western Union employed more than 300 operators during the day and 100 at night. American ingenuity and hard work had produced a land of economic plenty, leading to a class of wealthy industrialists, a burgeoning middle class, and a robust working class.[6]

Notwithstanding America's enormous economic expansion during the previous 100 years, the administration of President Ulysses S. Grant, the nation's eighteenth president, confronted a number of significant challenges in 1876. A deep economic depression had taken root three years earlier; known as the "Long Depression," the trouble started in Vienna, Austria, with the collapse of an economy pumped up by a rash of speculative money. The financial ripples rapidly spread across the Atlantic, causing, in part, the failure of Jay Cooke & Company, one of the largest financial enterprises in the United States. Soon the panic spread to other banks in Washington, DC, Pennsylvania, New York, Virginia, and Georgia, as well as the Midwest, including Indiana, Illinois, and Ohio. In all, more than 100 banks failed, leading to a nationwide economic depression.[7]

An even greater challenge confronting the United States in 1876 was the bitter legacy of the Civil War that had claimed the lives of more than 600,000 Americans and led to the destruction of countless homes and whole towns and cities, predominantly in the South. Perhaps even more worrisome than the regional destruction and economic disparity between North and South was the fact that notwithstanding the end of the devastating war a decade earlier, many Southerners continued to resent—and resist—the growing power of the national government in Washington, DC.[8]

Although Lincoln's presidency shaped American society in many ways, his policy of Reconstruction marked a turning point that ended a century of Black enslavement and profoundly transformed the nation's legal, economic, and political landscape.

In his annual message to Congress, submitted on December 8, 1863, Lincoln announced a policy of amnesty and reconstruction, offering to all rebels, with the exception of high-ranking Confederate officers, a "full pardon . . . with restoration of all rights of property . . . except as to slaves." He promised to readmit and recognize state governments if only 10 percent of all citizens in the state pledged allegiance to these terms.[9]

Lincoln's relationship with Native Americans was more complex and problematic. Lincoln had served as a militia captain in the Black Hawk War of 1832, but his views of Indigenous people were likely affected by the murder of his grandfather, whom he never knew: Abraham Lincoln Sr. was killed by Shawnee in Kentucky in 1786 as Lincoln's father, then only eight years old, watched. During his debates with Stephen Douglas in 1858, Douglas had declared the Declaration of Independence did not include "the savage Indians," but Lincoln responded that he believed "the authors of that noble instrument had included all men." Only three years later, however, President Lincoln, in a meeting with nine chiefs representing different Native nations, declared, "There is no way in which your race is to become as numerous and as prosperous as the white race except by living as they do, by the cultivation of the earth."[10]

BY 1876, GRANT WAS NEARING THE END of his second term in the White House. First elected in 1868, the president had been preoccupied with fulfilling Lincoln's policy of Reconstruction. He committed to using the full force of his government to ensure that Southern states readmitted to the Union had abolished slavery and that African Americans enjoyed the rights and privileges afforded to all under the Constitution. But the policy met with stiff resistance from White nationalists who launched armed attacks on African American communities. Reconstruction became not only a law enforcement mission but a military one as well: Grant recalled twelve companies of the 7th Cavalry from the West and deployed them throughout the South, where they worked alongside federal marshals to combat the rise of White supremacist organizations such as the Red Shirts and the Ku Klux Klan.[11]

During the first three years of the Grant administration, federal prosecutors indicted more than 3,000 Klansmen, a third of whom were convicted and jailed, often by mixed-race juries. Nevertheless, many Southerners continued to resist Grant's edicts and to defy the Constitution. The United States remained a deeply divided nation, and the South, a deeply segregated region. Nowhere was this more evident than in South Carolina, where twenty-one-year-old Ben Tillman committed himself to reversing what he viewed as the scourge of Grant's policy of Reconstruction.[12]

Tillman, born in Edgefield County to parents who owned a plantation and kept slaves, was an avowed racist who believed in the inherent inferiority of African Americans. At age sixteen in 1863, he had traveled to Georgia where he witnessed "death scenes and the horrors of war." Tillman hoped to join Edgefield's Company K of the Fourteenth South Carolina Volunteers, part of the Confederate army. But in 1864, after being diagnosed with a cranial tumor, Tillman was hospitalized with fever and convulsions. Gravely ill, he underwent an operation, and while surgeons were able to remove the tumor, Tillman lost his left eye. Nonetheless, he remained defiant and wrote of his "hatred and intense feeling of animosity toward those invaders of our homes and destroyers of our liberty," concluding, "They ought to be shot."[13]

That same year, 1864, an obscure professor named John Lyle Campbell from Wabash College in Indiana delivered a presentation at the Smithsonian Institution in Washington, DC, on the life and teachings of Galileo. As it turned out, his speech commemorating the 300th anniversary of the birth of the Italian astronomer would have an enormous impact on how Americans viewed themselves during the second half of the nineteenth century.[14]

Campbell, the son of a wealthy merchant, had graduated from Wabash in 1848. Five years later, after earning a master's degree in physics and a law degree, Campbell joined the Wabash faculty and taught physics, mathematics, and astronomy. He married a local woman and settled into a quiet and comfortable life of academia. Then, at 4:30 a.m. on April 12, 1861, the country came apart: Confederate troops fired on Fort Sumter in South Carolina's Charleston Harbor, and the next day Union forces surrendered. The Civil War had commenced.

Three days later, on April 15, President Lincoln, determined to quell the insurrection, called for a total of 75,000 volunteers to join the Union army. Governor Oliver P. Morton of Indiana immediately telegraphed to the president that Indiana pledged 10,000 volunteers to the fight, and several Wabash College students and faculty enlisted. Campbell, however, was one of only a handful of professors who continued to teach the few dozen male students who remained at Wabash. Convinced that the war was a glorious cause, Campbell nevertheless abhorred the widespread loss of life and worried what the great divisions within the population would mean for the future of the country.

Perhaps with this in mind, in his 1864 speech at the Smithsonian, Professor Campbell described Galileo as an astronomer, a physicist, and, significantly, an inventor who had worked in applied science and technology. Campbell was encouraged that during the Civil War a number of new inventions had emerged and taken root, including photography, the telegraph, and railroads. Almost as an aside in his speech in Washington, he mused to his audience that the United States should find a way to celebrate those new technologies as scientific advances that might bind people together wherever they lived.

In December 1866, Campbell decided to approach the mayor of Philadelphia, Morton McMichael, with a bold idea: a centennial exhibition to be held in the City of Brotherly Love in 1876 both to honor the

100th anniversary of the Declaration of Independence and to heal the nation in the aftermath of war. Campbell argued that the United States was experiencing a period of extraordinary innovation that would change the world: He envisioned a world's fair that would be about the nation's future rather than its divisive and bloody recent past. He noted that Philadelphia not only had been the setting for the signing of the Declaration of Independence in 1776 but had recently hosted the Great Central Fair of 1864, which had attracted tens of thousands of visitors.[15]

The concept of a world's fair was not particularly novel. Indeed, the first world's fair dated back to the end of the eighteenth century when Napoléon Bonaparte planned a national festival to celebrate his conquest after the 1797 Italian campaign. Later, various governments in France had used fairs to introduce new industries and encourage old ones. But Great Britain had improved on the French model by opening its doors in its 1851 fair to everyone in Europe, making it the first international exposition. America's Centennial fair would say a lot about how elites, principally East Coast politicians, bankers, and businessmen, viewed the nation in 1876.[16]

Mayor McMichael, a former police magistrate who had fought on the Union side at Gettysburg, wholeheartedly endorsed Campbell's vision. Although he left office only three years later, he both seeded and popularized the idea of a world's fair in Philadelphia with city government, with the city's business community, and with Pennsylvania's representatives in the US Congress. Ultimately, Congress established a national commission—with Campbell as its treasurer—to oversee planning and construction of a Centennial world's fair at Fairmount Park, a huge tract of land that encompassed some 2,800 acres on the outskirts of Philadelphia. While Congress did not initially provide federal funding, the commission raised over $11 million—the equivalent today of nearly $333 million. Construction for the fair began on July 4, 1873.[17]

The Centennial Exhibition at Fairmount Park was originally scheduled to open in April 1876 marking the 101st anniversary of the Battles of Lexington and Concord at the start of the Revolutionary War. However, construction delays caused the date to be pushed back to May 10. Although not likely considered by the exhibition's sponsors, the new date also had historical significance unrelated to the signing of the Declaration of Independence: A decade earlier, on May 10, only one year after the Civil War ended, the Eleventh National Women's Rights Convention had met in New York City to discuss what many viewed as a unique opportunity to rally for fundamental change and women's equality. One of the leaders was Elizabeth Cady Stanton, who, along with other women's rights leaders, primarily from the northeastern United States, had joined forces with leading abolitionists.

Born in 1815 in Johnstown, New York, Elizabeth Cady was one of eleven children. She excelled in both primary and secondary school and wanted to attend college, but at the time no institution of higher learning accepted female students. Although her father, a judge, was extremely conservative, he bought her law books so that she could participate in debates with his law clerks at the dinner table. In 1840, Cady married a prominent abolitionist, Henry Brewster Stanton, in a ceremony in which she refused to include the word *obey* as part of her vows. She began to speak out for women's rights and in 1848 helped organize the Seneca Falls Convention, considered the first major conference convened for the sole purpose of discussing women's rights. At the convention, Stanton declared, "We hold these truths to be self-evident: that all men and women are created equal."[18]

The National Women's Rights Convention officially merged with the American Anti-Slavery Society in 1866 to form the American

Equal Rights Association (AERA). Given the political climate in the South, the AERA was split over whether Black male suffrage should take precedence over universal suffrage. Some worried that political support for freedmen would be undermined by the pursuit of women's suffrage. AERA member Frederick Douglass insisted that the ballot was literally a question of life or death for Black men.[19]

May 10 held quite a different meaning for many White Southerners, especially the members of the Ladies Memorial Associations (LMAs)—again, a meaning completely unrelated to the signing of the Declaration of Independence. The women affiliated with the LMAs led the effort to memorialize the Confederate dead, praising their bravery and virtuousness through nationalist speeches and the erection of memorials. These women imagined new holidays during which White Southerners could reaffirm their allegiance to the Confederacy and express their opposition to Black rights. Many Southerners commemorated May 10, 1863, the anniversary of General Thomas J. "Stonewall" Jackson's death. Jackson, one of the Confederacy's most revered generals, and his troops had terrorized Union commanders during the first two years of the war. However, during the Battle of Chancellorsville in Virginia in May 1863, Jackson's own troops accidentally shot him, and one week later he died of complications due to pneumonia. Soon thereafter Jackson attained the status of hero and martyr in the South. Decades later, 50,000 people would attend the dedication of a seventeen-foot-high statue of Jackson in Richmond, Virginia, the first such statue to honor a Confederate general.[20]

President Grant, preoccupied with his policy of Reconstruction in the South, had not really focused on the upcoming Centennial fair. There is no written record of how he viewed the arc of America's first 100 years, though he did reply to two letters that referenced the impending celebration. When he received a congratulatory letter on America's achievement from the city council of Birmingham, England, the president penned a short note expressing his appreciation for the continuing "ties of kindred and interest" between the United States and Great Britain. And when he received an invitation from the United States Centennial Commission in late 1875 to open the World's Fair in Philadelphia, he replied simply that he would be honored to do so.[21]

~

DURING THE MONTH OF APRIL, CONSTRUCTION CREWS made final preparations for the opening of the Centennial fair, feverishly painting surfaces, laying floorboards, and installing glass windows and lighting fixtures in the more than 200 buildings at Fairmount Park. Two miles east, ground crews were also busy at the much smaller Jefferson Street Grounds, preparing for opening day of the National League baseball season. They resodded the field, erected a ten-foot, vertical-slatted fence, and built a pair of tiered pavilions abutting home plate.

The Jefferson Street Grounds ballpark was situated in a Philadelphia neighborhood called Brewerytown, near the Schuylkill River, and surrounded mostly by farms. *The Philadelphia Evening Bulletin* referred to the area as "a place for family bakeries and rich delicatessens, a neighborhood scrubbed to within an inch of its life and resounding to the guttural language of Goethe and Schiller." Streetcar lines provided the neighborhood with public transit, bringing fans to and from the ballpark.[22]

The park had been used for baseball since 1864 by White clubs, but in 1869 the first interracial baseball game between nationally prominent teams was played at the Jefferson Street Grounds: The Olympic Ball Club, an all-White team, and the Philadelphia Pythians, an all-Black team, squared off against one another. However, in 1876 the Pythians were not included in the newly constituted National League. Every player on each of the eight league teams was White.

On Saturday afternoon, April 22, the first ever National League game was played. By some estimates, as many as 3,000 fans packed the stadium. Every other National League game that day was rained out. In a game that lasted two hours and five minutes, Boston beat the Philadelphia Athletics 6–5. A combined twenty-six errors were committed.[23]

WHEN THE MORNING OF MAY 10, 1876, finally arrived, the sky was gray and overcast, but the torrential rain of the previous day had subsided. Workers had strewn yellow straw around the fairgrounds so that visitors, thousands of whom had been waiting for hours to enter, would not slip and slide in the mud.[24]

Drawing lessons from the failure of the Vienna exhibition a decade earlier, the twenty-six-year-old, Austrian-born chief architect of the fair, Herman Schwarzmann, had made certain the Philadelphia exposition would be easily accessible to the hordes of visitors. Dozens of hotels had sprung up in and around Philadelphia and within walking distance of Fairmount Park, including the grand United States Hotel, which charged $4 a night, including meals, and boasted 324 rooms, and the Hotel Aubrey, which operated on a European plan, charging a fixed rate for its 400 rooms; meals were extra. In addition to providing transportation to the fair by trolley, streetcar, and even docking facilities on the Schuylkill River, both the Pennsylvania and the Reading Railroads had laid track adjacent to entrances along the perimeter of the grounds. Trains departed New York City for Fairmount Park every thirty minutes, highlighting the nation's economic transformation, which had culminated with the completion of the nation's first transcontinental railroad in 1869.[25]

Once the gates at Fairmount Park swung open at 9 a.m. sharp, eager ticket holders poured through the turnstiles, quickly turning the golden straw on the pathways into a wet and matted black carpet. All day long droves of men, women, and children arrived to celebrate the first 100 years of the United States.

A fence nearly three miles long surrounded the more than 200 buildings constructed within the exposition's grounds. Five main buildings—the Main Exhibition Building, Memorial Hall, Agricultural Hall, Horticultural Hall, and Machinery Hall—housed nearly half of the fair's 30,000 exhibits. There were separate buildings celebrating each state's achievements, many others dedicated to foreign countries, and even a few that showcased corporate interests. The presence of so many buildings in one exposition set it apart from previous fairs around the world, which had relied on having one large building, or perhaps a few.[26]

While critics found little architectural harmony in the exposition, everyone agreed that the sheer scale and size of the achievement was impressive. Machinery Hall enclosed an area of more than 550,000 square feet. It had been constructed with 5 million board feet of lumber, 500,000 pounds of wrought iron, 750,000 pounds of cast iron, 7 million pounds of tin roofing, 6,000 perch of stone, and 175,000 pounds of double-thick, first-quality American glass.[27]

At 10 a.m., President Grant arrived with his wife, Julia, by horse-drawn carriage.

The president had been looking forward to this day of celebration—he was in the last year of his presidency, and the previous months had been stressful and at times downright unpleasant. In addition to the ongoing economic depression, political scandal had marred his administration. He was also facing challenges in the South, where White supremacists continued to flout the law and deny Black Americans their civil rights, as well as in the West, where Native Americans in the Dakota territory refused to sell their land to the government to make room for westward expansion. Grant's administration had previously given Native nations broad assurances that their ancestral lands would not be taken from them. However, as more and more settlers and miners flooded westward, the president decided that he would have to resettle many of the Indigenous groups. Only two days before arriving in Philadelphia, on May 8, he had tapped Lieutenant Colonel George Armstrong Custer to lead a campaign against the Sioux. In truth President Grant didn't much like Custer, who only a month earlier had publicly accused the president's friend and secretary of war, William Belknap, of taking bribes in the awarding of government contracts. However, Custer, a flamboyant self-promoter with a reputation as an Indian fighter, had a large following throughout the country. Grant likely thought to himself, at least Custer would be 1,000 miles away from Washington, DC.[28]

There to greet President and Mrs. Grant at the entrance of the exposition was the First Troop Philadelphia City Cavalry, a volunteer unit first organized in 1774 for defense of the colonies. Sitting astride magnificent steeds and smartly turned out in blue tunics, white breeches, and plumed helmets, the cavalry escorted the Grants to the Main Exhibition Building, where they were joined by Brazil's Emperor Dom Pedro II and Empress Teresa Cristina.

The presence of the emperor and his wife represented the first-ever visit by a reigning monarch to the United States. While generally favorably viewed, the imperial visit was not without controversy. The original invitation to visit the United States had come in 1871 from Louis Agassiz, a Swiss naturalist, zoologist, and professor at Harvard University. Agassiz had been a proponent of scientific racism, which posited interracial marriage as the main contributor to the decay of the human race. Brazil, the final destination for half of all enslaved Africans brought across the Atlantic, had the dubious distinction of being the last slaveholding nation in the Western Hemisphere.[29]

Before attending the Centennial's opening ceremony in Philadelphia, the emperor had traveled to every region of the United States.

Huge crowds had greeted his train in Chicago as he set out for a trip to the West six weeks earlier. Newspaper coverage had been extensive and overwhelmingly favorable. The emperor, or perhaps his courtiers, had the savvy to avoid any discussion of race relations—either those in their country or in the United States. The emperor's attendance at the Centennial fair was meant to be the capstone of his trip. His representatives tried to brush off questions about slavery in Brazil by claiming that the institution was "imposed by the force of circumstances" and "sure to disappear in a few years." Instead, Dom Pedro concentrated on boosting sales of his nation's most important commodity: coffee. A consortium of coffee distributors had prepared a pamphlet for the occasion that described Brazil "as an agricultural region possessing an extremely fertile soil" and Brazilians as "a peaceful, intelligent, and laborious people."[30]

AMONG THE PARTICIPANTS AT THE OPENING CEREMONY was Frederick Douglass. During the post–Civil War period, Douglass had been disappointed in his hope to be named US marshal for the District of Columbia, but for his service to the Republican Party, he received various political and diplomatic appointments, including US minister to Haiti.

Notwithstanding his prominence, Douglass was almost barred from entering the gallery on a stage reserved for guests of honor. The Philadelphia police monitoring the entrance simply had no idea who he was and had clearly been told not to allow Blacks to enter the VIP area. Douglass showed the police his ticket, but they still refused him admission. Eventually, US Senator Roscoe Conkling recognized Douglass and beseeched the guards to allow him to pass, causing the crowd in the gallery to erupt in applause. Douglass had barely taken his seat when the first chords of the Brazilian anthem were heard and applause broke out again—this time for the emperor entering the same stage arm in arm with Empress Teresa Cristina.[31]

After the guests were seated, an orchestra performed the anthems of more than a dozen foreign countries, closing with "Hail Columbia," the popular anthem often played during the Jubilee celebration fifty years earlier. The orchestra then performed "Centennial Inauguration March," which was dedicated to the Women's Centennial Executive Committee and written by renowned German composer Richard Wagner, who had been paid $5,000. Wagner was known for his operas, and his work sounded more like a dirge than a celebratory anthem. The orchestra's tempo picked up with the playing of a "Centennial Hymn," written by poet John Greenleaf Whittier. Then a thousand-voice choir sang various selections, ending with the "Hallelujah Chorus." Finally General Joseph R. Hawley, president of the United States Centennial Commission and a former US senator, stood to address the crowd. Before introducing President Grant, Hawley falsely claimed that despite "the remarkable and prolonged disturbance of the finances and industries of the country," the buildings and structures erected for the extravaganza had been completed "on time."[32]

President Grant then rose and walked slowly to the podium. He read a brief address in which he heralded American industry, innovation, and creativity, declaring that the fair provided an opportunity for "popular inspection." Though he never actually characterized the Centennial as a celebration of American democracy, the president noted that the country had now taken its place among the great nations of the world. Not known as a gifted orator, Grant might have seemed boastful, had he not spoken so softly that one newspaperman, sitting only a few yards away, "could not catch a single word." However, Grant's voice did rise momentarily at the conclusion of his ten-minute speech when he proclaimed, "I declare the international exhibition now open!" There was polite applause, which the writer William Dean Howells later characterized in the pages of *The Atlantic* as "indifference" to the remarks of the president.[33]

Grant finished his speech at noon; shortly thereafter, flags and banners were hoisted high on all the park's buildings, and a 100-gun salute reverberated throughout the fairgrounds. A master of ceremonies then directed the 4,000 "invited guests" to follow President Grant, Emperor Dom Pedro, and their wives into the Main Exhibition Building on the southern perimeter of the grounds. Constructed of iron, wood, and glass, the main building was 120 feet wide, 1,832 feet long, and 70 feet high, with four 75-foot towers at the corners and four 90-foot-high arcaded pavilions. Built in less than eighteen months at a cost of $1.76 million, it was reputed to be the largest building in the world, just as its builders had envisioned. Light poured into the building from huge glass panes, bathing the whitewashed walls and illuminating the numerous small, circular, stained glass portals that adorned the inner cornice. A number of foreign dignitaries joined the parade as the two leaders and their wives strolled through the building, admiring exhibits from a number of countries, including those from the United States, which occupied the largest and most prominent position in the middle of the edifice.[34]

After touring the main building, the presidential party proceeded to Machinery Hall, a sprawling thirteen-acre complex. In the middle of the hall, they stopped to ponder the massive Corliss duplex engine, designed by businessman George Corliss and manufactured by his company in Providence, Rhode Island. The gigantic engine, weighing more than 700 tons, was perhaps the most eagerly anticipated mechanical innovation of the entire exhibition. The engine packed 1,400 horsepower, making it one of the most powerful machines in the world. When activated, it powered all the exhibits in Machinery Hall through five miles of overhead belts, shafts, and pulleys. George Pullman would later buy it for his railroad sleeper car factory.

George Corliss's steam engine. (Credit: Courtesy of the Free Library of Philadelphia, Print and Picture Collection)

William Dean Howells, again writing in *The Atlantic*, marveled that the engine "did not lend itself to description. . . . [I]t rises loftily in the center of the huge structure, an athlete of steel and iron with not a superfluous ounce of metal on it; the mighty walking beams plunge their pistons downward, the enormous flywheel revolves with a hoarded power that makes all tremble, the hundred lifelike details do their office with unerring intelligence."[35]

President Grant offered the honor of starting the engine to Dom Pedro, though contemporary accounts suggest that both men pulled the lever together. The engine whirled and then roared; suddenly the entire building seemed to come to life as the Corliss powered hundreds of smaller machines in the grand hall. The president and the emperor both seemed delighted. Julia Grant, however, only forced a smile. She was annoyed that the empress of Brazil had also been invited—though it is not clear by whom—to put her hand on the "valve which started the great engine." While Julia's recollection of events was not reported or confirmed by any contemporary account, writing in her memoirs, she later complained, "I, the wife of the President of the United States—I, the wife of General Grant—was there and was not invited to assist at this little ceremony. . . . I wonder what could have prompted this discourtesy to the wife of the President of the United States and, at the same time, this honor to the wife of a foreign potentate." Perhaps misremembering the events of the day, she went on to write, "If General Grant had known of this intended slight to his wife, the engine never would have moved with his assistance."[36]

The Corliss engine was the largest and most powerful invention at the fair, but it was hardly the only innovation on display. In fact, the Centennial marked America's transformation into a major industrial power and its rise as the foremost center of innovation worldwide. As President and Mrs. Grant and Pedro II and his wife continued their tour of Machinery Hall, the emperor stopped to investigate Alexander Graham Bell's new telephone. "My God it talks!" the startled emperor is reported to have remarked as he dropped the black handset in disbelief.[37]

They also viewed Thomas Edison's new "automatic telegraph system." Born in 1847 in Milan, Ohio, Edison as a young man published a small newspaper called *The Grand Trunk Herald* and learned to operate the telegraph. Through this experience, Edison became fascinated with electrical science and began studying it intensively. After moving to New York City in 1869, he developed a stock printer by combining several different stock tickers and then sold the rights to his invention for $40,000. With his new wealth, he opened a lab and manufacturing facility in Menlo Park, New Jersey, where he continued to produce successful inventions. While his telegraph system was on display at the Centennial fair, Edison remained in Menlo Park, where he was perfecting the incandescent lightbulb. The inventions displayed at the fair inspired a number of future innovators, such as twenty-two-year-old George Eastman, who was in attendance and wrote to his mother, "The ingenuity that the innovators displayed is something marvelous." Only a few years later Eastman would unveil his new, improved camera.[38]

There were also impressive displays from America's firearms industry. In a massive glass case, inventor Samuel Colt had mounted more than 200 handguns in the shape of a giant pinwheel on a large wooden background. The Winchester Repeating Arms Company displayed more than 200 rifles and debuted the new Winchester 1876 model. The 1876 was an upgrade of the famous 1873 model and featured the ability to fire longer distances with larger ammunition, which made it ideal for game hunting. While it became the favorite rifle of future president and big-game hunter Theodore Roosevelt, in 1876 soldiers such as those in Custer's 7th Cavalry were armed with far less sophisticated and accurate weaponry.[39]

Another popular attraction was the right arm and torch of a proposed mammoth statue called *Liberty*—a gift of the French people to the people of the United States.

France had been America's ally in its war for independence from Britain, and the unfinished statue was perhaps the most obvious tribute to the events of 1776 of anything in the entire exposition. Since neither the French government nor the American government had agreed to pay for construction of the monument, funds had to be raised privately. For a fee of fifty cents, visitors could climb a ladder to a balcony adjacent to the top of the torch; the money raised would be used to build the pedestal for the statue.[40]

During his brief time at the fair, President Grant did not visit the building that housed displays of Native American culture, including

The *Colossal Hand of Liberty* on display at Philadelphia's Centennial Exhibition, 1876. (Credit: American Revolution Bicentennial Administration photo 452-G-13-2 / Still Picture Branch, National Archives)

life-size papier-mâché figures dressed in warrior clothing and holding weapons. Most White Americans had never seen a Native American and were completely ignorant of Indigenous cultures. However, if the goal was to educate the public about American Indians, the crude displays only reinforced racist stereotypes. William Dean Howells amplified this view: "The red man, as he appears in effigy and in photograph in this collection, is a hideous demon, whose malign traits can hardly inspire any emotion softer than abhorrence."[41]

Nor did President Grant tour the 30,000-square-foot Women's Pavilion, site of the first-ever women's exhibition at a world's fair. Financed by a team led by Elizabeth Duane Gillespie, great-granddaughter of Benjamin Franklin and head of the Women's Centennial Executive Committee, the building proved an extremely popular destination for visitors to the fairgrounds, with displays of women's contributions to the arts, sciences, education, and industry. All of the exhibits, ranging from art to needlework to new farming equipment, were created by women. There were also seventy-four inventions patented by women, including some designed to decrease the time and effort involved in performing household duties such as dishwashing, sewing, and cooking, thereby relieving women of some of their traditional burdens in the home. Gillespie's team also broke new ground by publishing an eight-page weekly paper, *The New Century for Women*, on a press powered by a steam engine in the pavilion. The newspaper advocated for women's rights both in the home and in the workplace and routinely criticized industry practices, such as unsafe and unhealthy working conditions, long hours, and poor compensation for female wage earners.[42]

Despite Gillespie's achievements at the fair, as well as in journalism, she and her inner circle eschewed political activism focused on a constitutional amendment guaranteeing a woman's right to vote as well as broader civil and political rights. As a result, the National Woman Suffrage Association, led by Elizabeth Cady Stanton and Susan B. Anthony, viewed Gillespie and her supporters as too complacent. Stanton and Anthony believed that, given the widespread press coverage of the Centennial Exhibition and the millions of visitors to Philadelphia, there might be an important opportunity to promote their agenda for greater women's equality.

The official count of first-day attendees was 186,272, with 110,000 entering with free passes. In the days following the opening ceremony, attendance dropped dramatically, with only 12,720 people visiting the exposition the next day. The average daily attendance for May was 36,000, climbing to 39,000 in early June. But then attendance fell off as a severe heat wave descended over much of the country in mid-June, including in Cincinnati, where nearly 400 delegates from across the country gathered on June 14 at the city's Exposition Hall for the Republican Party's convention.[43]

Some in the Republican Party encouraged President Grant to run for a third term. However, Grant was tired and would later remark on the "constant strain" he felt as president. He claimed not to be interested in a third term, but in truth he felt ambivalent: The job weighed on him, but he also worried that Reconstruction, about which he cared passionately, would be forsaken if he left the presidency.[44]

With President Grant on the sidelines, there were a number of aspirants for the nomination, but no obvious choice. After days of speechmaking and political horse trading, on the seventh ballot Republican delegates chose another son of Ohio, Governor Rutherford B. Hayes, to be the standard bearer. Hayes had served in the Union army and, after being wounded, had risen to the rank of brevet major general. The president admired Hayes for his service during the war and believed he would be a reliable successor in support of his policies, especially Reconstruction. But in his acceptance speech, Hayes made clear that should he win in November's election, he would follow a different course than his predecessor. He committed to serving only one term, pledged to reform the civil service, and in language that he claimed was designed to unify the country—but which many, including Grant, interpreted as a rebuke of Reconstruction—assured Southerners that he would "cherish their truest instincts" and work with them to obtain "the blessings of honest and capable local government."[45]

Nine days later, with the heat wave still blanketing the Midwest, the Democrats gathered in Saint Louis, Missouri, for their convention. After only two ballots, they nominated Samuel J. Tilden of New York for president and Thomas H. Hendricks of Indiana for vice president. Tilden, in many ways, was not so different from Hayes. He, too, had served as a governor. Having stood up to Boss Tweed and taken on the Tammany Hall political machine in New York City, Tilden, like Hayes, vowed to take on political corruption and promised a good and honest government. On the issue of Reconstruction, however, there was no equivocation or room to misinterpret Tilden's position: In his acceptance speech at the convention, he railed against the "rapacity of carpetbagging tyrannies."[46]

With only ten days until the July Fourth Centennial celebration and less than five months until the general election, the nominees were in place and the parties engaged in the contest for votes come November.

The race for the presidency in 1876, like the contests before it, would be decided by male citizens of the United States. Women were not permitted to vote, and White supremacists in the South would feel increasingly emboldened to stymie the voting rights of Black males, even though the Fifteenth Amendment had constitutionally protected those rights in 1870. Newspapers around the country focused on the presidential contest, unaware that in the days between the two conventions, a major calamity had befallen the US Army: the defeat of Custer's 7th Cavalry.

During the first weeks of June 1876, Lieutenant Colonel George Armstrong Custer, commander of the 7th Cavalry, was searching the northern Great Plains for Chief Sitting Bull, a Lakota Sioux leader. During the previous year the majority of Lakota had gone to reservations in search of food, but government rations were paltry, and many were starving. Now, in the early summer, several hundred Lakota and Cheyenne left the reservations each week to join Sitting Bull. Even if they had to travel far from the government encampments, they would take their chances and hunt the buffalo that still roamed the plains. With the arrival each day of more and more Native Americans, Sitting Bull's village more than doubled in size to 8,000 men, women, and children, making it one of the largest recorded gatherings ever of Native Americans.[47]

Custer had approximately 750 men under his command. Ironically, he was searching for Native Americans with a cavalry composed largely of men born outside the United States: 40 percent of the soldiers in the 7th Cavalry had immigrated from Ireland, England, Germany, and Italy, and the regiment also included troopers from Canada, Sweden, Norway, Spain, Greece, Poland, Hungary, and Russia. Nearly all of those born in America had grown up east of the Mississippi River.[48]

After days of riding without seeing any sign of Indians, on June 17 Custer and his troops came across a deserted Lakota village where a number of Native Americans had been laid to rest. The bodies of the dead lay on scaffolding around the campsite. Some of Custer's men desecrated the dead around the village by looting their bodies. One lieutenant recorded in his diary at the time, "Several persons rode about exhibiting trinkets with as much gusto as if they were trophies of valor, and showed no more concern for their desecration than if they had won them at a raffle."[49]

Three days later, on June 20, Custer's scouts located Sitting Bull's encampment on the banks of the Little Bighorn River. His scouts warned him that it contained as many as 4,000 warriors. Moreover, the scouts were convinced that Sitting Bull was aware of the presence of Custer and that the Lakota and Cheyenne and others would be prepared for any potential assault. Custer, however, didn't worry that Sitting Bull knew he was being hunted or that the 7th Cavalry was outnumbered. After all, Custer, as a Union cavalry officer, had played an important role in a number of engagements during the Civil War, including the Battle of Gettysburg. The key, he believed, was to develop a strategic plan of attack that relied on the element of surprise: a rapid assault and the capture of Indian women and children. Either Sitting Bull would surrender, or the Indian warriors seeking to rescue their families would be massacred.

Custer may have imagined that a great victory would have ramifications beyond opening the territory to miners and White settlers. Many political pundits at the time—and later some historians—believed that Custer had national political aspirations. Custer may have hoped to upstage Grant, preferably before the Democrats' convention on June 27, and at the very latest before the Fourth of July celebration at the Centennial Exhibition in Philadelphia. Custer envisioned a triumph over a last bastion of Indigenous resistance leading to a lecture tour back east, one that might propel him all the way to the Executive Mansion in Washington, DC. This was not just some private quixotic notion: In fact, Custer's father believed his son should be president and had written letters telling him so.[50]

Custer's confidence in himself inspired his troops. Camped on the banks of the Yellowstone, preparing to march into the valley of the Little Bighorn, the 7th Cavalry's spirits were high. A soldier in C Company claimed that it would all be over "as soon as we catch Sitting Bull." Another laughingly responded that Custer would then "take [them] with him to the Centennial." "And we will take Sitting Bull with us," added another.[51]

The following day Custer divided his regiment into three battalions; he prepared to go into battle with approximately 210 soldiers directly under his command. His troops carried limited ammunition on their horses, leaving 26,000 extra rounds on the pack mules. Custer told his company commanders to assign five or six men from each unit to fall back and guard the pack train that carried the additional supplies.[52]

When Custer led his troops into the valley of the Little Bighorn, they were quickly overrun by as many as 3,000 warriors. Of the 7th Cavalry's approximately 750 officers and enlisted men, 268 were killed, a number that included every member of Custer's battalion and an additional 58 men from the two other battalions. Those who died included not only their leader but almost half of their officers in the most devastating military defeat in the history of the US Army's war against American Indians in the West.[53]

The army reconnaissance party that found Custer's body a few days later discovered that he had been shot twice through the head—once between the eyes. Historians have speculated that Custer may have been badly wounded early in the fighting and that his brother, Tom, who fought by his side, may have shot him to keep him from being captured alive and tortured. General Custer's body was not disfigured by his enemies, but the body of Tom had been mutilated to prevent his soul from being reincarnated to make war in the future.[54]

Despite the heat wave that had hung over the East Coast since June, millions of Americans celebrated the Fourth of July, or "the Anniversary Day," as it was called. James D. McCabe, a nineteenth-century historian of the Centennial, characterized the celebration as "on a scale of splendor worthy of the glorious occasion." Beyond Philadelphia, nearly every corner of the country expressed pride in the nation's history as well as hope for the future.[55]

The city of Saint Paul, Minnesota, began the day with a 100-gun salute. In San Francisco a parade stretched four miles, while Omaha, Nebraska, featured a torchlight parade and "a grand electric display." In New Jersey, the city of Trenton's parade included a horse-drawn float carrying thirteen young ladies dressed in colonial-era costumes, and in Bristol, Rhode Island, nearly three times as many ladies crowded onto a parade float named "Goddess of Liberty" and waved to a crowd of onlookers. In Toledo, Ohio, the main streets were decorated with arches bearing the names of Revolutionary battles.

George F. Talbot, speaking in Portland, Maine, seemed to best summarize the pride that Americans felt: "The first century closes behind us," he said. "Let us enter upon the second with thankfulness for all that we have achieved, and with a determination to make our country worthier than ever of our highest love and holiest devotion."[56]

Curiously, a *New York Times* headline declared, "No Celebration in Washington: The City Nearly Abandoned for Points of Greater Interest on the Fourth." According to the article, "The public buildings are not decorated and the Government spends not one dollar to mark the fullness of the grand cycle of a hundred years." The *Times* explained that the Senate had adjourned on July 3 after scheduling a date for the impeachment trial for Secretary of War Belknap, and there had been "a large exodus of congressmen and private people on the outgoing trains to Philadelphia."[57]

As in 1826, Philadelphia was in 1876 the center of the nation's celebrations, with thousands flocking to Independence Hall to commemorate the 100th anniversary of the signing of the Declaration of Independence. The *Illustrated London News* described how some 10,000 troops marched from Chestnut Street to Independence Hall, remarking, "The most interesting and pleasing feature of the military program was the hearty reception given to the Southern troops who marched along with the men whom, a few years ago, they were fighting to the death."[58]

July Fourth had special meaning for President Grant: His third child and only daughter, Ellen ("Nellie"), was born on July 4, 1855. Additionally, on July 4, 1863, Confederate General John C. Pemberton had surrendered to General Grant, ending the Siege of Vicksburg and signaling a turning point in the Civil War. Only in 1870, during his first term as president, had Congress established July 4 as a legal holiday, finally officially recognizing the Declaration of Independence as central to the nation's identity. Nevertheless, President Grant did not view the 1876 celebration in Philadelphia as worthy of his attendance. Perhaps because he was now a "lame duck" president, perhaps because he had opened the Centennial fair only months earlier, or perhaps because he was worn down by the corruption investigations into his administration, he chose to remain in Washington. His absence was widely noted—and criticized. Senator Thomas Ferry, president pro tempore of the Senate and acting vice president since the death of Henry Wilson in 1871, appeared on the president's behalf. Ferry joined Philadelphia's luminaries on the crowded stage that had been constructed in front of Independence Hall.[59]

Independence Hall itself was festooned with red, white, and blue bunting, its entrance draped with American flags. Philadelphia philanthropist Henry Seybert had gifted a new bell to the city, known as the "Centennial Bell," a replica of the Liberty Bell, to hang in the steeple of Independence Hall. Manufactured by the Meneely-Kimberly Foundry in Troy, New York, the 13,000-pound bell had been cast by melting two cannons from the American Revolutionary War, one American and one British used at the Battle of Saratoga, and two cannons from the American Civil War, one Union and one Confederate used at the Battle of Gettysburg. The bell featured two inscriptions: "Proclaim Liberty Throughout All the Land unto All the Inhabitants Thereof" and "Glory to God in the Highest, and on Earth Peace, Good Will Toward Men." The only problem was that when rung, the bell sounded like an out-of-tune piano.

As a band played music, Mayor William Stokley raised the old colonial American flag atop the building. Five women from the suffrage movement, led by Susan B. Anthony, were in attendance and had received platform passes to witness the proceedings. Their presence was something of a symbolic acknowledgment of women's contributions to the nation over the past century. But the women had more than symbolism in mind that day. They had originally hoped that a declaration they had drafted proclaiming women's rights could be presented as an official part of the ceremony, perhaps at the close of the traditional reading of the Declaration of Independence. Elizabeth Cady Stanton, the group's driving force, wrote to Joseph Hawley, president of the United States Centennial Commission, "We do not ask to read our declaration, only to present it to the president of the United States (Ulysses Grant) that it may become an historical part of the proceedings." However, Hawley had turned her down. "Undoubtedly we have not lived up to our own original Declaration of Independence in many respects," he wrote. But "we propose to celebrate what we have done the last hundred years; not what we have failed to do." If Stanton's request were granted, the presentation of the women's declaration "would be the event of the day—the topic of discussion to the exclusion of all others." Therefore her petition was denied.[60]

With no speaking role, Stanton found no reason to celebrate the nation's first century and called for women to boycott the ceremony at Independence Hall. But five other leaders of the National Woman Suffrage Association, including Susan B. Anthony, viewed a boycott as an avoidance of politics and a concession to the patriarchal status quo. They decided to make their protest directly, in a style some of the original revolutionaries might have chosen. They accepted Hawley's consolation offer of platform passes.

The passes allowed the women to witness, but not take part in, the ceremonies. They stood quietly as an actor portraying founder Richard Henry Lee finished reading the original Declaration of Independence. Then, with an air of authority and without warning, the women marched down the aisle and past such distinguished guests as Emperor Dom Pedro II of Brazil, to the front of the platform, where they handed

Susan B. Anthony, the "Woman Who Dared," according to an 1873 illustrated newspaper. (Credit: Thomas Wust / Prints and Photographs Division, Library of Congress)

over their declaration—a "Declaration of the Rights of Women"—to a surprised Senator Ferry.

A sympathetic observer later wrote, "Mr. Ferry's face paled, as bowing low, with no word, he received the declaration, which thus became part of the day's proceedings; the ladies turned, scattering printed copies as they deliberately walked down the platform. On every side, eager hands were stretched; men stood on seats and asked for them." While a flustered General Hawley shouted, "Order, Order," Anthony and her colleagues left the platform and made their way to the courtyard of Independence Hall, where Anthony read aloud the four-page declaration to a crowd that quickly gathered around her. She began her presentation by saying, "While the nation is buoyant with patriotism, and all hearts are attuned to praise, it is with sorrow we come to strike the one discordant note, on this 100th anniversary of our country's birth. When subjects of kings, emperors and czars from the old world join in our national jubilee, shall the women of the republic refuse to lay their hands with benedictions on the nation's head?"

The crowd listened in hushed silence as Anthony continued her speech:

> And we do rejoice in the success, thus far, of our experiment of self-government. Our faith is firm and unwavering in the broad principles of human rights proclaimed in 1776, not only as abstract truths but as the cornerstones of a republic. Yet we cannot forget, even in this glad hour, that while all men of every race and clime and condition, have been invested with the full rights of citizenship under our hospitable flag, all women still suffer the degradation of disfranchisement.

She then recited a list of women's grievances against a government that practiced taxation without representation, denied women the right to trial by a jury of their peers, and imposed numerous unequal codes and laws. She concluded with a simple plea: "We ask justice, we ask equality. We ask that all the civil and political rights that belong to citizens of the United States, be guaranteed to us and our daughters forever."[61]

When Anthony finished, she looked up from the declaration she had been reading to acknowledge sustained applause from the crowd that surrounded her.

It was thirteen years to the day, July 4, since General Grant, in command of 70,000 troops, captured Vicksburg, thereby cutting the Confederacy's communication and supply lines and hastening the South's defeat. In the aftermath of the Civil War, the South suffered extreme economic devastation and desolation. The region's infrastructure had been demolished; cities had been leveled; plantations had been burned; railroad tracks had been destroyed. An economy once based on slave labor that was only partially replaced by tenant farmers and sharecroppers now suffered from an acute shortage of labor. Not surprisingly, Independence Day 1876 had a very different meaning for the citizens of the South.

In Greenville, South Carolina, with a mostly White population of nearly 3,000, the only reference to the Centennial birthday in the local paper, *The Enterprise and Mountaineer*, was a promotional advertisement titled "Our Centennial Offer." The newspaper promised to give away a sewing machine "to each of the five persons sending us the largest number of new cash yearly subscribers."[62]

A hundred miles west of Greenville, in Hamburg, South Carolina, a small town just across the Savannah River from Augusta, Georgia, the largely African American population viewed Independence Day as an opportunity to celebrate the rising freedom of Black South Carolinians. The main attraction in the town's Independence Day parade was the approximately 100-member Black militia led by a local activist named Dock Adams. Preparing to march down Main Street, the civilian volunteers had gathered in the town square.[63]

As the militia formed ranks, two young White men—Henry Getzen and Matthew Butler—both from wealthy, prominent local planter families, were driving a horse-drawn buggy down the street on their way to the market in Augusta. The street was not especially narrow, but Getzen and Butler demanded the Black soldiers step aside so that they might drive their buggy without interference. Adams argued that there was more than enough room for his soldiers to continue their march, and for the buggy to pass by them. A standoff ensued. Harsh words were exchanged. Getzen cracked his horsewhip, while Butler drew his pistol. Some members of the militia affixed bayonets to their rifles. Fearing that the situation might escalate to violence, Adams persuaded the militiamen to step off the road and allow the buggy to drive down the middle of the street.

However, the altercation was not finished: Instead, it was moved to the town's courts. Adams filed a legal complaint against Getzen and Butler, charging them with willfully disrupting his militia's parade. Getzen and Butler filed their own complaint against Adams, asserting that his militia had obstructed a public way; they demanded that the Black militia be disarmed. Butler's father would later recall, "We looked upon them as nothing more than a parcel of men, not a militia. . . . We did not think they had a right to have guns." Adams, on the other hand, argued that the militia had a valid charter and the legal right to march through the city. The judge in the case was an African American man named Prince Rivers, who had been a slave and had fought with the Union army. Rivers, aware of Getzen's and Butler's White supremacist affiliations, worried they wanted armed confrontation more than a victory in court. He summoned the two parties and implored them to settle their differences amicably. When both parties refused, Rivers ordered them to appear before him in court on July 8 for a hearing.[64]

On July 8 more than seventy armed members of the Red Shirts, a paramilitary White supremacist organization with chapters throughout the Carolinas and Georgia, marched into Hamburg to attend the hearing and show their support for Matthew Butler and Henry Getzen. Marching alongside Butler and Getzen was Ben Tillman, a leader of the Red Shirts, who later said he had told his followers "to seize the first opportunity . . . to teach the Negroes a lesson." Tillman, wearing a patch over the eye he had lost thirteen years earlier, viewed the confrontation in Hamburg as the perfect excuse for "whites [to] demonstrate their superiority by killing as many [Blacks] as was justifiable."[65]

When the Red Shirt mob reached the entrance to the courthouse, Butler stormed into the office of Judge Rivers, where Adams was already waiting. Seeing Rivers's clerk, William Nelson, sitting at a desk, Butler told Nelson to stop "just sitting down and fanning yourself" and demanded that the clerk relinquish his chair. When Nelson balked, Butler called him "a leather headed son of a bitch" and screamed, "God damn you."

As the Red Shirts chanted racial slurs and yelled demands outside the courthouse, Adams decided a public hearing might provoke confrontation and endanger the lives of his militia men, who were waiting in their drill room, located above a nearby general store. He quickly exited through a backdoor of the courthouse, returned to the drill room, and told his men to barricade the doors and to stay put: Perhaps Tillman's mob would leave, and they would settle the disagreement another day, hopefully without the threat of violence.

Butler, however, knew the location of the drill room and was undeterred. Surrounded by the Red Shirts, he marched to the general store and yelled from the street below, demanding that Adams and his militia surrender their arms and vacate the building. He insisted that Adams and his men apologize for their behavior on July 4. As townspeople became aware of the commotion, there was some attempt at mediation on the part of local African American businessmen. But Butler refused to compromise, and he ordered his White militia to bring up an old Confederate army cannon. If Adams and his men would not come out peacefully, Butler would blow a hole through the building.[66]

As darkness fell, with his militia outnumbered by more than two to one, Adams decided that his only option was to fight a rearguard battle. He opened the doors of the drill room, and several Black militia tried to escape. Shots were fired from both sides. One Red Shirt fell to the ground. A number of the militia scattered into the night.

The New York Times, which published a postmortem of the events, described what happened next based on a series of eyewitness accounts: James Cook, an African American militiaman and Republican town constable who in the past had fined and arrested White men, "attempted to jump a fence in the rear of the building, but was seen and in an instant fell dead, his head being literally honeycombed with bullets."[67]

Another Black man, Moses Parks, was also killed trying to escape.

At about 11 p.m., Butler and some of the Red Shirts climbed the stairs at the back of the general store and entered the drill room to arrest the remaining militia. After finding and capturing only a few men hiding there, they marched through the town and began breaking into houses and dragging out Black men. "Each fugitive when found was greeted with a yell and marched to a tree, where the other prisoners had been carried," the *Times* reported. "The moon and the torches gleamed on bright [gun] barrels, glittering bayonets and eager and determined faces."[68]

By 2 a.m. the Red Shirts had captured about twenty-five members of Adams's militia. Tillman's men surrounded their prisoners in a "dead ring." Getzen recognized a number of the Black militiamen and called them by name to step forward. The first to be called was Lieutenant Allen Attaway, who "begged hard for his life," *The Charleston News and Courier* reported. "A volley of five or six shots was his only reply, and he fell a corpse in the road." David Phillips "was next called and disposed of in the same way and then Albert Myniart, a ball being fired into each man," the *Courier* wrote. Hampton Stephens "was then called and told to run. He leaped over a low fence at the roadside . . . and was shot before he had gone five paces." Nelder Parker was shot in the back and died the next day. Pompey Curry's name also was called. "I knew what was coming, and I was running and dashed off through the high weeds at right angles," he told the *Courier*. He was wounded but managed to escape. Finally, the *Times* reported, the vigilantes "mounted their horses and rode rapidly away, and by 3 o'clock a.m. not a sound could be heard in the village where for six hours the work of death had been going on."[69]

Later that day, Judge Rivers's home was burned and his property stolen or destroyed by Tillman and his Red Shirts. Violence continued in the following weeks as Tillman and his henchmen worked to suppress Black voting in the upland counties, killing an estimated 30 to 100 African Americans over several days in September in nearby Ellenton township. A grand jury in Aiken, the county seat, subsequently indicted ninety-four White men for murder in the Hamburg Massacre. They were never prosecuted. In fact, Butler and later Tillman both became US senators from South Carolina as Southern Democrats regained control of the region's politics in the aftermath of Reconstruction and worked to establish a system of racial segregation that would rule the lives of Black Southerners for decades.

News of General Custer's defeat reached the American public on July 7, 1876, based on reporting from Clement Lounsbery, publisher of *The Bismarck Tribune* and the first civilian to write about the Battle of the Little Bighorn. For Americans across the country, many of whom were still celebrating the Centennial, the headlines came as a shock. Every major newspaper in the country ran a story based on Lounsbery's reporting: The *Boston Evening Transcript* described the battle as "Custer's Terrible Fate"; the *San Francisco Chronicle* bolded the caption "Brave Custer's Fate. His last engagement with the Sioux"; and, on the front page of *The Atlanta Constitution*, the headline screamed, "The Red Man's Revenge."[70]

The Battle of the Little Bighorn seemed to briefly shatter the notion of American exceptionalism. It also instantly elevated Custer to the status of national hero in death. While later accounts of the events at the Little Bighorn called into question Custer's judgment and military tactics, Custer's wife, Elizabeth ("Libbie"), used the newspapers to successfully burnish her late husband's gallantry and portray him as a courageous martyr for his country.[71]

The public outrage surrounding Custer's demise forced the Grant administration to push through measures that Congress would likely not have even considered only a few weeks before. Congress authorized the army to dramatically increase its presence and troop strength against Native Americans in the West, building forts and outposts on what had previously been considered tribal land.

The militarization of the West had a profound effect on the Native American population. Within a few years of Little Bighorn, all the major tribal leaders had taken up residence on Indian reservations, with one exception: Sitting Bull, the Lakota chief who had defeated Custer in 1876. But in 1883 he, too, would surrender and be confined to the Standing Rock Reservation in South Dakota. In 1890, a US government agent, James McLaughlin, acting on incomplete intelligence, feared the widely revered chief might be involved in plotting a Sioux uprising and ordered Indian police to arrest him at his small cabin on the Grand River. Indian police entered his cabin in the middle of the night; a struggle ensued, and Sitting Bull was killed in cold blood.

The presidential campaign of 1876 took a nasty turn after the July Fourth celebration. Maintaining the tradition of candidates not personally campaigning, neither Hayes nor Tilden ever made his case directly to the American people. But political operatives on both sides hurled invective at one another. Supporters of Hayes's campaign smeared Tilden as a drunk and a crook. Tilden's supporters tended to focus more on the Republican Party than Hayes personally. They pointed out that Hayes was the handpicked successor to Grant, whose administration had been tainted by corruption, and they claimed military occupation of the South amounted to nothing more than the imposition of a dictatorship.

Zachariah Chandler, the chairman of the national Republican Party and Hayes's campaign manager, sent a fundraising letter to every Republican appointee in the Grant administration, asking them—telling them—"to help bear the burden" by "promptly" remitting 2 percent of their salary. Chandler warned federal workers, "At the close of the campaign we shall place a list of those who have not paid in the hands of the head of the department you are now in."[72]

There was some irony in Chandler's bullying of federal workers given that one of Hayes's most prominent supporters was Samuel Clemens, the famous author better known as Mark Twain, who had recently published his novel *Tom Sawyer*. After marching through downtown Hartford, Connecticut, on September 30 in support of Hayes, the legendary writer called for an end to the "spoils" system: the politicization of the civil service system that had occurred under President Grant. Standing on the steps of Hartford's city hall, Twain declared, "We will not hire a blacksmith who never lifted a sledge. We will not hire a schoolteacher who does not know the alphabet. . . . But when you come to our civil service, we serenely fill great numbers of our minor public offices with ignoramuses." The speech landed on the front page of *The New York Times*.[73]

Republican operatives nicknamed Tilden "Slippery Sammy" and "Soapy Sammy." They accused him of evading taxes while making millions as a lawyer who represented ruthless, unethical industrialists, also known as "robber barons," of coddling corrupt officials in New York City's Tammany Hall, and of praising slavery and planning to pay off the Confederate debt if he became president. Before the campaign was over, he had been called a thief, a liar, a drunkard, a syphilitic, and a swindler. One campaign pamphlet dismissed Tilden as little more than a common criminal and claimed he was not only a disgrace to New York state but a "menace to the United States."[74]

Tilden disapproved of smear tactics in political campaigns, but the Democrats also trafficked in lies and character assassination, claiming falsely that Hayes had stolen the pay of dead soldiers in his regiment during the Civil War, that he had cheated Ohio out of vast sums of money while governor, and that he had shot his mother "in a fit of insanity."[75]

When November 7, Election Day, finally arrived, it was marred by widespread election interference, voter suppression, and even race riots. The improprieties and irregularities were especially rampant in the South, where reports circulated of local party bosses standing by the ballot boxes and tearing up ballots marked for the "wrong" candidate. Some Blacks were killed attempting to exercise their right to vote, while some Whites were allowed to vote multiple times.

At midnight on election night, it seemed clear that Tilden had won the presidency, receiving 4.3 million votes to Hayes's 4.036 million, a difference of some 264,000 votes. Notwithstanding his advantage in the popular vote, Tilden was still one short of the necessary majority in the Electoral College count, and Republicans claimed that the elections in Florida, Louisiana, and South Carolina were fraudulent because of intimidation and other illegal practices. The Republican Party formally challenged the legitimacy of the votes in those three states and demanded a recount.

Local election boards began to disqualify many of Tilden's votes for unspecified "irregularities." Democrats had no doubts that Republicans had stuffed ballot boxes; they claimed in some places the number of votes exceeded the population. Hearing reports of voter intimidation by White "rifle clubs," President Grant dispatched federal troops to the contested states to make certain that violence did not break out while the election was still undecided. He also ordered federal troops into the streets of Washington, DC.[76]

On December 6, the presidential electors were scheduled to meet in their respective state capitals, but they faced conflicting and irreconcilable sets of returns submitted by local election boards. Grant decided to establish a bipartisan electoral commission of fifteen members, composed of five members from the Senate, five from the House, and five from the Supreme Court.

The presidential election would not be decided until early the following year, 1877. There was no doubt that the Democrats and Tilden had won the national popular vote. However, the Electoral Commission decided 8–7 that Hayes had narrowly won the states in dispute and should be awarded their electoral votes. Hayes, according to the commission, had therefore won the election. There were allegations of a Faustian bargain claiming that Hayes had been awarded the highest office in the land in exchange for the Republicans' commitment to discontinue the policy of Reconstruction in the South.[77]

THE CENTENNIAL EXHIBITION IN PHILADELPHIA CAME TO a close in November 1876. The fair had been an enormous success. Cooler temperatures, newspaper publicity, and word of mouth had increased attendance in the final three months of the exposition, with many late visitors arriving in Philadelphia from great distances. In September the average daily attendance rose to 94,000; in October, to 102,000. The highest daily attendance of the entire exposition came on September 28, Pennsylvania Day, when nearly a quarter million people visited the fair. That day marked the 100th anniversary of the Pennsylvania Constitution of 1776, and exposition events included speeches, receptions, and fireworks. The final month of the exposition, November, had an average daily attendance of 115,000. By the time the exposition ended on November 10, more than 10 million people, nearly a quarter of the entire population of the United States, had visited the fair. Among the attendees who were duly impressed by the exposition was Princeton University sophomore Woodrow Wilson, who, with his minister father, Dr. Joseph Ruggles Wilson, had traveled from North Carolina.

Not long after the closing of the fair, the buildings in Fairmount Park were torn down and sold for scrap.

In late 1876, the Centennial Bell was removed from the steeple of Independence Hall and shipped back to Troy, New York, for recasting to improve its sound. It seemed a fitting metaphor for Americans who could legitimately celebrate their many achievements over the past 100 years but were not yet in harmony with the lofty ideals expressed in the Declaration of Independence. And as the US Army waged war against Native Americans in the West, and Jim Crow, a system of racial apartheid, emerged to replace slavery in the South, that dissonance between the American creed and American realities rang truer still.

4

Sesquicentennial

> America must be kept American.
>
> —CALVIN COOLIDGE (1923)[1]

THE INVISIBLE EMPIRE WAS VISIBLE IN 1926. Led by Imperial Wizard Hiram Evans, it stood, 15,000 white-robed members strong, atop Capitol Hill, poised to march down Pennsylvania Avenue to the White House. Its ranks were thinner than the last time the Ku Klux Klan (KKK) had massed in the nation's capital. A sex crime involving the head of Indiana's state Klan had stripped the national organization of much of its professed moral authority since 30,000 racists, anti-Semites, and anti-Catholics strode down America's Main Street in 1925. But the 1926 klonvocation was representative of the hate group's wide reach. Delegations traveled from Texas, Tennessee, Mississippi, Alabama, Louisiana, and other former Confederate strongholds, where the first KKK originated after the Civil War to terrorize Blacks. Contingents also came from every other state in the union. Pennsylvania's and New Jersey's were the largest, a sign of the second Klan's rapid growth since

1915, when sixteen Southerners, inspired by D. W. Griffith's incendiary film *The Birth of a Nation* (based on a 1905 novel, *The Clansman*), gathered on Georgia's Stone Mountain to found the group.[2]

"Native, white, Protestant supremacy," Evans wrote. These were the essentials of "One Hundred Percent Americanism," the new Klan's nativist platform that wrapped White nationalism in the American flag to target a wider array of people. "First in the Klansman's mind is patriotism—America for Americans," said Evans, who performed dentistry in Dallas when he wasn't wizarding. Old immigrants—English, Scottish, Dutch, German, Irish, those who had long inhabited the land—were fully American, so long as they were Protestant. New immigrants, tens of millions of whom had poured into the United States since 1880, mostly from southern and eastern Europe, were not. Jews and Catholics, not to mention Blacks, were excluded. Any attempt to include them in the body politic amounted to treason.[3]

Such red, white, and blue bigotry was mainstream in the 1920s. Some 100,000 spectators lined Pennsylvania Avenue, many cheering as Evans led the KKK down Capitol Hill on a late summer afternoon, followed by grand dragons, exalted cyclopses, and "a platoon of fascisti-attired men" who, *The Washington Post* reported, were clad in black. Behind them came the rank-and-file members marching in white robes, including some dressed as Uncle Sam or Columbia, the goddess of liberty; the floats, none more impressive than New Jersey's, topped by "Miss 100 Percent America," a young woman who regally waved to admirers with one hand, a Bible clutched in her other; and the American flags that passed, the *Post* remarked, "in a well-nigh unbroken stream. Tiny flags, large flags, and huge flags," all carried by state klonvocation delegates. The Virginia delegation's flag, the largest, measured seventy-eight by twenty-six feet.[4]

Evans and his gang of flag-waving Ku Kluxers passed within reach of a prospering national bank, the headquarters of organizations lobbying on behalf of American Indian and women's rights, and a rowhouse where historian Carter G. Woodson was working to change the conversation about race in America. Located on 9th Street in Washington, DC's northwest quadrant, the rowhouse, Woodson's home, doubled as the offices of the Association for the Study of Negro Life and History (ASNLH). Known today as the Association for the Study of African American Life and History, the learned society published *The Journal of Negro History* (now *The Journal of African American History*) as part of a broader effort to popularize Black history, which at the time hardly figured into the historical record, as documented by non-Black scholars. Few history books devoted much space to the Black presence in America, and those that did often made derogatory references to African Americans, depicting them, according to Woodson's influential text, *The Mis-education of the Negro*, "in menial, subordinate roles, more or less sub-human." This "tradition" suggested that Black individuals had not contributed meaningfully to human progress. Schooled into children, it taught African Americans to despise themselves and non-Blacks to hate Black people. Lynching, Woodson insisted, began in the schoolroom.[5]

The association's efforts, as important as they were, reached only a limited audience. So, Woodson, fifty, the son of former enslaved people, proposed a new initiative to broaden the appeal: Negro History Week.

First celebrated in February 1926, Negro History Week sought to "crown [the Black individual] as a factor in early human progress and a maker of modern civilization," Woodson wrote. A weeklong commemoration of Black accomplishment in schools and communities across the country would instill racial pride, he hoped. More broadly, the event aimed to include African Americans in the story of America, to demonstrate that, for better or worse, Black history was American history, and vice versa, and that Black Americans deserved the same rights and responsibilities as other Americans. As Woodson wrote in his 1922 book *The Negro in Our History*, his purpose was to present "the history of the United States as it has been influenced by the presence of the Negro in this country." The book recounted the history of Blacks in America from the moment African slaves arrived in Jamestown in 1619 to the victory African American soldiers helped win in the Great War of 1914 to 1918.[6]

This, then, was a snapshot of America in the Sesquicentennial year 1926, a nation in which African Americans, Native Americans, women, and millions more, buoyed by the prosperity, progress, and promise for which the Roaring Twenties were known, struggled for inclusion, for realization of the principles laid down in the Declaration of Independence 150 years earlier. America circa 1926 was a nation in which racial violence, Jim Crow poll taxes, and literacy tests prevented non-Whites from exercising their unalienable rights. It was a nation of immigration quotas that excluded newcomers from legally pursuing life, liberty, and happiness in the United States, and it was a nation traumatized by a costly foreign war, an even costlier global pandemic, and rapid demographic and technological changes that were upending society. And yet it was also a nation brimming with hopefulness.

"Well, I opened the Sesqui!" said Jacob J. Henderson, shaking raindrops from his derby as he entered the turnstiles. The sixty-year-old Woodbury, New Jersey, resident had visited Philadelphia's 1876 Centennial Exhibition as a child, deciding then and there that he wanted to attend another world's fair. Stayed by neither the morning downpour nor scaffolding that marred the entrance, he realized his boyhood dream a half century later, becoming the first paying customer of the city's Sesquicentennial International Exposition. Fifty cents, the cost of admission, seemed a small price to pay, he said, for being a part of history.[7]

Pushing past the turnstiles, Henderson walked south on the fairgrounds' main thoroughfare, the Forum of the Founders, a 250-foot-wide boulevard lined with thirteen ornamental columns memorializing the representatives of the colonies who signed the Declaration of Independence in 1776. To his left, he saw Building No. 1, the white-stuccoed Palace of Liberal Arts and Manufactures, an immense rectangle measuring 970 feet long and 392 feet wide that would eventually house, once construction was complete, nearly 200 exhibits. Sponsored by businesses and corporations, these displays showcased the mighty progress of American industry, which had pushed the gross national product to a record $97 billion in 1926, a 1,200 percent increase since 1876 ($7.4 billion), thrusting the United States to the very forefront of the world's economies.

Telecommunications had advanced since Alexander Graham Bell premiered the telephone at the Centennial Exhibition, the American Telephone and Telegraph (AT&T) exhibit reminded visitors. Thirty-nine percent of US households now had telephones, on 17 million of which Americans held more than 49 million daily conversations. Modern switchboards connected callers, like the working switchboard displayed in AT&T's exhibit, where a team of female operators wowed observers by fielding thousands of calls per minute.[8]

Westinghouse Electric and Manufacturing Company displayed a miniature model of the Luminous Liberty Bell, an eighty-foot-high replica of the Liberty Bell illuminated by 26,000 fifteen-watt lightbulbs that straddled Broad Street, near the expo's entrance.

A popular attraction, especially at night, the Luminous Liberty Bell was a conspicuous display of electric power, which had developed into a key driver of the American economy. (Between 1902 and 1926, the production of electric energy multiplied more than fifteen times in the United States—from six billion to ninety-four billion kilowatt hours.) Another such display was the fair's tallest structure, the 175-foot-tall

The Luminous Liberty Bell guards the entrance to Philadelphia's Sesquicentennial exposition, 1926. (Credit: US Information Agency photo 306-PSE-82-339 / Still Picture Branch, National Archives)

Tower of Light, designed to emit the Light of Independence, a beacon so intense, promoters warned, "that it would instantly ruin any human eye accidentally touched by it at close range."[9]

Electricity had business applications, according to the International Business Machines Corporation (IBM), founded in 1911. IBM's exhibit displayed forty types of machines enabling businesses to save time, raise productivity, and increase profits. These included accounting machines, electric timekeeping systems, job time and cost recorders, time stamps, security devices, production-control mechanisms, computing scales, tabulating technology, and sorters capable of cataloging IBM's latest innovation—punched cards—at the rate of 360 per minute.

Electricity had home uses too, though service was unevenly distributed. Only about 3 percent of American farms enjoyed its benefits on the August 1923 night when a messenger arrived at Vice President Calvin Coolidge's family home in rural Vermont, which lacked a telephone as well as electricity, to report that President Warren Harding had died of a heart attack just hours earlier in San Francisco. Coolidge took the presidential oath of office by the light of a kerosene lamp in a scene that became central to the president's rustic image. But Americans were moving. The 1920 census marked the first time in US history in which over 50 percent of the US population resided in urban areas. Almost all dwellings in cities were wired for electricity, which powered not just lights, though they were critical, but household appliances as well, including those displayed by Westinghouse—from an electric kettle, a toaster oven, and an automatic range outfitted with a cook timer to cooling fans, clothes washing machines, and a plug-in iron equipped with "a million-dollar invention" that regulated temperature.[10]

These and other modern miracles, manufacturers said, aimed to alleviate the burdens of housework, which fell almost entirely on women, especially middle- and working-class women who expended considerable effort just doing laundry—hauling and heating water, scrubbing items by hand, pressing almost every individual piece with a heavy iron—not to mention cooking and cleaning and everything else. "Some women," observed historian Ruth Schwartz Cohen, "determined to keep their homes as orderly and healthful as they could make them, exhausted themselves in the task; while large numbers of others—perhaps less optimistic, perhaps less brave, perhaps more realistic—just gave up and rarely attempted it."[11]

More Americans than ever before could afford to purchase consumer goods. Income, like electricity, was unevenly distributed. While workers' income went up 11 percent from 1923 to 1929, corporate profits skyrocketed 62 percent and dividends 65 percent, widening a gap to which some economists would point as a root cause of the Great Depression that began in 1929. But per capita income rose to a record

$681 in 1929 even as working hours fell—automaker Henry Ford introduced the five-day workweek in 1926—to foster a sense of prosperity that underwrote much of the optimism characteristic of the Roaring Twenties. "Prosperity," wrote historian William Leuchtenburg, "held the promise not merely of personal gain but of eliminating poverty, spreading knowledge, making American society more urbane, and resolving class bitterness." The country was infused with a feeling of "benevolent materialism."[12]

Visitors who followed Jacob J. Henderson to his next stop, Building No. 2, the Palace of Agriculture and Foreign Exhibits, would see examples of this material abundance on display. They would observe how margarine manufacturers combined vegetable oil with rendered animal fat to put a butter substitute on the table, and how the Jell-O Company mixed gelatin with sugar, water, and artificial coloring to form wiggly-jiggly salads, relishes, and desserts that enlivened almost any meal. Michigan's Battle Creek Food Company, a forerunner of Kellogg's, would showcase almost 100 products—crackers and biscuits, cereals and confections, diet and other "reducing" foods—all selected for their "health-giving propensities."[13]

This and more was available at one's local grocery store, claimed the Great Atlantic and Pacific Tea Company (A&P). Operator of 13,961 red-front stores, with annual sales totaling $437 million in 1925, A&P, the low-price, high-volume Walmart of its day, was well on its way to becoming a symbol of American affluence—the place where consumers went to purchase one of every seven cups of coffee, one of every fourteen pounds of butter, and one of every twenty-eight eggs sold in the United States. Ten cents of every dollar Americans spent on food crossed A&P counters. The grocery giant's Sesquicentennial exhibit included a model A&P store stocked with samples of every product handled by the company, including free cups of "Eight O'Clock Coffee," a Brazilian blend like the one Brazil's emperor had hawked at the Centennial.[14]

Building No. 2 also held international exhibits. President Coolidge continued many of Harding's policies, including his fellow Republican's foreign policy of steering clear of entangling alliances and other international commitments that, they believed, limited US freedom of action. Termed isolationism by some, independent internationalism by others, this stance was a reaction to the international activism of Harding's Democratic predecessor, Woodrow Wilson, who led the United States to war in 1917 to make the world "safe for democracy" and headed the ensuing peace conference in Paris in hopes of establishing an international peacekeeping organization, the League of Nations. However, in March 1920, the Republican-led US Senate rejected the Treaty of Versailles, arguing that the League covenant's collective-security clause infringed on national sovereignty, particularly on Congress's constitutional power to declare war. Weeks later, Harding, one of the senators who voted against the treaty, gave a campaign speech in which he declared that Americans wanted "normalcy," not the type of Wilsonian "nostrums" that had misled (in his view) 116,516 Americans to their deaths in the Great War, the deadliest foreign conflict in US history to that point. Harding's words came at the end of the 1918–1920 Spanish flu epidemic, which killed an additional 550,000 Americans and sickened tens of millions more. In November's presidential election, Harding won 60.4 percent of the popular vote, 26.2 percentage points more than James Cox, the Democratic nominee. His decisive victory confirmed that voters had indeed grown weary of overseas causes; normalcy, a word Harding popularized, entered the American lexicon.[15]

Yet the United States, winner of two foreign wars since 1876—starting with the Spanish-American War of 1898, which left the United States with colonial possessions stretching from the Caribbean (Cuba and Puerto Rico) to the Pacific (Guam and the Philippines)—had grown to become a world power by 1926. It had extensive business and other overseas interests, and the Coolidge administration remained engaged with the wider world, signing peace pacts, convening arms-control conferences, and promoting American exports and investments abroad, especially in the Western Hemisphere. Fittingly, then, forty-three nations participated in the Sesquicentennial International Exposition. The list ran from *A* (Argentina) to *V* (Venezuela), with the likes of China, Egypt, Great Britain, Persia (Iran), Spain, and Uruguay in between. Some sent ambassadors, ministers, or chargés d'affaires to the opening ceremonies. Others mounted displays in the Palace of Agriculture and Foreign Exhibits. Still others sponsored their own pavilions on the fairgrounds. Japan's million-dollar pavilion was the costliest, including not only a lakeside Japanese teahouse but displays of decorative arts in lacquerware, cloisonné, porcelain, silk, bamboo, and pearls valued at $500,000.[16]

Stepping south once more, Henderson must have been in awe upon arriving at Philadelphia's new Sesquicentennial Stadium, where twenty-one-gun salutes welcomed visitors to the fair's opening ceremonies. Attendance was lighter than expected due to the rain. Spectators occupied only 20,000 of the venue's 84,000 seats. But the skies cleared briefly, and after a Memorial Day moment of silence, Mayor W. Freeland Kendrick opened the exposition on behalf of Philadelphia, the birthplace of the Declaration of Independence.

US Secretary of Commerce Herbert Hoover, the miracle-working engineer who modernized the Commerce Department after feeding hungry Europeans during the Great War, took the microphone, his voice amplified by the kind of devices displayed in the Palace of Manufacturers. Such marvels, he said, demonstrated the mighty progress the United States had made since its founding. "We have multiplied ten times in national wealth. We have progressed vastly in science, in invention, in art and industry, and in our social and national life."

Take the Corliss steam engine: Centennial visitors were amazed that a single engine could generate 1,400 horsepower. Now steam engines produced 70,000 horsepower, fifty times as much. They were rapidly giving way to electric engines that powered locomotives and gasoline engines that propelled automobiles and airplanes. Hoover was confident that "men of science"—the noun was assumed—were pushing ever forward, putting Americans "on the threshold of other great discoveries, the bare beginnings of which" were visible throughout the fair.[17]

After a burst of fireworks, fairgoers spilling out of the southern end of the stadium found another major structure, Building No. 5, the Palace of United States Government, Machinery, and Transportation, where Bethlehem Steel would display the iron and steel that built the skyscrapers that were rising in America's cities. Gulf Oil would display, in the same building, a model of the company's drive-up gas stations that serviced the nation's growing fleet of automobiles, 26.7 million of which were registered in 1929, up from 9.3 million in 1921. And Wright Aeronautical, founded by aviation pioneers Wilbur and Orville Wright, would exhibit the engine that would power Charles Lindbergh and his *Spirit of St. Louis* across the Atlantic in 1927.

Federal agencies also would demonstrate how government served the growing needs of the American people. No booth would represent the Social Security Administration, or the Environmental Protection Agency, or the Civil Rights Division of the Department of Justice. They and many other federal agencies and offices did not yet exist. Pro-business Republicans who commanded the White House and both chambers of Congress throughout the 1920s sought to limit the size and regulatory power of the federal government, which had grown significantly during the war years. Harding and Coolidge had managed to shrink the size of the federal workforce to 548,713 employees in 1926, down from a record 854,500 in 1918.[18]

Even so, dozens of federal agencies would participate in the Sesquicentennial. The US Census Bureau, created in 1902, displayed a large electric chart with images of a stork at the top, the Grim Reaper at the bottom, and steamships on either side, each timed to illuminate at certain intervals set to approximate prevailing demographic trends. The stork celebrated a birth every twelve seconds. The Grim Reaper collected a death every twenty-four seconds. And the steamships blinked in two- and six-second intervals to mark in- and out-migration. In the center of the chart, a white light flashed every twenty seconds to indicate a net population gain of one person. It all added up to a youthful, dynamic nation that, swollen by immigration, had grown to include 117 million people, two and a half times more than the 1876 population of 46 million.[19]

Physically, too, the United States had grown, as the General Land Office would demonstrate by means of maps and charts. Eleven states—the former territories of Colorado, North Dakota, South Dakota, Montana, Washington, Idaho, Wyoming, Utah, Oklahoma, New Mexico, and Arizona—had entered the union since the Centennial, each of them on July 4, raising the number of US states to forty-eight. Their addition completed the process of continental expansion, closing a chapter of American history that had begun with the Louisiana Purchase of 1803.

Sesquicentennial plans called for more, much more. They called for a lagoon where gondoliers ferried passengers; for a midway stocked with carnival games, rides, and amusements; and, though Independence Hall was just minutes away, for a historical area designed to look and feel like Philadelphia circa 1776.

Yet little of it was open when Jacob J. Henderson entered the turnstiles on May 31. Crews worked around the clock to complete the exposition in time for opening day. “Overalled men dash about like characters in a rapid-motion movie film,” wrote a reporter who visited the site in April. Hammers pounded. Saws buzzed. Foremen swore. Steam shovels hissed and groaned under capacity loads.[20]

But the whirl of activity came too late. Mayor Kendrick had decided only in 1925 to hold the exposition on 300 acres of marshy land in South Philadelphia occupied by trash dumps, freight yards, and oil refineries. Draining, grading, and improving the remote site, which had received low marks from city engineers and architects in terms of aesthetics, accessibility, and healthfulness, raised the fair's cost, which ballooned to $33 million. Much of it was pocketed, critics alleged, by Philadelphia's political boss, Congressman William S. Vare, who owned at least two plots in the area, known locally as "Varesville." According to *The New York Times*, "The whole enterprise is no more than a gigantic real estate scheme to boost realty values in South Philadelphia, a lagging realty section which has been for many years and which still is the stronghold of the Vare Republican machine."[21]

Locating the fair in Varesville also delayed construction, with the result that the Palace of United States Government, Machinery, and Transportation remained closed on opening day. Both the Palace of Liberal Arts and Manufactures and the Palace of Agriculture and Foreign Exhibits were empty shells. Visitors who ventured within their cavernous walls saw only an army of workers building booths and unpacking crates. The Tower of Light, the 175-foot-tall structure that was supposed to project the Light of Independence, the beam so intense that it would ruin the eyes of any human who dared behold it, consisted of five large holes dug for its foundation between the two main palaces. Scaffolding covered the stanchions of the Luminous Liberty Bell. Even the sidewalks remained unpaved, forcing fairgoers to slog through mud from one unfinished site to another. "Isn't the mud terrible?" they complained.[22]

No record of Jacob J. Henderson's reaction to the disarray survives. But the five-member McHenry family certainly came away disappointed. They had driven all the way from Dubuque, Iowa, bumping for days along the nation's patchwork system of roads to reach

Philadelphia by opening day, only to pay $1.75 (children were admitted for twenty-five cents each) for a limited number of sights. "This thing reminds me of a guy I knew out in Ioway [*sic*]," Mr. McHenry said as he loaded his family back into their Model T for the long journey home. "He invited a raft of friends and relatives to a big birthday dinner and surprise party one time. He got so darned excited about how many he was going to have, invitations, his speech of welcome, and the program of entertainment, he plumb forgot to order any grub. When he thought of it, everybody was there, the stores closed, and he in a heck of a fix!"

Even the Sesquicentennial's official history, cowritten by the expo's publicity director, acknowledged that "all seemed confusion" during the fair's early days.[23]

THOMAS JEFFERSON UNDERWENT A RESURRECTION OF SORTS in 1926. Once hailed as the father of American independence, the author of a declaration "pregnant with . . . the fate of the world," as he himself wrote in 1826, Jefferson had fallen into disrepute following the Civil War. His fall was due less to his stance on slavery (though that reckoning would come) than to his support of states' rights, which had sowed disunion, critics said. And his ideal of a rural republic of yeoman farmers seemed irrelevant in a rapidly industrializing, rapidly urbanizing society. Jefferson faded in the shadow of his rival, Alexander Hamilton, whose economic vision foresaw manufacturing and investment. Hamilton's stature surged each time the Dow Jones Industrial Average index ticked a new high: 120 in 1924, 156 in 1925, 160 in early 1926.[24]

The 1929 stock market crash would change the equation. Embraced by President Franklin D. Roosevelt, Jefferson would emerge as a hero of the common man during the Great Depression. Yet the Sesquicentennial played a critical role in renewing interest in Jefferson, more so as it coincided with the centennial of his death. Sculptor Gutzon Borglum selected Jefferson to appear alongside George Washington, Theodore Roosevelt, and Abraham Lincoln on a memorial he was beginning in South Dakota. Congress introduced a resolution authorizing the construction of a memorial at a location to be determined in Washington, DC, near the Washington Monument, which had loomed over the National Mall since 1884, and the Lincoln Memorial, which had opened on the Mall's western end in 1922. And the Thomas Jefferson Memorial Foundation dedicated Monticello, his home near Charlottesville, Virginia, to the nation in a ceremony held on the grounds.

Sold soon after Jefferson's death to cover his debts, the property—much like Jefferson's brand—had fallen into serious disrepair over the years. Jefferson's gravestone was missing fragments, vandalized by souvenir hunters who chipped away at the obelisk. The foundation, a private nonprofit, purchased Monticello in 1923 with the goal of restoring the estate to serve as a shrine to Jefferson and the timeless values he espoused. "Here," the foundation's director said at the 1926 dedication ceremony, "the faithful may repair in days of discouragement to gather strength and inspiration for the never-ending battle against autocracy and privilege."[25]

The spirit of '76 was very much alive in the aftermath of World War I. Woodrow Wilson's call for self-determination amid the breakup of the Ottoman, Romanov, and Hapsburg empires had inspired movements for autonomy across the globe. Many national leaders again looked to the United States and its founding documents for guidance. Dozens of declarations of independence issued by states from Europe to Africa to Asia imitated the American version in some form or fashion. Czechoslovak leader Thomas Masaryk signed a 1918 declaration in Philadelphia's Independence Hall with a pen dipped in an inkwell used by many of the framers in 1776. India's 1930 declaration, drafted by Mahatma Gandhi, stated, "We believe that it is the inalienable right of the Indian people, as of any other people, to have freedom and to enjoy the fruits of their toil and have the necessities of life, so that they may have full opportunities of growth."[26]

Most declarations were limited to proclaiming national sovereignty and listing grievances against whichever power held their authors in thrall; the human rights potential of Jefferson's preamble ("We hold these truths . . . ") would not be fully realized for some time yet. But the words of 1776 continued to provide language for Americans seeking change as well. Labor unions and socialists, suffragists and feminists, abolitionists and civil rights activists all issued alternative declarations of independence in the nineteenth and twentieth centuries with the aim of completing the unfinished work of the American Revolution—or, as a group of New York farmers once put it, to "take up the ball of revolution where our fathers stopped it and roll it to the final consummation of freedom and independence of the masses."[27]

American Indians bore the brunt of the physical expansion of the United States, the very advance that had accelerated since 1876 and was so proudly hailed by the General Land Office in its Sesquicentennial exhibit. The federal government dispossessed Native nations of hundreds of millions of acres of land through more than 300 treaties. Disease and warfare with settler militias and US armed forces decimated Indigenous peoples, reducing their total population to fewer than 300,000 in 1926 from an estimated 4 million in 1776. These truths, argues historian Ned Blackhawk, disprove America's central thesis. Native American history, no less than African American history, dims any vision of American exceptionalism.[28]

Zitkala-Ša lived much of that history. Born Gertude Simmons on South Dakota's Yankton Sioux Reservation in 1876, the year Lakota Sioux and other Plains Indians defeated George Armstrong Custer's forces at the Battle of the Little Bighorn, Zitkala-Ša came to national attention in 1900 when she published under that name (meaning Red Bird in Lakota) a series of articles in *The Atlantic* documenting the cruelty of Indian boarding schools. Semi-autobiographical, these pieces were based on her own experiences as a student at White's Manual Labor Institute in Wabash, Indiana, and as a teacher at the nation's preeminent Indian school, the Carlisle Indian Industrial School in Pennsylvania. Carlisle's motto, "Kill the Indian, Save the Man," expressed the assimilationist mission of such schools, which sought to "civilize" Indian children by Americanizing them. She wrote of children, removed from their families, being forced to cut their hair, give up their traditional clothing, and stop using their Native names. She wrote of pupils being punished, often corporally, if they spoke their own languages rather than English, as required. And she wrote of youth being subjected to an "iron routine," a strict discipline imposed by Euro-American teachers who were determined to break Indian resistance.[29]

Dismissed from Carlisle in 1901, Zitkala-Ša emerged as an important voice, part of a new generation of activists who laid the groundwork for future breakthroughs by empowering Native Americans. She published collections of traditional Sioux tales, including *Old Indian Legends* (1901) and *American Indian Stories* (1921), to counter racist stereotypes that commonly portrayed Native Americans as ignorant savages. She composed *The Sun Dance Opera* (1913), the first American Indian opera. As secretary and treasurer of the Society of American Indians, the first national Indian rights organization run by and for Native Americans, and editor of its flagship publication, *The American Indian Magazine*, she lobbied for US citizenship for American Indians. "The Red man asks for a very simple thing—citizenship in the land that was once his own, America," she wrote in 1919, citing the 12,000 Indigenous soldiers who had served in the American Expeditionary Forces during the Great War. Native Americans deserved the same rights as other American citizens.[30]

Congress passed the Indian Citizenship Act in 1924. Signed into law by President Coolidge, who proudly claimed Indian heritage, the act extended US citizenship to all Native Americans born within the United States. Although some Indian leaders opposed citizenship, concerned that it would reduce tribal sovereignty, the act represented a significant step. Under the law, some 40 percent of the 300,000 American Indians then living in the United States gained citizenship status, a status previously denied to them despite the Fourteenth Amendment to the US Constitution, which, adopted in 1868, stated, "All persons born or naturalized in the United States . . . are citizens of the United States and of the State wherein they reside."

Still, the act was limited. It did not close the boarding schools, end the loss of Native land, or solve the many other problems that plagued Indigenous communities. Nor did it guarantee voting rights. Arizona, New Mexico, and Utah all continued to prevent Indigenous people from voting based on a claim that residents of reservations were wards of the federal government and therefore ineligible to vote under state law. It would be decades before all Native Americans gained the ability to vote, and even then, many of them faced the same Jim Crow barriers as African Americans.[31]

In 1926, Zitkala-Ša, now fifty, cofounded the National Council of American Indians (NCAI) to succeed the Society of American Indians, which had recently disbanded. According to its mission statement, the NCAI had but one purpose: "to better the Red Race and make its members better citizens of the United States. These objects it cannot attain unless the Indians are accorded the rights essential to racial self-respect and a spirit of loyalty of the United States." It was for that reason that the NCAI petitioned Congress during the Sesquicentennial year.[32]

Signed by council president Zitkala-Ša, who headed the group until her death in 1938, the petition began by invoking the Declaration of

Independence: "When in the course of human events a civilized state asserts by virtue of an alleged right of discovery the power of preemption in an aboriginal territory, it assumes before the Great Spirit who rules over the destinies of mankind, and under the Law of Nations, an obligation for those whose possession it displaces which neither emperors nor sovereign peoples may avoid."

Though incomplete, the struggle for empowerment continued.[33]

Toasts, the July Fourth tradition of drinking alcoholic beverages in honor of independence, were illegal for the most part in 1926. The Eighteenth Amendment to the US Constitution, which went into effect in 1920, prohibited the manufacture, sale, or transportation of intoxicating liquors for beverage purposes. Violations of the law were punishable by fines of as much as $5,000, imprisonment up to one year, or both.

Tell that to the hundreds who jam-packed Texas Guinan's Manhattan speakeasy, the 300 Club, in the predawn hours of Saturday, July 3, 1926. They were there to exercise their unalienable right to inebriation, to ring in Independence Day weekend with Guinan, a Jazz Age hostess known for ruling her midnight realm, as one British visitor, writer Stephen Graham, put it, "like a queen, like the sun, like a big firework."[34]

"Hello, suckers!" she hollered her trademark greeting. Buxom, brassy, and bottle-blond, Guinan wasn't a conventional feminist icon. She wasn't a suffragist like Susan B. Anthony or Elizabeth Cady Stanton, thanks to whom half the nation, some fifty-two million Americans, finally gained the franchise in 1920, when states ratified the Nineteenth Amendment stating that the right of citizens to vote "shall not be denied or abridged by the United States or by any State on account of sex." She wasn't an activist like Alice Paul or Crystal Eastman, who had drafted a proposed Equal Rights Amendment (ERA) to the

Constitution. Introduced in Congress in 1923, the ERA read, "Men and women shall have equal rights throughout the United States and every place subject to its jurisdiction." She certainly wasn't a prohibitionist like Carrie Nation or Frances Willard, who had succeeded in pushing through the Eighteenth Amendment banning alcohol.

No, Guinan wasn't like any of those more famous women. But she did make history, for the new woman who emerged in the 1920s to achieve greater levels of independence and freedom than her Victorian forebears came in many forms: flapper, capitalist, outlaw, and speakeasy hostess, no less than suffragist, socialist, clubwoman, and prohibitionist. And Guinan was nothing if not a flesh-and-blood archetype of a new kind of woman. A brazen performer who modeled "transgressive femininity," to quote scholar Angela Latham, Guinan was a third-wave feminist (before third-wave feminism existed) who evinced sex positivity, as well as a thrice-divorced businesswoman who worked outside the law. She wasn't afraid to break the rules, written or unwritten, and her disobedience encouraged others to defy Prohibition laws—which many Americans, women included, believed unduly infringed on their freedom to drink, on their Declaration-given right to pursue life, liberty, and happiness. For many Jazz Age women, writes historian Martha Patterson, "liquor became a flag of their new freedom." As such, Guinan entered the ranks of unruly women who blazed trails in US history. *Vogue* magazine would profile her nearly a century later as "the Original 'Nasty Woman,' the kind of wild American woman who in her time enthralled and inspired a generation of night crawlers."[35]

Born in 1884, Mary Louise Cecilia Guinan fled Waco, Texas, at a young age to pursue a career as a singer, showgirl, and vaudeville performer in New York. "Miss Guinan has looks, and dresses well," *Variety* noted in 1909. "Her well-trained soprano does the rest."[36]

Her next stop was Hollywood, where she starred in silent westerns, including *The Gun Woman* (1917), *The Lady of the Law* (1919), and *The*

Boss of the Rancho (1919). "She rode hard" across the celluloid plains, an observer noted, pursued by villains over precipices, only to be saved by fate. Cowgirl roles came naturally to Guinan, who boasted of her rodeo skills, "I could twirl a lariat, rope a steer, ride and shoot to beat any tobacco-chewin' cowpoke."[37]

Weary of "kissing horses in horse operas," she returned to New York in 1922. By then, Prohibition was in full swing, dotting Manhattan with illegal bars, speakeasies where Guinan found her true calling as a hostess, first at clubs owned by gangsters and later at places in which she herself held stakes. "Miss Guinan's particular function was to make whoopee," a prosecutor explained. "She made everybody feel at home in a jovial way. There was entertainment, the silliest of songs and jokes and the thumbing of noses at the law." These exhibitions of "whoopee" went on while guests of the establishment got sloshed, thanks to the bootleg liquor they purchased on the premises.[38]

Guinan's 300 Club, located in Midtown Manhattan on West 54th Street, was vulgar and rowdy, wrote journalist Lois Long, who chronicled the city's nightlife for *The New Yorker*. "Oh, it is a tough and terrible place, but everybody should go once in a lifetime." She recommended going because Guinan's was the spot to see and be seen, the kind of place frequented by everybody who was anybody, and some who were not. People from all walks of life rubbed shoulders, from millionaires, college boys, and members of high society to movie stars, athletes, rumrunners, and politicians, including New York City Mayor Jimmy Walker, who was once spotted there. The "Queen of the Nightclubs," as admirers called Guinan, lorded over them all. "Jimmy Walker rules New York by day; Texas Guinan by night," wrote Graham, the British visitor. To gain admission to her nightclub was to enter a state of freedom ungoverned by the rules of daily life.[39]

"Two Senators See Guinan Club Raided," read *The New York Times* on Independence Day 1926. When Prohibition began, temperance leaders did not expect to open newspapers on America's 150th birthday to find prominent citizens openly defying the law. They figured the "respectable classes" would rally around the cause. Yet there they were: two US senators, a British sea captain, and famous golfers celebrating the great Bobby Jones's first British Open Championship, all present at 3 a.m. when New York City police and federal agents raided the 300 Club. Policewomen disguised as flappers accompanied by policemen wearing evening clothes had cased the club in advance of the raid, gathering evidence for the search warrant. Raiding officers made several arrests and seized four bottles of liquor: two of gin, one of rye, and one of scotch.

Club representatives complained that they and their guests had been "roughly" treated by police. Many of those present expressed indignation at what they termed an "unwarranted intrusion" by authorities, who acknowledged that "some of the patrons became very boisterous and . . . several men offered to 'fight it out man to man' with them." Officers forcibly ejected twenty of the most pugnacious patrons.[40]

The July 1926 incident at the 300 Club, among New York's more fashionable nightspots, was not isolated. As the decade progressed, resistance to Prohibition enforcement, once limited mostly to working-class drinkers, climbed the social ladder to reach establishments like the 300 Club that served middle-class and wealthy guests. On numerous occasions in the latter half of the 1920s, speakeasy and nightclub patrons grew angry when Prohibition agents interrupted their drinking. Raids on Midtown establishments increasingly degenerated into violent melees, complete with flying chairs, thrown bottles, and fisticuffs. Patrons regularly jeered at or threatened officers of the law. "Such open resistance to Prohibition enforcement efforts among the city's 'better classes' contributed significantly to the eventual demise of the noble experiment," writes historian Michael Lerner.[41]

Guinan soon reopened the club, as she always did. If anything, the crowds grew larger. Police raids turned out to be good for business, producing free advertising, the kind of notoriety that attracted thrill seekers who, as the prosecutor put it, enjoyed thumbing their noses at the law. Though often arrested, Guinan never spent more than a few hours in jail. Nor was she ever convicted on a Prohibition charge. Her legend grew each time she emerged from behind bars; she became a folk hero, a symbolic leader of the rebellion against Prohibition, a wet counterpoint, Lerner writes, to the "great women drys" of the early twentieth century.[42]

"What, again?" Guinan asked in February 1927 when a dozen federal agents raided the 300 Club. "I hope I can ride in a taxi." Afforded that courtesy, she threw an ermine cloak over her evening gown and, wearing an elaborate headdress from the night's performance, walked out to the curb for the ride to the precinct house, where Guinan, playing the role of an irreverent speakeasy hostess, did some of her best work.[43]

"How sweet," she said when she learned she would have to spend a night in jail. "What a thrill! Texas Guinan going to jail!" She certainly took the news in stride, entertaining the reporters who followed her to the precinct with songs, jokes, and barbs aimed at Prohibition authorities. "You boys have all been very lovely," she told them. "But get me a magazine, won't you? I want to read or something. Now, can I have a hand?" The crowd duly applauded as police led Guinan, still wearing the ermine cloak and headdress, to her cell, where she passed the next few hours flipping through the pages of a magazine.[44]

Her act extended to court, where she arrived dressed in a peach-colored gown, cloaked in mink, decorated with diamonds and pearls, topped with a modish hat, and surrounded by an aura of perfume. Guinan, a devout Catholic, denied that she drank alcohol (which was true), much less served it. "I certainly did not order any waiter to serve liquor to any patron at the 300 Club," she testified.[45]

"You didn't think it was tea, did you?" the prosecutor asked.

"I don't know—I don't drink tea, either," Guinan cracked. "I drink coffee."

"Tex had a swell time," the *Chicago Tribune* reported. The jury had an even better one. Acquitted, as usual, she adopted the padlock, a symbol of Prohibition enforcement, as her personal brand. She began wearing a charm bracelet made of tiny gold padlocks. She also staged an irreverent revue, "The Padlocks of 1927," at the 300 Club.[46]

Following more run-ins with the law, Stephen Graham found her at a different location, ruling another giddy crowd.

"Who is the greatest flapper on the American stage?" she asked guests.

Louise Brooks, the flapper icon who was then appearing on Broadway? they guessed.

No, teased Guinan.

Clara Bow, the "it girl" who topped Hollywood box offices in the 1920s?

Nope, not her either.

You, Tex! Is it you?

"No," she replied, "the greatest flapper on the American stage [is] the American flag." At which point, she reached between her breasts, pulled out a flag, and cheerfully waved it. The crowd roared with laughter.[47]

Calvin Coolidge, the thirtieth president of the United States, did not appear at the Sesquicentennial exposition on Sunday, July 4, 1926. Nor did the president appear anywhere in public that day, beyond attending church, and even then he did not take questions or make a statement in honor of the nation's 150th birthday. Coolidge, the first and only president born on July 4, remained in the White House quietly celebrating his fifty-fourth birthday with a friend, Boston merchant Frank Stearns, and with First Lady Grace Coolidge and their son John, nineteen.

The Coolidges' younger son, Calvin Jr., had blistered a toe playing tennis with John on the White House courts two summers earlier. The toe became infected. Without penicillin, first used successfully to treat an infection in 1930, he went into septic shock and fell dead within a week. President Coolidge blamed himself for his son's July 1924 death. "He was a boy of much promise, proficient in his studies, with a scholarly mind, who had just turned sixteen," Coolidge would recall in his autobiography. "We do not know what might have happened to him under other circumstances, but if I had not been President he would not have raised a blister on his toe, which resulted in blood poisoning, playing lawn tennis in the South Grounds."[48]

Calvin Jr.'s death devastated the president, who, according to one account, afterward suffered from clinical depression. Coolidge withdrew from regular activity, sleepwalking through the demands of office, a broken man. Coolidge himself recalled, "When [Calvin Jr.] went the power and the glory of the Presidency went with him."[49]

Yet demands there were, so on Monday, July 5, Coolidge stood on a stage in rainy Sesquicentennial Stadium before a battery of microphones ready to carry his words to millions of listeners.

Tightlipped, Silent Cal, as he was known due to his well-documented reputation for brevity, did not explain why he avoided Philadelphia on Independence Day. But many believed it had something to do with Sesquicentennial officials' recent decision to open the fairgrounds on Sundays—starting on July 4, no less. By keeping the fair open seven days a week, exposition leaders hoped to boost attendance, which lagged well below expectations due to the construction delays, foul weather, and poor word of mouth that dogged the fair from the moment Jacob J. Henderson entered the turnstiles on day one. It rained on 107 of the

President Coolidge delivers a memorial address, 1927. (Credit: US Signal Corps photo 111-SC-100337 / Still Picture Branch, National Archives)

fair's 184 days of operation. When it wasn't raining, it was uncomfortably hot and humid. A deadly heat wave gripped much of the United States that summer. Philadelphia temperatures regularly soared above 90 degrees, hitting 101 degrees in July. Though organizers anticipated welcoming thirty million guests before the fair closed in the autumn, paid admissions would not reach one million until early August, by which time the exposition was drowning in red ink, almost $4 million worth, forcing officials to halt construction on the still unfinished Tower of Light, whose skeleton loomed over the exhibition grounds, a reminder of ambitions past.

Sunday openings did raise attendance somewhat. More than 54,000 guests entered the grounds on July 4, climbing to almost 100,000 on July 25, the most since opening day. But the decision was highly controversial at a time when religion played a deeply meaningful role in many

Americans' lives. To many Catholics, conservative Protestants, and evangelical Christians, a seven-day Sesquicentennial represented not only contempt for the Sabbath but a victory for the forces of secularization that were then sweeping the country, changing it for the worse, in their view. "Philadelphia," said one pastor, "stands indicted before God and Christian-thinking men." A Methodist group charged the Sesquicentennial's controller with violating Pennsylvania's blue laws of 1794, which banned most amusements and commercial activities on Sundays. A judge agreed, fining the controller for allowing concessionaires to charge fees on the Sabbath.[50]

Coolidge, a devout Congregationalist, had worked to become a model of rectitude since taking the oath of office by the light of that kerosene lamp in August 1923. Numerous political scandals had emerged soon after former President Harding's untimely death, involving federal agencies headed by members of the Ohio Gang, a group of cronies who played late-night poker with Harding in the White House. The most serious of these scandals involved Harding's secretary of the interior, Albert Fall, accused of accepting more than $400,000 ($7.6 million today) in loans and gifts from oilmen for single-bid leases on naval oil reserves located at Teapot Dome in Wyoming and Elk Hills in California.

Coolidge acted decisively in response to Teapot Dome, as the scandal became known. In January 1924, he stated, "If there is any guilt it will be punished; if there is any civil liability, it will be enforced; if there is any fraud, it will be revealed; and if there are any contracts which are illegal, they will be canceled. Every law will be enforced and every right of the people and the Government will be protected."[51]

The president subsequently appointed two special prosecutors, one Republican and one Democrat, to investigate. He also took internal action. According to his naval aide, Vice Admiral Wilson Brown, he discouraged even his closest friends from "taking liberties with the president of the United States." He made clear that they would not have the type of influence previously enjoyed by Harding's cronies or even President Wilson's advisor, Edward House, who lived in the White House for a time before Wilson broke with him over a foreign policy difference. These friends included the Coolidges' July Fourth guest, Frank Stearns, the Boston merchant who underwrote Coolidge's political rise. "I'll have you know, Mr. Stearns," said Coolidge, "I will have no Colonel House in my administration."[52]

Mindful, too, of how the Ohio Gang's late-night poker parties had besmirched the White House, Coolidge was determined, Vice Admiral Brown recalled, "that there should be no critical gossip about any of his household." He would not allow his son John, when home on vacation from college, to entertain friends or even to accept invitations to parties lest it lead to gossip about White House shenanigans, as had happened in previous administrations.[53]

These measures, strict as they were, put Teapot Dome, arguably the biggest scandal in US history prior to Watergate, safely in the past by mid-1924. All Harding administration officials involved had resigned from office or been fired or were on their way to prison, including Secretary Fall, who was found guilty in 1929 of accepting a bribe, the first cabinet officer ever convicted of a crime. Coolidge, the accidental president, a relative unknown, an apparent lightweight when he assumed office, cruised to victory in the 1924 presidential election, winning 54 percent of the popular vote, based largely on the perception that he had cleaned up Washington. No president, wrote Brown, who also served Herbert Hoover, Franklin Roosevelt, and Harry Truman, "ever tried more faithfully to preserve the prestige of the presidency."[54]

In many respects, Coolidge was the very antithesis of the Roaring Twenties, or at least the popular image of them. The Twenties spent money purchasing the automobiles, radios, refrigerators, and other consumer goods that poured out of American factories; Coolidge saved, annually running budget surpluses that reduced the national debt from $22.3 billion in 1923 to $16.9 billion in 1929. The Twenties danced the Charleston and drank bathtub gin in defiance of Prohibition; Coolidge did neither, though Admiral Brown once saw him and Mrs. Coolidge, in an unguarded moment, "solemnly dancing a minuet with exaggerated bows and curtsies." The Twenties also talked at the movies, talked on the phone, talked of the town in *The New Yorker* magazine; Coolidge kept mum. Dorothy Parker, the writer, seated next to him at a White House dinner, once tried to draw him into conversation by wagering that she could get more than two words out of him. "You lose," he responded.[55]

Though perhaps apocryphal—Coolidge insisted he never said any such thing—the story contained a kernel of truth, for Silent Cal was famously uncommunicative, especially in comparison to the garrulous Warren Harding, who, for all his faults, was regarded as an accomplished orator, someone who had spent years on the lecture circuit honing an ability to make each audience member feel as if he were speaking directly to them. Coolidge had no such ability. Even friends described his delivery as cold, proceeding, one wrote, "in a rather flat manner, with very little of the 'light touch.'" He typically read from a manuscript, seldom departing from the text, varying his cadence, changing his tone, looking at his audience, or conveying much in the way of emotional warmth. Standing ramrod straight, the very picture of uprightness, he employed few physical gestures, only occasionally chopping his right hand to emphasize a point or unleashing his arm, also his right, to illustrate the grand sweep of history. Even his 1925 inaugural address stuck to the script. Stepping to the podium, Coolidge paused to look down the Capitol steps at the sea of upturned faces below. "Then," *The Atlanta Constitution* reported, "his eyes dropped to the manuscript before him on the stand and he went on steadily, quietly to his [inevitable conclusion]" in a monotone seldom betraying any sense of feeling.[56]

Coolidge, though, had the advantage of being the first radio president, the first to make extensive use of the medium to communicate with voters. Via radio, Silent Cal reached more Americans than did any previous president, probably more than all his predecessors combined. In 1924, his first full year in office, he delivered 265 addresses, speaking an average of 9,000 words a month to audiences that numbered in the millions: ten million for a press association address in 1927, twenty million on George Washington's birthday that year, thirty million when he feted Charles Lindbergh for crossing the Atlantic alone.[57]

His delivery worked better on the radio. Listeners couldn't see him avoid eye contact or move awkwardly on the stage. They could only hear him speak clearly and directly in short sentences, using simple language and familiar words that, according to the Kansas newspaperman William Allen White, "went straight to the popular heart." Subscribers to a radio magazine ranked Coolidge among their favorite personalities, ahead of entertainer Will Rogers.[58]

Silent Cal was considerably more loquacious when it came to the founding fathers, a term coined by his predecessor, Warren Harding. As an undergraduate at Amherst College, Coolidge wrote an 1894 essay, "The Principles Fought for in the American Revolution," that won a national gold medal from the Sons of the American Revolution. He returned to the topic again and again, first as lieutenant governor and governor of Massachusetts and later as vice president and president of the United States, giving dozens of speeches, addresses, and proclamations in small towns and big cities alike honoring everyone from George Washington, Alexander Hamilton, Patrick Henry, and Paul Revere to the Declaration of Independence, the Constitution, and the Battle of Bunker Hill. "No modern president," writes author David Pietrusza, "has spoken so much—or so well—of America's providential genesis."[59]

And no such speech won more applause than Coolidge's Sesquicentennial address. As a navy band ended its rendition of "The

Star-Spangled Banner," the president, with trembling hands, opened a black leather portfolio he carried and read, eyes down, the text inside, bound as if it were an important historic artifact. "Fellow Countrymen," he began, his high-pitched voice, accented with New England twang, carrying to 35,000 people listening in person and millions more by radio. "We meet to celebrate the birthday of America."[60]

By "celebrate," Coolidge—who addressed audiences, a biographer wrote, "like an affable though strict schoolmaster"—meant "study," study and learn the lessons of history, starting with the origins of the Declaration of Independence. Americans searching for the document's roots needn't look far, said the president. For they were located not abroad, in the teachings of Jean-Jacques Rousseau, French thinkers, or English philosopher John Locke, as scholars claimed. Rather, they were located on American shores, in the texts, sermons, and writings of colonial clergy such as Thomas Hooker and John Wise. "Whatever else we may say of it," said Coolidge, giving voice to the nationalist worldview that informed the times, "the Declaration of Independence was profoundly American."[61]

Inspired by clergy, beginning with a reference to Nature's God, and ending with an appeal to the Supreme Judge, the Declaration was also divine. "In its main features the Declaration of Independence is a great spiritual document. It is a declaration not of material but of spiritual conceptions," Coolidge said. No one who studied the historical record could escape the conclusion that it was the product of seventeenth- and eighteenth-century clerics who preached equality by testifying to human brotherhood, who justified liberty by praising the divine creation of all people. Quoting Wise, he said, "Democracy is Christ's government in church and state." Even Thomas Jefferson, said Coolidge, acknowledged that "his 'best ideas of democracy' had been secured at church meetings."[62]

If America's existential statement was divinely inspired, as Coolidge insisted, then it was immutable. "About the Declaration," he said, "there is a finality that is exceedingly restful." Americans celebrated July Fourth not to adopt new policies but to "reaffirm and reestablish those old theories and principles which time and the unerring logic of events have demonstrated to be sound." Measures to perfect the union were unnecessary, harmful even. Government's role should be limited.[63]

Coolidge's words didn't leave a particularly strong impression on those who suffered through his forty-minute speech in Philadelphia's open-air Sesquicentennial Stadium, sweating in the summer afternoon heat, dodging the rains that intermittently dumped several additional inches on the city that day. But *The New York Times* said it was the most notable speech on a patriotic theme Coolidge had given in his administration. That was saying something, because his tenure included many such speeches, including a talk marking the 150th anniversary of the First Continental Congress in 1924, an address celebrating George Washington's birthday in 1925, and remarks honoring the sesquicentennial of Virginia's call for independence in 1926.[64]

Coolidge credited radio for whatever success he enjoyed as a public speaker. "I am very fortunate that I came in with the radio," he told Senator James Watson of Indiana. He couldn't make a stemwinding speech like other politicians could. But, he said, "I have a good radio voice, and now I can get my messages across to [audiences] without acquainting them with my lack of oratorical ability or without making any rhetorical display in their presence."[65]

His lack of pretense, his authenticity, and his old-fashioned faith in the country and its foundational texts made Americans feel secure in a rapidly changing world, in which advertisers, publicity agents, promoters, and hucksters increasingly vied for public attention during the ballyhoo years, as journalist Frederick Lewis Allen called the Coolidge era. Some listeners might disagree with his message: More than 45 percent of voters opposed his candidacy in the 1924 presidential election. But nobody ever doubted Coolidge's sincerity. "The truth about it is that everybody heard him with keen pleasure," Senator Watson mused, "because they felt that they were listening to an honest man who was giving them his sincere thoughts on the questions under discussion." In an age of uncertainty, such steadfastness was reassuring.[66]

CARTER WOODSON'S 1926 CALL FOR NEGRO HISTORY Week received an enthusiastic response from educators. It was the age of the "New Negro," wrote Harlem Renaissance philosopher Alain Locke, a time when African Americans were busy pursuing new opportunities, migrating in search of greater freedom, striving to realize American ideals. State education officials in Delaware, North Carolina, and West Virginia encouraged their teachers to participate in Negro History Week, as did city administrators in Baltimore and the District of Columbia. Some private school principals and college and university presidents voiced their support as well, with the result that requests for instructional materials poured into the 9th Street NW headquarters of the Association for the Study of Negro Life and History, the professional organization Woodson founded in 1915.

ASNLH staff scrambled to meet the demand. They distributed study materials—lessons for teachers, plays for historical performances, and posters depicting important people and dates—along with suggestions on how best to commemorate the occasion. In honor of the Sesquicentennial, the 1926 program, scheduled in February to coincide with the birthdays of Abraham Lincoln and Frederick Douglass, emphasized the importance of Black individuals in the founding and development of America—as laborers, soldiers, and inventors, as well as artists, businesspeople, and educators.[67]

Teachers documented how their communities celebrated the week. In 1927, Julia Davis of Saint Louis reported that fifth graders performed as Frederick Douglass and cosmetics entrepreneur Madam C. J. Walker and sang jubilees made famous by the Fisk Jubilee Singers, an a cappella ensemble founded in 1871 whose lyrics spoke of hope, deliverance from tribulation, and the promise of a brighter tomorrow. Richmond, Virginia's 1930 activities, wrote Alice Harris, included student speeches on themes in African American history and a pageant attended by 800 people. By 1931, over 80 percent of Black high schools celebrated Negro History Week. "The celebration has become one of the important objectives of the school year," Woodson wrote. "No other single thing has done so much to dramatize the achievements of persons of African blood."[68]

But the Invisible Empire was never far away. Led by Hiram Evans, the Texas dentist–cum–imperial wizard, it appeared in Washington,

A bird's-eye view of the Ku Klux Klan's march down Pennsylvania Avenue, Washinton, DC, September 13, 1926. (Credit: National Photo Co. / Prints and Photographs Division, Library of Congress)

DC, on that late summer day in 1926, just steps from Woodson's home—marching, 15,000 members strong.

The KKK was a nationwide force, as popular above the Mason-Dixon Line as below it. At its peak, the Klan boasted three million to four million dues-paying members. Klansmen numbered 35,000 in Detroit, 55,000 in Chicago, and 200,000 in Ohio, comprising, writes historian Kevin Boyle, "a veritable army of proud Anglo-Saxons kluxing in their local klaverns."[69]

The KKK spread in reaction to the Great Migration, the movement of millions of Black Southerners to Northern cities starting in the 1910s, as well as to the new immigration that brought millions more southern and eastern Europeans to American shores, prompting a nativist backlash that influenced society at large. "America must be kept American," President Coolidge proclaimed prior to signing the Johnson-Reed Act into law in May 1924. Passed with strong congressional support, the law imposed a national-origins quota limiting annual immigration from any country to 2 percent of the number of its nationals resident in the United States as determined by the 1890 census. (The act barred all immigration from Asia.) By setting 1890 as the baseline, the quota favored the homelands of the old immigrants. Great Britain and Ireland together could send about 62,000 immigrants a year and Germany over 50,000; no other nation exceeded 10,000. Italy's great flood of immigration slowed to a trickle of less than 4,000 a year; all southern and eastern Europe together could scarcely muster 20,000.[70]

Klan members were not unwelcome by many White residents of the nation's capital, which remained racially segregated when the KKK arrived in September 1926. *Washington Post* coverage of the Klan's rally said little about the group's espousal of hatred. Nor did the *Post* have much to say about the Klan's grim record of violence, including in Alabama, where a 1928 report found "a lad whipped with branches until his back was ribboned flesh; a Negress beaten and left helpless, to contract pneumonia from exposure and die; a white girl, divorcée, beaten into unconsciousness in her own home; a naturalized foreigner flogged until his back was a pulp because he married an American woman; a Negro lashed until he sold his land to a white man for a fraction of its value."[71]

Rather, the *Post* lovingly detailed the warm reception Klansmen, women, and even children, some as young as three, received from residents of the District's Capitol Hill neighborhood, where marchers assembled prior to the parade. As Klan members, sweating in their robes, searched for shade or respite from the late-summer heat, children helped the weary travelers pass the time by dancing the Charleston. Neighbors handed out soft drinks and sandwiches. Vendors sold ice water. "Penny a glass," they cried.[72]

One marcher's 100 percent Americanism was beyond reproach, declared the *Post*. J. M. Fraser, a seventy-seven-year-old resident of Houston, Texas, claimed membership in the original Klan, "famous," the paper said, for its activities during Reconstruction. His ancestors came to the United States from the highlands of Scotland in the late seventeenth century. He proudly hailed from "a long line of patriots," some of whom participated in the Boston Tea Party, others of whom fought in the War of 1812, the Mexican-American War of 1846 to 1848, or the Indian Wars of the late nineteenth century. Fraser himself was a Confederate veteran, and he wore a hero cross commemorating his "work," as the *Post* put it, in the first Klan, which he joined in 1866. The septuagenarian, described as "a diminutive old gentleman with a grizzly beard and a great deal of pep," duly occupied a place of honor, accompanying the chief flag bearer at the head of the Klan's parade down America's Main Street.[73]

Importantly, Fraser walked with his hood raised, face exposed for all the world to see. So did most others, including Dallas, Texas's district attorney, who posed for a photograph. Published in the morning newspaper, the photo appeared over a caption that identified him by name. Black newspapers promised that any public officials who were positively identified as Kluxers would be voted out of office. But the fact that so many marched unmasked suggested that the group, responsible for lynchings and other acts of terror, felt empowered to operate with impunity. With its millions of members, the Klan exerted considerable influence on both major political parties. Critics dubbed the 1924 Republican National Convention, held in Cleveland, the "Kleveland Konvention" because the party rejected a proposed anti-Klan plank. (Weeks later, delegates to the Democratic National Convention, held in New York City, defeated a similar measure denouncing the Klan by name.) Seventy-five members of the US House of Representatives reportedly owed allegiance to the Klan. The year 1926 saw a former Klansman, Hugo Black, win election to the US Senate, a seat he would hold until winning confirmation to the US Supreme Court in 1937. There was even talk of electing a Kluxer president.[74]

At the state level, the Klan operated political machines in Oregon, California, Colorado, Kansas, Texas, Oklahoma, Arkansas, Alabama, Georgia, and Indiana strong enough, in some cases, to elect governors and control legislatures. At the local level, Klansmen served as moral watchdogs: whipping wayward wives, breaking up bootleggers' stills, and purifying public schools, mostly by demanding that Catholic teachers be fired. "We are ready after these many years to snatch the banner of Americanism from the ramparts we have so ably defended and go over the top against Romanism, alienism, bolshevism, and anti-Americanism of all kinds," Imperial Wizard Evans declared.[75]

Muskogee, Oklahoma, was among the locales where the Klan wielded clout. Exactly how much is unclear, though Oklahoma's governor was removed from office in 1923 after attempting to oust Muskogee's exalted cyclops, the leader of the city's chapter of the Klan, as part of a broader effort to tame the state's KKK, which boasted as many as 105,000 members, reportedly including prominent political, religious, and civic leaders. In any event, the city's all-White school board sprang into action when it discovered, in 1925, that Negro Manual and Training High School teachers had adopted Carter Woodson's text, *The Negro in Our History*, for classroom use. After examining the book's contents, board members expressed "horror and surprise that such a work should have crept into our Negro schools." Woodson's depiction of a mixed-race jury in Washington, DC, offended segregationists, as did his criticism of the US government for its mistreatment of African American soldiers. His discussion of a race riot in the nation's capital in 1919, one of dozens that flared across the country that year, rankled as well. The board decreed that no book should be "instilled in the schools that is either klan or antiklan," insinuating that Woodson's work was anti-Klan.[76]

Woodson inaugurated Negro History Week in hopes of countering the ignorance that he saw as the root cause of the violence that shaped the Black experience in America. It was often in the schoolroom, he wrote, where students learned that Black lives did not matter, that "the Negro [was] nothing, ha[d] never been anything and never [would] be anything but a menace to civilization." Greater knowledge of Black history, of the challenges faced and contributions made by persons of African descent, could "bring about a reign of brotherhood through an appreciation of the virtues of all races, creeds and colors."[77]

Muskogee's Black residents, though, like many African Americans nationwide, lived with the reality of racial violence. Muskogee was located just fifty miles from Tulsa, where in 1921 White mobs destroyed "Black Wall Street," as the city's Greenwood District was known, killing at least thirty-six people, most of them Black. This event was never far from the minds of Muskogee's African American educators, not when thousands of Klansmen were marching unmasked in the nation's capital. Muskogee's Black teachers, writes scholar Jarvis Givens, "were always on notice about their vulnerability. Their local realities were tethered to an expansive history of so-called uppity Negro educators being physically whipped or having their homes bombed." Angry Whites, they knew, sometimes shot into schoolyards where students played. Schoolhouses mysteriously burned down in the middle of the night. Stories of such violence were engrained in the consciousness of Black educators.

So the response was muted when Muskogee's school board banned Woodson's "anti-Klan" book. The board confiscated all outstanding copies and prohibited teachers from using the book moving forward. It also forced the school's principal to resign. The consequences for challenging White supremacy, educators knew, could have been more severe. "Violence and terror were central to the ways in which Black people were conscripted into the sociality of the American school," writes Givens. Threats shaped Black educators' professional reality in many locales. Muskogee was no different.[78]

PHILADELPHIA'S SESQUICENTENNIAL EXPOSITION WAS SAVED BY THE bell. Not the Liberty Bell, though the illuminated replica that straddled the fair's entrance certainly attracted attention. Rather, the bell that rang ringside as 102,757 paying customers crammed into Sesquicentennial Stadium on a soggy September night to see heavyweight boxing champion Jack Dempsey defend his crown for the first time in three years.

"I ain't never seed anything like it," promoter George "Tex" Rickard said of the crowd, the largest ever gathered until then to witness an American sporting event. High rollers shelled out as much as $27.50 ($510 today) for ringside seats. According to *The Philadelphia Inquirer*, the "diamond and pearl brigade" comprised a veritable who's who of the Roaring Twenties, including Treasury Secretary Andrew W. Mellon, steel magnate Charles M. Schwab, publishers William Randolph

Hearst and Joseph Pulitzer, and heirs to the Rockefeller, Astor, Harriman, and Whitney fortunes. New York Yankees slugger Babe Ruth headlined the famous athletes present. Movie stars Charlie Chaplin, Norma Talmadge, and Tom Mix traveled from Hollywood. Gamblers, including Arnold Rothstein, the man suspected of fixing baseball's 1919 World Series, sat close to the action as well.[79]

The rain that had soaked the Sesquicentennial from the outset beat down on fans, softening the men's broad-brimmed fedoras, plastering the women's short skirts against their legs, and generally dampening the mood. "It was the sort of fight night nobody enjoys save those who were unable to be present," wrote novelist Katharine Brush, who braved the conditions. "They tell you afterwards, smugly, 'Well we thought of you! There we were, all warm and cozy, hearing it *perfectly* on the radio—.'"[80]

Dempsey entered the Philadelphia ring bareknuckled. Judges supervised the taping of his hands in full view of the crowd to ensure that his gloves did not conceal weights or other foreign objects, which he was rumored to have used to wrest the championship from Jess Willard seven years earlier. Dempsey had entered that contest relatively unknown, a native of tiny Manassa, Colorado (population 642), brought east by Rickard to vie for the title based on the strength of his record fighting in saloons, clubs, and theaters across the American West. Though physically unimposing even by the standards of the day—at his peak Dempsey stood no more than 6'1" and weighed 185 to 190 pounds—he exited the July 4, 1919, bout as the "Manassa Mauler," the brawler who knocked down Willard seven times in the first round alone, forcing the 6'6", 245-pound "Pottawatomie Giant" to throw in the towel after the third round, reportedly with a broken jaw, a fractured cheek, cracked ribs, missing teeth, and hearing loss in one ear. Dempsey's fearsome legend, as told and retold by sportswriters, only grew with each of his five successful title defenses, such that he stood with Babe Ruth atop the galaxy of star athletes—including footballer Red Grange, golfer Bobby Jones, tennis players Bill Tilden and Helen Wills Moody, and swimmers Gertrude Ederle and Johnny Weissmuller—who distinguished the 1920s as a golden age of sports.

Some boos rained down on Dempsey from the cheap seats because he had not defended his title since knocking out Luis Ángel Firpo in 1923. Critics claimed he was ducking a top challenger: Harry Wills, holder of the World Colored Heavyweight Championship. Black boxers could compete with Whites for the world title in lower divisions. But a color line, drawn in 1892 by the first heavyweight champion of gloved boxing, John L. Sullivan, aka the "Boston Strong Boy," prevented heavyweights from competing for the ultimate prize, just as a line barred Black baseball players from playing in the major leagues. "I will not fight a Negro. I never have and I never shall," said Sullivan.[81]

Since fighting Firpo, Dempsey had appeared in Broadway plays and starred in Hollywood movies. Sporting a monocle, an accessory he had affected while traveling in Europe, the champ stood before a gaggle of reporters and insisted, "I'll fight Wills." Notwithstanding his yearslong hiatus from boxing, he was fully confident that he could lick anyone who entered the ring. Organizers needed only to set the price. "I'll be ready," he said. "All I want now is some money, some exercise, and a fight."[82]

But Dempsey had been quick to redraw the color line in 1919 when he wrested the title from Jess Willard, the White boxer who had dethroned the first Black heavyweight champion, Jack Johnson, four years earlier. Johnson's exceptional reign only reinforced exclusionary practices in boxing's uppermost reaches. Dempsey, sounding much like Sullivan, announced in 1919 that he would "pay no attention to Negro challengers." Only White heavyweights need apply.[83]

Black journalists called Dempsey yellow, a coward, for ignoring Wills. The champion's refusal to settle things in the ring represented a step backward in the struggle for equal opportunity, declared the editors of *The Chicago Defender*, a leading African American newspaper. For a moment, during the days of Jack Johnson, the heavyweight title "was a fair and square proposition, to be earned and held by anyone capable of annexing it." Since then, the championship had been lily white. No Black heavyweight had gotten a shot at the crown, not even the great Harry Wills, the three-time World Colored Heavyweight Champion who had defeated several top contenders, including Firpo, the Argentinian famous for knocking Dempsey out of the ring in 1923 before getting knocked out himself. Wills's exclusion was unjust, un-American even, *Defender* editors suggested.[84]

Wills himself called out Dempsey in March 1926. "The only thing I can figure from the way he's ducked fighting me is simply that he doesn't want my game. Call it fear or what you like." Wills trained with calisthenics every day. He was prepared to fight Dempsey.[85]

Bowing to public pressure, the New York State Athletic Commission issued a ruling in June 1926. Authorized to regulate boxing and other combative sports in the state, the commission barred Dempsey from fighting in New York, boxing's richest market, unless he defended his title against Wills.[86]

Tex Rickard, boxing's kingpin, greeted the news with mixed emotions. On the one hand, he hated to miss out on a big payday. On the other hand, he refused to promote a Dempsey-Wills bout under any circumstances. Rickard had promoted the "Fight of the Century," the July 4, 1910, contest in which Jack Johnson successfully defended his title against the "Great White Hope," former champion Jim Jeffries, who had been coaxed out of retirement specifically to unseat Johnson. Johnson's victory triggered race riots across the country that ended with at least nineteen people dead and hundreds more injured—most of them Black. In 1926, the measurables showed that Dempsey, thirty-one, enjoyed a six-year age advantage over Wills, who at thirty-seven was well past his athletic prime. But the 6'2", 220-pound Wills outweighed Dempsey by thirty-plus pounds. The "Brown Panther," as Wills was known, had a puncher's chance. Rickard did not want to risk another great White champion going down to defeat, not in the heated ethnoracial climate of the 1920s. Besides, Rickard claimed that unnamed "powerful forces" in Washington had directed him not to schedule a Dempsey-Wills fight.[87]

With New York no longer an option, Rickard decided to look elsewhere for a match between Dempsey and someone other than Wills. Sesquicentennial officials invited him to consider Philadelphia. In August, Rickard announced that Dempsey would meet a White contender, Gene Tunney, in Sesquicentennial Stadium on September 23, 1926. Rickard pledged to do his utmost "to make the bout contribute to the good of the city and the sesqui."[88]

Pennsylvania's three-person boxing commission approved the match over the objection of its lone Black member. Editors of *The Philadelphia Tribune*, an African American newspaper, criticized state officials for allowing the contest to be held, especially in conjunction with the Sesquicentennial. Sanctioning a segregated title match in the home of the Declaration of Independence represented "a disgrace to the historic celebration."[89]

Philadelphia leaders were jubilant though. Despite opening Sundays, "America's Greatest Flop," as *Variety* called the Sesquicentennial, remained in serious financial distress. Fewer than 1.6 million of the estimated 30 million visitors had entered the gates by late August, and the exhibition was well on its way to being $10 million in debt. Rickard offered a lifeline. Under the terms of the deal, the city's Sesquicentennial Exhibition Association was slated to receive 10 percent of gross receipts, which Rickard predicted would reach $2 million. At $200,000, the commission's cut would help satisfy creditors, hundreds of whom were threatening legal action to recover their monies. Plus,

Gene Tunney (dark trunks) and Jack Dempsey (crouched low) square off in Philadelphia's Sesquicentennial Stadium, September 23, 1926. (Credit: Hulton Archive / Getty Images)

the additional visitors the title fight was expected to draw to the city would generate millions of dollars in concession sales, hotel fees, and tax revenues. "This is the greatest thing that ever happened for the Sesqui," Mayor Freeland Kendrick proclaimed. He was confident the bout would boost the expo's fortunes.[90]

Aside from the drenching rain—a remnant of the Great Miami Hurricane of 1926 that devastated South Florida, killing hundreds—the opening moments of the fight went as expected. Dempsey, a heavy 3.5:1 favorite, charged his opponent from the bell, crowding Tunney into the corner, against the ropes. Crouched low, Dempsey unleashed his furious attack, fists flying: A left hook to the jaw. A quick right and left to the body, followed by another combination to the face. A jab to the head. Two more rights to the body.

Few expected Tunney, a light puncher, to last the full ten rounds. But the challenger was smart (too smart for some sportswriters, who commented, disapprovingly, that "Gentleman Gene" liked to read, and not the *Police Gazette* but literature by the likes of George Bernard Shaw, Thornton Wilder, and Somerset Maugham). He had carefully studied Dempsey. And he had concluded that a skillful boxer could thwart the champ's frontal assaults. He also noticed that Dempsey was susceptible to a straight right-hand punch. Firpo had nailed him with a right in 1923. So had another challenger, Georges Carpentier, in 1921.[91]

Tunney's preparation paid off in Philadelphia. As Dempsey launched yet another left in his first-round fusillade, Tunney stepped in toward the champion and snapped off a straight right hand to the face. The punch landed high, on the cheek. It was tough to tag Dempsey square on the jaw, fighting as he did in a crouch, with his chin tucked into his left shoulder. But it shook the champ, taking some of the starch out of him. Dazed, he staggered back, and then clinched Tunney, holding his opponent's arms for a moment to steady himself. Tunney, noticing Dempsey's hesitation, followed with another right, a good left, and four quick clips—right, left, right, left—to the head before the bell. Sitting in his corner breathing smelling salts after the round, won easily by Tunney, Dempsey thought, "I'm an old man."[92]

A proud champion, Dempsey continued to press, aiming for a knockout. In the fourth round, "Jack rushed from his corner with a semblance of his old-time fury," according to one ringside observer, sportswriter Nat Fleischer. Reaching Tunney almost before the challenger was off his stool, Dempsey knocked him almost over the top rope with hard right and left hooks to the head. In the sixth, he landed a left to the throat so hard that Tunney ended up hoarse and coughing blood for days.[93]

But that straight right to the cheek that Tunney landed in the first round was the blow that won the fight. "Thereafter," Tunney recalled, "it was a methodical matter of outboxing him, foiling his rushes, piling up points, clipping him with repeated, damaging blows, correct sparring."[94]

Tunney, onlookers agreed, probably would have knocked out Dempsey had the fight gone longer than ten rounds, so thorough was his dominance. Displaying "fine generalship," "The Fighting Marine," as Tunney was also known due to his service in the US Marine Corps during the Great War, made Dempsey look "as helpless and bewildered as a raw crude street corner fighter," wrote legendary sportswriter Grantland Rice. He made him look like a "selling plater," a racehorse so slow as to be sold at auction, Nat Fleischer agreed.[95]

As it was, Tunney won by unanimous decision, scoring one of the biggest upsets in heavyweight history. "I have realized all my ambition," exclaimed Tunney. He promised to defend the crown "as becomes a Marine."[96]

As fans squished out of Sesquicentennial Stadium, Philadelphia officials counted their receipts. Officially, the fight grossed $1.895 million, a record high for a sports gate. At 10 percent, the Sesquicentennial association received $189,500. In addition, fans rang up taxi, restaurant, and hotel bills, bringing Philadelphia's total windfall to $5 million—the price of crowning a White champion in the Cradle of Liberty. "Merchants, café owners, and hotel officials were all smiles yesterday," reported *The Philadelphia Inquirer*, praising "the best money spending crowd that this city has ever played host to."[97]

As the Sesqui drew to a close, Americans paid tribute to a man once considered an enemy of the state, labor leader Eugene V. Debs, who died in a Chicago-area sanitarium on October 20, 1926, after a lengthy illness. He was seventy years of age.

But the founders had the courage to stand up and speak out, to declare the birth of a new age in which governments were instituted among citizens, deriving their just powers from the consent of the governed.[103]

At first, Debs continued, these rebels faced stiff opposition. They were denounced. They were condemned. Had the American Revolution failed, they almost certainly would have been executed as traitors. But the Revolution had succeeded, and those self-same rebels were revered 150 years later as the founders of American democracy. "Debs's thought and the actions that flowed from it were firmly rooted in the American experience," observed Salvatore.[104]

Found guilty in September 1918 despite his appeal to the jury, Debs was sentenced to ten years' imprisonment. He refused to seek a pardon from President Wilson or from Wilson's successor, Warren Harding, because Debs did not believe he had committed a crime: "If I should apply for pardon it would be in my eyes an acknowledgement that I was wrong when I stood my ground for the right of free speech in the United States."[105]

Even so, President Harding released Debs (without pardoning him) and twenty-three other political prisoners on Christmas Day 1921. Debs returned by train to Terre Haute, where he was met, *The New York Times* reported, by "red fire, blaring bands, and fully 50,000 men, women, and children." As soon as he set foot on the station platform, he was lifted on the shoulders of his welcomers and carried to a waiting automobile that whisked him to the humble abode on Terre Haute's Eighth Street that he shared with Kate, his wife of thirty-six years. He was back home again in Indiana.[106]

There he remained, in failing health and mostly out of the public eye, until October 1926. "Gene Debs, Socialists' Chief, Dies," read Nebraska's *Omaha Morning Bee* headline. Debs's death came as a blow to the American Left, which was already in considerable disarray following the Red Scare. Outside the Rand School of Social Science, a socialist institution based in New York City, the American flag flew at half-staff. Buildings housing *The Jewish Daily Forward* and other leftist publications were draped in black. Many union headquarters bore placards with expressions of grief.[107]

Fifteen thousand mourners attended a hastily arranged memorial meeting at New York's Madison Square Garden. Norman Thomas presided. A rising star who would go on to be the Socialist Party of America's candidate for president of the United States in 1928, the first of six unsuccessful bids for the nation's highest office, Thomas said of Debs, "No leader in our generation had so deep and true a hold of the affection of millions of men and women as Gene Debs." He engendered such admiration because no leader "so sincerely loved mankind."[108]

As Thomas suggested, Debs's loss was felt across the political spectrum. Mourners from many walks of life came to pay their respects at the Terre Haute home where Debs's body lay in state in the family's flower-embowered parlor. Lines stretching for blocks converged on the Eighth Street address from three directions—left, right, and center. Grievers included neighbors who had known Debs since he was a pink-cheeked youth, friends who had stood shoulder to shoulder with him in some of his early unionization efforts, and Main Street businesspeople and community leaders who respected the sincerity of his convictions even if they themselves disagreed with them. "Rich and poor, lofty and humble, it was a brotherhood of man such as Debs hoped for," reported the Associated Press.[109]

While Debs had powerful enemies, many people remembered him as a great American—a leader who had gone to prison for stating his views, however unpopular they might have been at the time; a martyr who had suffered in the name of freedom; a civil libertarian who had dared to exercise his rights in a country at war. Arthur Brisbane may have put it best. An influential columnist employed by publisher William Randolph Hearst, whose newspapers were known for taking conservative editorial positions on both domestic and foreign policy matters, Brisbane wrote in an obituary, "Eugene V. Debs, a sincere and honest man, is dead, killed by imprisonment inflicted upon him for saying what he thought about the War."[110]

TESSIE MCGEE ADDRESSED HER CLASS, READING FROM a copy of Carter G. Woodson's "book of the Negro" that rested in her lap, tucked safely behind the teacher's desk. McGee, twenty-eight, taught history during the 1933–1934 academic year at the only secondary school open to African American students in Webster Parish, Louisiana. The state's all-White education department had set clear expectations: Teachers were to keep a preapproved lesson plan openly displayed on their desks, which they were to follow closely in acquainting students with the required learning objectives. But McGee deviated from the script when she, in her professional judgment, felt it was in her students' interest to do so. She often read passages from Woodson's book, which she kept hidden from administrators. Though subject to the disciplinary practices of Jim Crow authorities, McGee was undeterred. "She read to us from that book," a former student recalled. Whenever the principal appeared in the doorway, she would lift her eyes to the outline displayed on her desk and teach from it. When the principal left, her eyes returned to the Woodson text in her lap.[111]

McGee's act of defiance was not isolated. Black teachers across the country supplemented US history with African American history to foster the next generation. "Children," Houston A. Baker Jr. remembered his Kentucky elementary school teacher, Ms. Carter, saying, "you must never be ashamed of being Negroes! Dr. Woodson wants us to be proud of our history."[112]

Introduced in 1926, that message would sustain students as they marched for freedom and struggled to realize the Declaration of

Independence's principles. "I could not move, because history had me glued to the seat," Montgomery, Alabama's Claudette Colvin, fifteen, thought in March 1955 when a driver ordered her to move to the back of the bus. "It felt like Sojourner Truth's hands were pushing me down on one shoulder and Harriet Tubman's hands were pushing me down on another shoulder, and I could not move." Colvin and her classmates at Montgomery's segregated Booker T. Washington High School had studied America's founding texts during February's Negro History Week. She knew she had rights—unalienable ones.[113]

"We were standing on the shoulders of others," remembered Carlotta Walls LaNier, who in 1957 desegregated Arkansas's Central High School as one of the Little Rock Nine. "We had Negro History Week in the segregated Black schools." She was always proud to read and hear about what African Americans did for the country.[114]

Teachers in John Lewis's rural Alabama school displayed "photographs and pictures of great African Americans for Carter G. Woodson's Negro History Week," Lewis recalled many years later. Such images started Lewis on a path that led to making "good trouble" at Selma's Edmund Pettus Bridge in 1965 in support of voting rights for African Americans. They led to Atlanta, where Lewis embarked on a political career that would take him to Washington, DC, where he represented Georgia's Fifth District in the US House of Representatives, rising to a leadership position in the Democratic caucus. And as 1976 approached, they led Lewis and other civil rights activists to build on these hard-won gains by working, not just in the South but across the nation, to organize voters, achieve economic justice, and secure full inclusion in schools, the workplace, and other national institutions—to realize, in other words, the American promise made in 1776.[115]

5

Bicentennial

I must say to you that the state of the Union is not good.

—GERALD FORD (1975)[1]

"EASTWARD HO!" CRIED A TEAMSTER AS THE horse-drawn covered wagons moved out of Blaine, Washington, in June 1975. "Somehow," he admitted, "that just doesn't have the right ring to it." Yet east was the direction the wagons were headed on a yearlong journey to Valley Forge, Pennsylvania, where George Washington's army had wintered in 1777–1778.[2]

The Blaine wagons were the first to depart on a route that reversed the westward treks thousands of nineteenth-century settlers had made along the Oregon Trail. Averaging twenty miles a day, they crossed the state border in July 1975, where they were joined by wagons representing Oregon and, later, Idaho. In September, they added wagons from Nevada and Utah retracing the historic Mormon Trail. And in October, they added more still from Montana and Wyoming crossing the Rocky Mountains along the old Bozeman Trail.

After wintering the horses—"We're not trying to recreate the hardships of the original wagon trains, just the steps," a traveler explained—the wagoners got moving again in the spring of 1976, meeting in Missouri a train of wagons coming from California on the Gila and Santa Fe Trails through Arizona, New Mexico, Colorado, and Kansas. Other wagon trains appeared on the horizon as well. One snaked from the Dakotas down to Iowa, back up to Minnesota, and across Wisconsin, Illinois, Indiana, and points east. Another moved south from Maine, New Hampshire, and Vermont through Massachusetts, Rhode Island, Connecticut, and New Jersey. Still others headed north from Texas, Louisiana, Georgia, and other Southern states.[3]

Fifty wagons total representing each of the states, plus chuck wagons, lead wagons, and a phalanx of pickup trucks, horse trailers, mobile homes, and other support vehicles, were all part of the Bicentennial Wagon Train Pilgrimage, a modern-day Wild West show of sorts that aimed to circle up in Valley Forge to celebrate Independence Day 1976.

Conceived by Thelma Gray, an advertising executive, the wagon train sought to draw tourism to Pennsylvania, the birthplace of not only the Declaration of Independence but the Conestoga—the wagon that, she said, had helped win the Revolutionary War and (later, in modified prairie schooner form) settle the American West. Gray envisioned the wagon train as a grassroots "demonstration of the fiber, the pioneer spirit, that made America great"; of the grit that enabled "America to survive wars, depressions, epidemics."[4]

Americans living in 1976 needed such a demonstration because the national mood had soured. Truth be told, the country was on a losing streak, and losing was not something to which most Americans were accustomed—not in the decades following World War II, anyway. After all, victory in 1945 had propelled the United States to superpower status and launched a sustained period of economic growth that powered a confident belief that Americans could "pay any price, bear any burden, meet any hardship" to reach for the stars, as President John F. Kennedy had said in his 1961 inaugural address.

But 1976 found Americans still mourning the loss of President Kennedy, as well as his brother, Senator Robert F. Kennedy, and civil rights leader Dr. Martin Luther King Jr., all killed by assassins. National unity was fraying. Dr. King's 1968 shooting, by a White man, triggered urban riots that reached within a stone's throw of the US Capitol in Washington, DC, one of many cities left scarred. Divided by the Vietnam War, which ended in defeat in 1975 with over 50,000 US soldiers dead, many more wounded, and others traumatized, Americans were also reeling from Watergate, a scandal–cum–constitutional crisis that shook public faith in government. And they were suffering through a deep economic recession, the deepest since the Great Depression of the 1930s, that ended the period of prosperity and much of the confidence it underwrote. Economists introduced a new statistic, the "misery index," to measure the real-world pain inflicted by stagflation, another new term coined to describe the economy's unusual combination of high unemployment and high inflation. The state of the union was not good, President Gerald Ford acknowledged in his annual address to Congress, saying out loud what everybody already knew.

After years of bad news, the country's 200th birthday celebration presented an opportunity to change the subject, to talk about something, anything other than stagflation, Watergate, or Vietnam. The Bicentennial Wagon Train, for instance, an official commemorative event sponsored by Pennsylvania's state Bicentennial Commission, encouraged citizens to rededicate themselves to the country's founding principles. Volunteers could demonstrate their pioneer spirit by driving wagons cross-country, and many people self-funded the journey. "We're going all the way," said Marie Scufiel of Fiddletown, California. "We sold our ranch to finance the trip."[5]

Others could show their mettle by signing "rededication scrolls" distributed to schools, youth groups, and businesses by 4-H clubs, Boy Scout and Girl Scout troops, and other service organizations. Printed by Encyclopedia Britannica, a corporate sponsor, the scrolls invited signers to avow their belief in the Declaration of Independence's ideals: "To commemorate this nation's Bicentennial we hereby dedicate ourselves anew to the precepts of our Founding Fathers . . ." A "pony express" consisting of members of local riding clubs collected signed scrolls for carriage to Valley Forge, where they would be catalogued and preserved.[6]

Many Native Americans, galvanized by an upsurge of rights activism that saw protestors occupy the US Bureau of Indian Affairs building in 1972, opposed the wagon train. To them, the event recalled a painful history of theft, genocide, and defeat. "We felt the invitation was like the Germans inviting the Jews to celebrate Hitler's rise to power," the director of Portland, Oregon's Urban Indian Program said of his decision not to participate.[7]

Undaunted, the wagoners forged ahead on a Bicentennial journey they hoped would work wonders. "I don't know whether all this wagon train business will make any difference in this country," said Ken Wilcox, a fifty-seven-year-old wagon master. "Whether anyone will actually rededicate himself to America's ideals, we'll never know. But it's a pretty dream, I reckon."[8]

Gerald Ford, a president whom no one had voted for, was emblematic of the nation's woes. Richard Nixon, not Ford, was supposed to have been president in 1976, of course, and Nixon began his second term in office fully expecting to end his tenure bathed in red, white, and blue Bicentennial glory. But Nixon—faced with almost certain removal from office after the House Judiciary Committee adopted articles of impeachment for his coverup of White House ties to the June 1972 break-in at the Democratic National Committee (DNC) headquarters in Washington, DC's Watergate office complex—announced his resignation on August 8, 1974.

Ford, Nixon's sixty-one-year-old vice president, assumed office the next day. A former congressman from Grand Rapids, Michigan, Ford had served as House minority leader for almost nine years before Nixon named him vice president in October 1973 to replace Spiro Agnew, who himself had resigned in disgrace as a result of an unfolding bribery investigation. Like Calvin Coolidge before him, Ford sought, as president, to heal the nation's wounds. "My fellow Americans," he remarked upon taking the oath of office as president, "our long national nightmare is over. Our Constitution works; our great Republic is a government of laws and not of men."[9]

Among his first major acts as president was to grant Nixon an unconditional pardon for all offenses he had committed or "may have committed" while in office. Pardoning Nixon served the country's interests, Ford claimed. Any trial or other legal actions Nixon might face for obstructing justice, abusing power, or holding Congress in contempt were likely to be prolonged, with no clear end in sight, during which time the Watergate nightmare would have continued, polarizing society and challenging the credibility of America's governing institutions. Ford said it was time to move on: "My conscience tells me it is my duty, not merely to proclaim domestic tranquility but to use every means that I have to insure it."[10]

Watergate resisted easy closure, though. Critics complained that Ford's hasty pardon allowed Nixon to escape justice. Telegrams, letters, and phone calls poured into the White House denouncing Ford's decision. Protestors jeered him when he appeared in Pittsburgh the day after his announcement.[11]

More seriously, Ford's action fueled speculation that, as vice president, he had agreed to a secret deal with Nixon to trade the presidency for a pardon. Outside the White House, picketers hoisted a bedsheet reading, "Promise Me Pardon and I'll Make You President." These charges were never fully substantiated. But they recalled previous allegations of backroom deals in American history, including the "corrupt bargains" that supposedly decided the 1824 and 1876 presidential elections. And they irreparably harmed Ford's standing. His approval rating plummeted from 71 to 49 percent, the biggest drop ever measured. Suddenly, an ally said, Ford "was vulnerable. And he was vulnerable because he had pardoned Nixon."[12]

Distrust of the executive branch deepened. "Huge CIA Operation Reported in U.S. Against Antiwar Forces, Other Dissidents in Nixon Years," read a December 22, 1974, *New York Times* headline. Although the news article itself did not implicate Ford directly—the misdeeds the *Times* documented occurred before he assumed office—the paper's claim that the Central Intelligence Agency had conducted, under previous administrations, "a massive, illegal domestic intelligence operation" against anti–Vietnam War protestors, civil rights activists, and other dissident groups subjected the presidency to closer scrutiny. Congress opened investigations of the CIA, the Federal Bureau of Investigation (FBI), and other portions of the US intelligence community, or "secret government," as some called it. Ford tried to limit the damage by appointing a blue-ribbon commission chaired by Vice President Nelson Rockefeller. But when Ford voiced concern in a January 1975 meeting with journalists that Rockefeller's commission might discover additional activities such as foreign assassination attempts that would "blacken the name of every president back to Harry Truman," the "son of Watergate," as CBS News correspondent Daniel Schorr termed the intelligence furor, grew bigger still.[13]

Skeletons came spilling out of the deep state's closet. Congressional investigators discovered that the CIA and FBI had withheld key evidence from the Warren Commission, the panel tasked with investigating President Kennedy's 1963 assassination. Investigators also discovered that the FBI had aimed COINTELPRO, a vast counter-intelligence program, against Martin Luther King Jr. and other civil rights leaders. These shocking disclosures followed those previously unearthed by Watergate investigators, including the discovery of CIA ties to the June 1972 DNC break-in. Together, such revelations fueled public cynicism and disillusionment, popularizing conspiracy theories holding that sinister forces were behind many events, including the JFK and MLK assassinations. By 1976, the overwhelming majority of Americans, 81 percent, believed that people beyond a lone gunman were responsible for Kennedy's murder. A journalist reported, "American society has gone buggy on conspiracy theories of late because so many nasty demonstrations of the real thing have turned up."[14]

As the intelligence drama showed, norms governing the press and its handling of sensitive information were rapidly changing. Journalists grew more assertive in the wake of Vietnam and Watergate—a scandal uncovered by *Washington Post* reporters Bob Woodward and Carl Bernstein. Secrets that the news media once safeguarded were now being exposed. These included personal as well as state secrets. During the 1930s and 1940s, the press tactfully avoided taking, much less publishing, photographs of a polio-stricken President Franklin D. Roosevelt using a wheelchair. Even during the Kennedy administration, reporters never mentioned the president's womanizing in print. But times had changed. Now that Watergate had exposed the president's failings, the media, with public support, began highlighting instances of presidential awkwardness or weakness.[15]

And in June 1975, when President Ford slipped and fell while exiting an airplane in Salzburg, Austria, critics found their mark. It had rained in Salzburg, Ford's defenders noted, just before the president landed in Air Force One in the middle of a weeklong diplomatic swing through Europe. He had slept poorly the night before, and the damp weather stiffened his arthritic knees. As he helped his wife, Betty Ford, down the airplane's slick metal steps—one arm around the First Lady and the other clutching an umbrella—he lost his footing and tumbled to the tarmac in full view of cameras.

In reality, Gerald Ford was a gifted athlete, probably the best who has ever manned the Oval Office. A star football player at the University of Michigan, he remained physically active throughout his presidency, enjoying tennis, swimming, and golf. A superb skier—better at it at sixty-plus years of age than most of the younger reporters assigned to cover him—he regularly hit the slopes in Vail, Colorado, with family and friends.

Nevertheless, Ford, the accidental president, continued to stumble and bumble his way through his tenure. He fell skiing in Vail. He crashed into the end of the White House pool while swimming laps. He bumped his head entering the presidential helicopter. Working a crowd, he tripped over the outstretched leg of a woman in a wheelchair.

Each incident made the news and, worse, became the butt of jokes by late-night comedians. In October 1975, a new comedy program, *NBC's Saturday Night*, premiered on television. Later renamed *Saturday Night Live*, the show's original cast included Chevy Chase, a thirty-two-year-old physical comedy specialist who rocketed to fame based largely on his satirizing of Gerald Ford. Chase's slapstick impressions of Ford falling off airplanes, stumbling into lecterns, and hitting golf balls with tennis rackets made audiences laugh. They also conveyed the impression that Ford was clumsy, physically as well as intellectually. According to historian Yanek Mieczkowski, they communicated "the image of a man who was mentally obtuse, prone to making policy blunders as well as physical ones."[16]

Ford shrugged off the jokes. As a former college athlete, he said he was used to public criticism. But he could never shake the impression of being an oaf—a congenial oaf, to be sure, but an oaf, nonetheless. His press secretary lamented, "I could never change Ford's image; I could never convince the press that he wasn't clumsy and a bumbler."[17]

Bicentennial planners sought to flip the script. "We were turning a page," recalled a former US public affairs officer. By forgetting the "bad war" in Vietnam and remembering the good works the Declaration of Independence had performed in the world, planners tried to convey the impression that America "was basically a good society."[18]

At 200 years, the Declaration remained vibrant. Almost 100 declarations of independence had been issued by newly independent nations around the world since 1776. Twenty-eight appeared between 1945 and 1975 alone, when quantitatively the Declaration achieved its greatest-ever relevance. To be sure, many of those declarations took inspiration from sources other than the American original. The United States had squandered much of its moral capital as a force for good in the world since the Democratic Republic of Vietnam issued its declaration of independence in 1945. Authored by Ho Chi Minh, the document began by paraphrasing Thomas Jefferson's famous lines: "All men are created equal. They are endowed by their Creator with certain unalienable rights, among them are Life, Liberty, and the pursuit of Happiness."[19]

Yet Jefferson's identification of self-evident rights provided a basis for much of the human rights talk that emerged in the second half of the twentieth century. Together with 1789's French Declaration of the Rights of Man and of the Citizen, the American Declaration of Independence invented human rights insofar as those texts first gave direct political expression to the modern conception of human rights as natural, equal, and universal. The American and French declarations combined with the United Nations Universal Declaration of Human Rights (1948) and the European Convention on Human

Rights (1950) to create the first—and still ongoing—global rights moment in world history. In 1975, President Ford joined thirty-five world leaders in signing accords in Helsinki, Finland, that would prove important in guaranteeing human rights in Eastern Europe and the Soviet Union.[20]

Bicentennial plans drew on America's Revolutionary heritage to boost the nation's image. In 1966, Congress had established a federal agency, the American Revolution Bicentennial Commission, to plan, develop, and coordinate commemorative activities nationwide. Ambitious early plans called for full-throated celebrations of American history. Philadelphia was supposed to host an exposition, as the city had done in 1926 and 1876. "The American Revolution Bicentennial should be developed into the greatest single peacetime public opinion mobilization effort in our nation's history," said a public relations executive involved in early planning efforts.[21]

But Watergate cast a pall over the commission's plans. In 1972, *The Washington Post* published the "Bicentennial Papers," leaked commission files documenting close communication among commission staff, White House political operatives, and Republican Party campaign officials. According to the *Post*, the commission—chaired by businessman David J. Mahoney, a self-described "drinking and football buddy" of Nixon's, and composed largely of "white, middle-aged conservative Republicans and staunch supporters of the president"—sought to exploit the national holiday for partisan political purposes.[22]

Corporate interests dominated the Bicentennial Commission, the papers also showed. The commission's chairman, Mahoney, headed a conglomerate, Norton Simon Inc., that owned a number of major consumer brands. He handpicked a fellow business executive to serve as the commission's director, and together, critics alleged, they were busy selling the "Buycentennial" to the highest bidders. Commission officials were in talks with firms to produce all manner of commemorative kitsch, from sparkling new red, white, and blue Mack Trucks bearing the official Bicentennial logo to special Hallmark cards and Baskin-Robbins ice-cream flavors like "Betsy Ross Twirl" and "George Washington Cherry Tree."[23]

Someone had to pay for Bicentennial events, insisted commissioners, who sold licenses to businesses to market official Bicentennial items. General Motors, IBM, American Airlines, and other corporations contributed millions of dollars in sponsorship fees. These revenue streams offset official operating costs. Besides, said the executive secretary of the New York chapter of the Sons of the American Revolution, "There's nothing wrong with making a buck. Free enterprise is the thing that has made this country go zowee."[24]

The People's Bicentennial Commission was not mollified. Founded in 1971 by Jeremy Rifkin, a twenty-six-year-old schooled in the tactics of New Left protest, the people's commission sought, in contrast to the "Tory celebration" proposed by officials, to put the Revolution back into the American Revolution Bicentennial. Rifkin's group aimed to honor the nation's Revolutionary heritage in such ways as to expose the new breed of "corporate monarchs," economic royalists, and other forces of concentrated power who were allegedly perverting American democracy.[25]

Members of the people's commission fired the Bicentennial's first volley in Boston, a hub of commemorative activity due to the city's rich Revolutionary history. On December 16, 1973, an estimated 40,000 people gathered at Boston Harbor for ceremonies marking the 200th anniversary of the Boston Tea Party. Official proceedings, organized by the city of Boston, began as expected. Historical reenactors wearing tricorn hats and knee breeches boarded the *Beaver*, a freshly refurbished replica of the Tea Party ship that city officials hoped would draw visitors to the wharf for years to come, and dumped crates of ersatz tea into the harbor. But things veered off course when protestors seized the

Beaver and unfurled a banner over its side that read, "Impeach Nixon." They also dumped empty oil drums into the harbor to protest the grip high energy prices then had on American consumers due to an Organization of the Petroleum Exporting Countries embargo. Meanwhile, another people's commission group circled the brig in a rowboat. One crew member wearing a Nixon mask waved his hands high in Nixon's familiar "V for victory" style. Other crew members hanged a tarred-and-feathered Nixon dummy in effigy.

The day's events made news—just not the kind public officials and corporate sponsors wanted. "The first anguished attempt to make something—anything—out of one of America's most meaningful historic events," opined *The Washington Post*, resulted only in the sort of "commercial and ideological hucksterism that seems pandemic to this land today."[26]

That month, Congress replaced the federal commission with the American Revolution Bicentennial Administration (ARBA). Directed by Secretary of the Navy John Warner, soon to gain fame as actress Elizabeth Taylor's sixth husband, the new Bicentennial administration kept the same basic mission: to coordinate, facilitate, and promote events commemorating the nation's 200th anniversary. But its aims were downsized. Philadelphia's federally funded exposition was scrapped, as were plans to construct public housing, parks, and other projects with tax dollars. Economic hard times prevented such grand schemes, authorities said. Instead, the administration turned over planning—and payment responsibility—to local governments and voluntary associations. The Bicentennial would be celebrated primarily at the local level—a development organizers hailed as a feature, not a bug. Henceforth, the Bicentennial would be "a hometown affair," they said, working to "bring dissidents as well as neighbors and friends together in common purpose."[27]

"JESUS, MARY, AND JOSEPH!" A BOSTON OFFICIAL cried the morning of March 5, 1975. "It could be another massacre all over again." According to reports, Restore Our Alienated Rights (ROAR), a White-led segregationist group, planned to disrupt the day's events marking the 205th anniversary of the Boston Massacre, including a ceremony honoring Crispus Attucks, an American sailor of African and Native American descent who was among those killed by British troops in 1770. ROAR's plans were among the latest salvos in the "Battle of Boston," a multiyear tumult that followed a federal judge's 1974 order requiring Boston schools to desegregate by busing students. The judge's finding that schools in Boston, the "Cradle of Liberty," were segregated—intentionally so by local authorities, the decision noted—shattered any illusion that racism was confined to Birmingham, Little Rock, or any number of other Southern locales where action was required to desegregate public facilities. And it demonstrated that the civil rights struggle was not over; while significant progress had been made since the US Supreme Court issued its landmark *Brown v. Board of Education of Topeka* decision in 1954, a great deal of work remained undone in many areas, Boston included.[28]

Participants in the busing battle, recalled journalist J. Anthony Lukas in his Pulitzer Prize–winning account *Common Ground*, drew historical parallels with the American Revolution. Many African Americans were skeptical of Bicentennial cheeriness, insisting that not all Americans had realized liberty, equality, and the other self-evident truths espoused by Thomas Jefferson in 1776. "It's a birthday party for a 200-year-old white man," said Byron Rushing, director of Boston's Museum of African American History. "When he was a baby he had a black nanny and when he got older he had black servants and blacks working his land. Now that he's 200, the black man still doesn't sit down at his table. He serves the cake." Rushing hoped the nation would eventually make good on its promises, including providing equal access to educational opportunity in Boston and elsewhere. But words were not enough. "Blacks don't respond much to all this Bicentennial talk," he said. "We want some reality."[29]

Busing proponents saw themselves as modern-day patriots determined to complete America's unfinished revolution. "Each person," an activist wrote, "whether his skin is black, white, brown, yellow or red, must be accepted as a person and given every chance to share the blessings that this country could give."[30]

Opponents—representative of the grassroots conservatism that swept the country in the transitional 1970s—imagined themselves as patriots as well. They claimed to be fighting against arbitrary power, the same force that had driven American colonists to declare independence from Britain in the first place. W. Arthur Garrity Jr., the judge who issued the 1974 desegregation order, stood in for King George III. "He's not elected by the people. He rules for life. He reigns just like a king," one critic complained. Garrity's decision amounted to "forced busing," imposed on parents by jurists, bureaucrats, and other outsiders who little appreciated how busing might negatively impact their children and their communities. South Boston's state representative said, "The sacred principles on which this nation was founded are threatened by a new tyranny, a tyranny dressed in judicial robes."[31]

Bicentennial celebrations of American democracy seemed misplaced in the face of such arbitrary power. "How can we celebrate our country's history when we are being denied the very rights we fought for in the Revolution?" asked an opponent, Nancy Yotts. Escorted by police, buses carrying Black students invaded her neighborhood on a regular basis, bringing the daily rhythm of life to an abrupt halt. "They even stopped an ambulance—an ambulance with a sick person in it—so those damn buses could get by," she said.[32]

Led by Louise Day Hicks, an outspoken fifty-eight-year-old city councilwoman with a bouffant hairdo and a thick South Boston accent,

ROAR did not interrupt the Crispus Attucks ceremonies, as feared. Some 150 attendees gathered peacefully to honor Attucks. His blood, among the first spilled for American liberty, one speaker noted, inspired a fight for human freedom that continued from Boston and Concord to Little Rock and Selma and back again.

Later, however, some 400 ROAR members marched toward the massacre site in downtown Boston for a scheduled reenactment. Led by two drummers beating a funeral dirge, eight black-clad pallbearers carried a coffin marked "RIP, Liberty—Born 1770–Died 1974." Some marchers chanted anti-Garrity slogans. Others carried placards reading, "Boston Mourns Its Lost Freedom" or "You Think This Is a Massacre, Just Wait." Behind them came still more marchers, Lukas wrote, some keening for their lost liberty "in the high-pitched wail long used to mourn the Irish dead."[33]

When they reached their destination, a man wearing a "No Forced Busing" sweatshirt led renditions of "The Star-Spangled Banner," the patriotic song "America (My Country, 'Tis of Thee)," and ROAR's anthem. To the tune of the "Colonel Bogey March," members intoned,

> *Boston was first in liberty.*
> *Boston, the one that first was free.*
> *Boston, again in Boston,*
> *The people will lead the whole country.*[34]

ROAR quieted as the reenactment began. Redcoat reenactors portrayed the squadron of British soldiers who in 1770 fired into a crowd of colonials, killing five, Attucks included. When the reenactors fired blanks, the sounds of which echoed off the glass and steel skyscrapers that now ringed the historic site, all 400 ROAR demonstrators dropped to the pavement en masse, Lukas recalled, "lying there for a moment as still as liberty in her coffin, as if to say: We, too, are victims."[35]

TED LANDSMARK DID NOT INTEND TO MAKE history on April 5, 1976. A twenty-nine-year-old Yale-trained lawyer employed by local contractors, he was running late to a meeting to discuss minority hiring in construction jobs. Preoccupied, he rounded a corner in Boston's City Hall Plaza, only to come face-to-face with a crowd of antibusing demonstrators coming in the other direction from a ROAR-sponsored rally.

"Get [him]," one demonstrator shouted, using a racial slur. Landsmark tried to escape. But assailants kicked and punched him, breaking his nose and bruising his body. One attacker, a young man, assaulted him with a pole bearing an American flag, as a news photographer, Stanley Forman, snapped pictures nearby.[36]

Forman's photograph, titled *The Soiling of Old Glory*, appeared on page one of the next morning's *Boston Herald American* under the headline "Youths Beat Black Lawyer at City Hall." It appeared on the front pages of newspapers across the country, from *The Washington Post* to the *Chicago Tribune* and the *San Francisco Chronicle*. And it made network television news.[37]

The image of a White youth assaulting a Black man with the Stars and Stripes changed the trajectory of Boston's busing crisis. It contradicted, in black and white, protestors' claim that issues other than race motivated their opposition to busing. Why did attackers single out Landsmark? "Because I'm Black," he answered. "It was racism pure and simple," Boston's mayor agreed. Discredited, ROAR leaders, Hicks included, lost their city council seats in 1977. Protests eased, and Judge Garrity would eventually relinquish control of city schools.[38]

The racially motivated attack would have been a matter of concern regardless of its circumstances. But the fact that it occurred in Boston, the cradle of the American Revolution, on the eve of the nation's

The Soiling of Old Glory showing Ted Landsmark being assaulted by a White man wielding a flagpole. Boston, April 5, 1976. (Credit: Stanley Forman)

Bicentennial, close to Faneuil Hall, the Boston Massacre site, and other historic attractions, prompted a reckoning with history. Landsmark, his broken nose heavily bandaged, appeared at a press conference days after his assault. He observed that he had been attacked not far from the site "where Crispus Attucks . . . got his."[39]

Editors of *Ebony* magazine noticed the connection as well. Despite claims to the contrary, the attack on Landsmark showed that some things had changed little since Attucks's killing in 1770. Inspired by musician Gil Scott-Heron's 1976 spoken-word poem "Bicentennial Blues," *Ebony*'s editors offered a blues verse of their own:

> *If you see Crispus Attucks and the blacks who died to make us free.*
> *If you see Crispus Attucks and the blacks who died to make us free.*

Tell 'em it's business as usual in Boston and the land of liberty.[40]

"We cannot celebrate the country," the magazine's editors concluded, "where an American citizen can be singled out because of his color and denied employment and education. This is still a country where an American can be abused and violated because his foreparents came from Africa. This is still a country riven by tribalism." Only the true spirit of '76, combined with strong moral leadership, could change the equation.[41]

"My name is Jimmy Carter, and I'm running for president." Carter, fifty-one, was a fresh face on the national scene in 1976, so fresh that he needed to introduce himself to voters at every stop in his fledgling campaign. Gerald Ford, Richard Nixon, Lyndon Johnson, indeed all presidents since World War I, had some sort of Washington experience prior to taking office. Even Dwight Eisenhower, though he never held elective political office before becoming president, was a household name thanks to his World War II generalship. Carter, though a US Navy veteran, was different. His political résumé was relatively thin, consisting of one term as Georgia's governor, two terms in its state senate, and service on county boards. In short, he was an outsider.

The very idea of Carter seeking the Democratic presidential nomination struck even his closest staff members as absurd. "We all knew it looked kind of preposterous," recalled Chief of Staff Hamilton Jordan. An early poll did not list Carter among thirty-five likely candidates. *The Washington Post* misidentified him as "Governor Jimmy Collins" and "Jimmie Carter."[42]

But Carter's team realized that being an outsider had certain advantages in 1976, for it freed him of Vietnam, Watergate, and other baggage that weighed down Washington insiders like Ford. So, Carter—Jimmy, not James or Jim—leaned into his biography as a smiling, down-to-earth peanut farmer who taught Sunday school back home in Plains, Georgia, on the side. He carried his own bags on the campaign trail. He spoke earnestly about the importance of integrity, decency, and good government. And he told Americans that he would always tell the truth. In TV ads, Carter said, "I'll never tell a lie. I'll never make a false statement. I'll never betray the confidence you have in me."[43]

Some voters struggled to hear past Carter's syrupy Georgia accent. His evangelical Christianity—a Southern Baptist, he spoke at one campaign stop about having "a deeply profound religious experience that changed [his] life dramatically"—struck others as odd, even concerning. Still others assumed, according to Carter, "that since [he was] a southern governor, [he] must be a secret racist."[44]

But he declared that the time for racial discrimination was over. He enjoyed the unwavering support of a fellow Georgian, Martin Luther King Sr., father of the slain civil rights leader. "I love and believe in [Jimmy Carter]," said King at an Atlanta rally. Popular musicians such as James Brown, Johnny Cash, and members of the Allman Brothers Band backed him too. ("If it hadn't been for Gregg Allman, I never would have been president," Carter said later.) And he was well acquainted with the work of the great folk star Bob Dylan, whom Carter hosted at the governor's mansion for late-night scrambled eggs and grits after an Atlanta concert.[45]

Carter's idealism appealed to younger voters. In remarks at Harvard Law School, he described his campaign as a "healing process" that would draw on the character of the American people to restore hope and confidence in the American system. Carter's "healing southernness," a scholar writes, held broad appeal well beyond the South, bolstered by popular TV programs like *The Andy Griffith Show* and *The*

Waltons, which went some way toward rehabilitating the region's image in the wake of the civil rights movement. Plus, with racism flaring in Boston and other parts of the North, Carter could plausibly argue that the South had weathered such strife in the past and was now moving toward a more inclusive, welcoming future.[46]

To the surprise of many, Carter, the dark horse candidate once considered laughable by many Washington experts, won the Iowa Democratic caucuses in January 1976, earning twice as much support as the second-place finisher. In February, he won the New Hampshire primary. And in March he defeated Alabama Governor George Wallace to win in Florida. Now the clear frontrunner, Carter withstood a late challenge from California Governor Jerry Brown to secure the Democratic nomination, which he formally accepted at the 1976 Democratic National Convention, held in mid-July in New York City's Madison Square Garden. There his running mate in the general election, vice presidential nominee Walter Mondale, made a bold prediction: "The year of our 200th birthday, the year of Jimmy Carter's election, will go down as one of the greatest years of public reform in American history."[47]

President Ford faced a strong challenge for his own party's nomination from former California Governor Ronald Reagan, a conservative who often spoke of the nation's traditions of limiting government, advancing individual freedom, and pursuing free market principles. America's founders, he said in a widely noted 1964 speech, "knew that governments don't control things. A government can't control the economy without controlling people. And they knew when a government sets out to do that, it must use force and coercion to achieve its purpose."[48]

Ford won the early primaries. Reagan's last shot came in North Carolina, where he won a surprising victory in March, mainly by attacking his fellow Republican's foreign policies. Success in the Tar Heel State breathed fresh life into Reagan's campaign. He followed with big victories in Texas, Alabama, Georgia, Indiana, Nebraska, and other states, garnering enough delegates to take the nomination fight all the way to that summer's Republican National Convention in Kansas City, Missouri.

Ford prevailed at the convention, albeit just barely, winning 1,187 delegates to Reagan's 1,070 to earn the GOP nomination. But Reagan's surprising performance electrified supporters. "We want Reagan!" they cheered, envisioning victory—in 1980, if not in 1976.[49]

THOUGH THE BICENTENNIAL WAGON TRAIN HAD OPENED to great fanfare, by spring 1976 the novelty had worn off for many wagoners. Still, Azusa, California, residents Larry and Pauline Asmus remained committed to the journey east. Both had been actively involved in their community's Bicentennial programs: Pauline chaired Azusa's planning committee, and Larry, a forty-four-year-old construction worker, managed California's state wagon train project. Seeing the trip as a once-in-a-lifetime opportunity, a chance to relive the romance of the Old West, they took their three teenage children out of school and headed to Pasadena, where they drove the California state wagon in the Tournament of Roses Parade on January 1, 1976. Flowery tributes, television cameras, newspaper reporters—it was all very exciting, and Larry spoke glowingly about his reasons for participating: "I served my time in Korea and I didn't believe in it. A lot of people served in Vietnam and didn't believe in it. But I believe in the 200 years it took us to get this far. I love this country. Hell, guys have given their lives—I'm just giving a little time and money."[50]

Traveling roughly twenty miles per day, the Asmuses, like other wagoners, stopped at predetermined destinations on the winding road to Valley Forge: Yuma, Arizona; Las Cruces, New Mexico; Garden City, Kansas, and points in between. At every stop, they collected rededication scrolls signed by residents. (One California town closed its elementary schools for "Pledge of Rededication Day," during which children brought their families to school for signing ceremonies.) They participated in daily parades, fairs, and other special events organized by local groups. They also hosted nightly renditions of the *Wagon Train Show*, a forty-five-minute program of song and dance performed on a portable stage by a troupe of college-aged actors who traveled with each wagon train. Audiences enjoyed the shows, so much so that crowds often gathered near the wagons for hours afterward to swap stories. "It's infectious," said Al Mavis, who escorted another part of the train across Illinois. "This is the real Bicentennial. You can hardly go to bed at night because people stay to sit around the campfire and sing."[51]

Each day offered a fresh adventure, a new opportunity to discover the majesty of America, a nation that had grown since 1926 to include fifty states (Alaska and Hawaii entered the union in 1959). Heading east, Pauline Asmus recalled seeing "the eerie beauty of the Arizona desert at sunset, the red clay and craggy mountains of New Mexico, the snowfalls of Colorado, the shimmering plains of Kansas in the rainy spring, the beauties of the Missouri, Mississippi, and Ohio Rivers."[52]

But the daily grind grew exhausting as the miles piled up. Organizers made some concessions to modernity. Mobile kitchens, chemical toilets, and other conveniences unavailable to nineteenth-century migrants eased the burdens of cross-country travel. Twentieth-century travelers, though, faced some challenges their forbears had not. Toxic herbicides prevented horses and mules from feeding on roadside grasses. Tin cans, broken glass, and other debris littered the pavement. An endless stream of gawkers clogged the roads, automobiles belching exhaust into the polluted air. Author Rachel Carson had raised environmental awareness with her 1962 book *Silent Spring*. Congress passed the Clean

Air Act in 1963, among the first modern US environmental laws. Activists marked the initial Earth Day in 1970. Yet the hazards remained. "I'm tired of waving to all those people with their cameras," groused wagoner Dale Wolford of Cottondale, Florida.[53]

The weather took a toll as well. Exposed to the elements, the riders pressed ahead, despite the wind that blasted their bodies, the rain that soaked them to the bone, the mud that caked everything, and worse. "There was a terrific thunderstorm here today," noted Grace Ritchie of Rigby, Idaho, who copiloted her state's wagon with her husband, Fred, as they neared Ogallala, Nebraska, on April 7, "then a great downpour of hail and rain that lasted twenty-four hours." Local farmers were pleased because the rains provided relief from drought. But it was hell on wagoners, who had to soldier through. "8:00 am—Through the mud and rain we went," Grace Ritchie wrote in her diary the next morning. The Ritchies gained a better appreciation of what it must have been like to be a pioneer, traveling by day in wet clothes, sleeping at night on bedding soaked with rain. "Another day in the life of a modern pioneer," Grace remarked a week later, as she and Fred struggled yet again to unstick their wagon from the mud.[54]

Some folks weren't in it for the long haul. They had jobs and kids—lives—to get back to. Besides, trail driving was dangerous. Horses bucked. Wagons overturned. Injuries occurred along the way, even deaths—two people suffered fatal heart attacks, and one person driving a support vehicle was killed when a fuel tank exploded. At least four horses died, including two that had to be euthanized after suffering extensive burns when their owners' trailer caught fire in Arizona.[55]

Native American protestors harried the travelers. Although American Indians had achieved significant legislative victories since 1924's Indian Citizenship Act, a great deal of work remained to reverse two centuries of federal Indian policy. One protest group appeared near Ogallala flying the American flag upside down—"not to be ornery,"

American Indian activist Russell Means speaks in Gordon, Nebraska, 1972. (Credit: Bill Ganzel)

Grace Ritchie noted in her diary, "but as [a] distress signal of their plight." They may have been part of the Trail of Self-Determination Caravan, which set off from the Yakima Nation in Washington state. Joined by members of other Native nations, including the Sisseton-Wahpeton Sioux of South Dakota and the Wolf Point Sioux and Blackfeet of Montana, the caravan followed the wagon train east in hopes of presenting Congress and President Ford with a list of grievances, Declaration of Independence style. The grievances highlighted the federal government's failure to honor past treaties with and commitments to Native peoples, with the goal of replacing the Bureau of Indian Affairs with an agency elected by and for Indians. Self-determination was key, a participant said, if Native Americans were to gain full control of tribal lands and resources.[56]

Many American Indians opposed the Bicentennial's celebratory spirit. "Who would want to participate in the 200th year of the rip-off of our country?" asked Grace Thorpe, daughter of noted athlete Jim Thorpe. "If the government would say, 'okay, we'll honor all your treaties on water and fishing rights and we'll give back land that was stolen,' that would give the Indians something to celebrate."[57]

Some Indigenous leaders proposed a counter-commemoration marking the 100th anniversary of the Battle of the Little Bighorn in which Lakota Sioux, Northern Cheyenne, and other tribes defeated George Armstrong Custer in 1876. "While the rest of the United States celebrates the bicentennial," author Beverly Badhorse announced, "Northern Cheyenne will hold the traditional victory dance so long denied them." Some Indians would celebrate the centennial of a legendary Indian victory; others would mourn the unrealized principles on which the United States was founded.[58]

Nevertheless, wagoners, thousands of them, pressed forward. As they entered each new state, additional wagons, including that state's official schooner, joined in. "The wagon train is growing longer each day," Grace Ritchie noted in May. For every one wagon that dropped out, two more arrived.[59]

Crowds, too, kept coming, day after day, week after week, because the wagon train captured people's imagination. Their reactions refreshed the riders. As the Ritchies approached Sutherland, Nebraska, for example, they heard that spirits were "real low until [residents] learned that the Wagon Train was coming to town, then everyone joined in and really spruced up their town." When the Ritchies arrived, they found Sutherland's level of enthusiasm to be quite high. "Flags were out all over town, the band met us and escorted us through town. Programs and a meal were prepared and the spirit here was really great." This was what the Ritchies were aiming for: "to bring to our nation the spirit of the Bi-Centennial as we head eastward for the Re-Dedication of the Declaration of Independence and hope to renew all it stands for." Participants were proud of the energy and goodwill their work seemed to be generating.[60]

So, on they went. Eastward ho!

Alex Haley's Bicentennial gift to America, as the writer and civil rights activist James Baldwin called it, originated on the front porch of Haley's childhood home in Henning, Tennessee. After supper, his grandmother, aunts, and other relatives would often go out to visit in the summer evening air. As dusk deepened into night, and "the lightning bugs flicker[ed] on and off around the honeysuckle vines," the subject of conversation sometimes turned to what, Haley grew to realize, was their family history—a centuries-long tale that was as old as America itself.

The story began with "the African," an ancestor named Kin-tay who was brought to America on a slave ship sometime in the late eighteenth century. Kin-tay tried again and again to escape from the Virginia plantation where he was held in bondage. Each time, however, he was captured—at last by slave catchers who maimed his right foot to prevent future runaway attempts. Hobbled, Kin-tay remained enslaved on another plantation for the rest of his life. There he met a woman, Bell. They had a daughter, Kizzy, who told her son George tales about their African lineage. And those oral stories got handed down from one generation to the next until they ended up on the front porch in Henning, where they made an indelible impression on Haley, inspiring years of genealogical research that led to the 1976 publication of *Roots*, his celebrated novel tracing the descendants of Kunta Kinte, an African who arrived in North America aboard a slave ship just prior to the American Revolution, as they struggled for freedom across more than two centuries of US history.[61]

Roots' acknowledgment of the harsh existence in America, a nation that prized individual liberty, of a people who had been brought to its shores in chains—the unforgiveable crime against humanity that forever stained the American experience—hardly seemed likely to achieve wide readership amid 1976's patriotic ebullience. Yet "Haley's Comet," as *Time* magazine called it, made an instant impact when the novel arrived in bookstores that summer. It topped *The New York Times* bestseller list for twenty-two weeks, reportedly selling fifteen million copies in less than a year. A television adaptation premiered in January 1977 and quickly became a smash hit. Watched by an estimated 130 million Americans—more than half of the US population of 215 million—the series was the most-watched TV program ever.[62]

Roots' reception spoke to the remarkable journey America had taken in the fifty-some years since Alex Haley heard his family's stories sitting on that porch back in Jim Crow–era Henning, Tennessee. In 1939, he enlisted at the age of seventeen in the US Coast Guard—which, like all US armed forces, remained racially segregated at the time—initially serving as a steward, the only entry rank then open to Black Americans. As a guardsman, he helped score a double victory in World War II: victory abroad over authoritarianism but also victory at home against segregation and other forms of institutionalized racism that, said the African American *Pittsburgh Courier*, denied Black Americans the same experience of democracy that White Americans had long enjoyed.[63]

Displaying remarkable writing ability, Haley rose up the ranks, becoming in 1950 the first journalist, Black or White, to attain the rank of chief petty officer in the (now racially integrated) US Coast Guard. Retiring in 1959 as the guard's chief journalist, he reentered civilian life just as the civil rights movement was inching closer to realizing the nation's founding principles. "Our nation in a sense came into being through a massive act of civil disobedience," Martin Luther King

Jr. wrote, "for the Boston Tea Party was nothing but a massive act of civil disobedience." The 1964 Civil Rights Act, proponents said, finally realized the Declaration of Independence's promise of equality for all. The 1965 Voting Rights Act ended taxation without representation.[64]

Not all activists sought integration. Black nationalists insisted that America was irredeemable, that it was, writes historian Gary Gerstle, "too beholden to its racialized tradition ever to welcome blacks into the national community on terms equal to whites." Black American progress could come only through racial separation culminating in the establishment of independent Black institutions.[65]

The Autobiography of Malcolm X, coauthored by Haley and published months after the civil rights leader's 1965 assassination, spoke to this rejection of the melting pot, the amalgamating metaphor that has served to unify the multiethnic nation throughout much of American history. As Malcolm X famously said, "We didn't land on Plymouth Rock, my brothers and sisters—Plymouth Rock landed on us!" Or, as he told a Cleveland audience, echoing Frederick Douglass's 1852 "What to the Slave Is the Fourth of July?" address, "No, I'm not an American. I'm one of the 22 million black people who are the victims of Americanism. One of the 22 million black people who are the victims of democracy, nothing but disguised hypocrisy. So, I'm not standing here speaking to you as an American, or a patriot, or a flag-saluter, or a flag-waver—no, not I. I'm speaking as a victim of this American system." Inspired by Malcolm X, many African Americans became ardent students of Black history in search of an authentic past on which to build a proud identity.[66]

After completing Malcolm X's *Autobiography*, Alex Haley set out to address a set of profound existential questions: Who am I? Where do I come from? How did I get here? The poet Maya Angelou wrote that these questions haunted Black consciousness because African Americans often lacked the genealogical data required to answer them satisfactorily. Such basic facts as dates of birth, names of ancestors, and places of origin had been systematically withheld from enslaved people and their descendants, splitting family trees and fostering generational self-doubt but also, Haley noted, nourishing "a hunger, marrow-deep, to know our heritage—to know who we are and where we came from."[67]

Haley's family saga fed that hunger. Though some critics questioned his scholarship, *Roots* sparked a phenomenon of Black self-discovery that continues to this day. Finding one's roots can lead to grim discoveries. And Haley's warts-and-all account of the ways in which slavery's disfiguring reach harmed generations of African American families provided a counterpoint to the Bicentennial's celebratory view of US history. Yet, as historian Michael Eric Dyson put it, *Roots*' appearance in the jubilee year of 1976 effectively "wrote black folk into the book of American heritage," reminding readers that "the black story is the American story."[68]

Appreciation of Black history grew. The National Register of Historic Places listed sixty Black history sites by 1977, up from just two in 1970. They included the Michigan gravesite of nineteenth-century abolitionist Sojourner Truth, the New York offices of activist W. E. B. Du Bois, and the Montgomery, Alabama, church pastored by the late Dr. Martin Luther King Jr. in the 1950s. They also included the homes of historically important persons such as Harriet Tubman, Ida B. Wells, and Carter G. Woodson, whose home on 9th Street NW in Washington, DC, entered the registry in 1976—the same year Negro History Week, the event he pioneered in 1926, became Black History Month after years of lobbying by civil rights leaders. Such developments, officials said, represented a desire on the part of Americans, Black and non-Black alike, to go "back to our roots" during the Bicentennial era.[69]

"Hey, hey, what do you say, ratify the ERA," chanted the 400 protestors who marched along Philadelphia's Chestnut Street on

Independence Day 1976. Organized by a coalition of women's rights groups, the marchers called for ratification of the Equal Rights Amendment to the US Constitution outlawing sex discrimination. Introduced in Congress in 1923, the ERA made little headway until the arrival of second-wave feminism in the 1960s. Approved by lawmakers in 1972, the ERA went to state legislatures for ratification. Dozens of states signed on, putting the amendment on the verge of gaining the three-fourths necessary for ratification.

Roy Potts, an engineer from Audubon, New Jersey, wearing a red, white, and blue baseball cap, said he was marching for freedom. "I think we all have to get behind freedom for everybody," he said. "When women are free, then men are free to really be themselves." Virginia Barrett traveled from Rowe, Massachusetts. "I think it all is very moving, very moving," she said through tears.

One Philadelphian was unimpressed, though. Mary Johnson was waiting for a bus to take her to Sunday church services when the march passed by. "That's it, that's the Bicentennial, isn't it?" she asked. She hadn't really been paying attention to the Bicentennial, as she'd "been following Jesus." With that, Johnson turned her back on the marchers and walked away.[70]

That scene encapsulated the status of the women's rights movement, circa 1976. Significant advances had been made since Betty Friedan launched the second wave with her 1963 best seller *The Feminine Mystique.* That year's Equal Pay Act required equal pay for men and women who performed comparable work. Title VII of the Civil Rights Act of 1964 prohibited employment discrimination based on sex, race, and other characteristics. Title IX of the Education Amendments of 1972 prohibited sex discrimination in any federally funded education program or activity, opening unprecedented opportunities for women and girls in sports. And the US Supreme Court's 1973 *Roe v. Wade* decision determined that the Constitution generally protected a woman's right to an abortion. These and other developments led *Time* magazine to declare 1975 the "Year of Women." According to the editors, feminism had reached a tipping point: 63 percent of Americans now favored efforts to strengthen and change women's status in society, whereas just 42 percent had expressed support five years earlier.

Across the country, female truck drivers, electricians, pipefitters, doctors, business executives, and more were busy living the new reality, symbolized by *Time*'s Women of the Year. They included First Lady Betty Ford, a Republican who spoke out in support of the ERA and the *Roe* decision; US Secretary of Housing and Urban Development (HUD) Carla Hills, just the third woman ever to serve in the cabinet; and Congresswoman Barbara Jordan (D-TX), the first Southern Black woman ever elected to the US House of Representatives. In sports, they included Billie Jean King, who in 1975 won the ladies singles tennis title at Wimbledon, her twelfth major singles title overall. In literature, Susan Brownmiller was honored by *Time* for raising awareness with her much-discussed book *Against Our Will: Men, Women, and Rape*. And in the workplace, Addie Wyatt, women's affairs director of the Amalgamated Meat Cutters Union, was recognized for fighting to eliminate wage differentials between male and female employees. The list went on.

Human equality, the unalienable right asserted in the Declaration of Independence, seemed just around the corner. Author Elizabeth Janeway was certainly optimistic. "The sky above us lifts, the light pours in," she said.[71]

But "women's lib," as some dismissively called the movement, faced headwinds. Factional disputes divided the leading women's rights organization, the National Organization for Women (NOW). Friedan, NOW's cofounder, spurned lesbians and younger, more radical feminists, fearing they would marginalize the organization. NOW prioritized the needs of White middle- and upper-class professionals over those of women of color and working-class women.

Despite legislation, the gender pay gap remained wide. Female workers earned fifty-nine cents per dollar of male earnings in 1975, slightly *less* than they had before the passage of 1963's Equal Pay Act. This disparity stemmed in part from the fact that most working women held pink-collar jobs: teachers, nurses, salesclerks, receptionists, secretaries, and other service or caregiving positions that commanded less pay. But it also arose from the fact that women were simply denied equal pay for comparable work.

A glass ceiling prevented women from reaching the highest echelons of power. The 1,300 largest US companies employed only about 150 women directors. With rare exceptions, women had not risen as high as vice president in heavy industries such as steel, automobiles, oil, and railroads. "At the top," *Time* observed, "business is almost wholly a men's club."[72]

Wherever they worked, women often faced sexual harassment and other forms of workplace discrimination: comments about their physical appearance, touching of their bodies, sexual propositions backed by the threat of job loss, forced sexual relations, human resources complaints that went nowhere. These were just some of the realities commonly experienced by working women. "Sexual harassment is one of the few sexist issues which has been totally in the closet," said NOW President Karen DeCrow. "It is an issue that has been shrouded in silence because its occurrence is seen as both humiliating and trivial."[73]

"When I think about it, I get real worked up . . . men thinking they have a right to touch me, or proposition me because I'm a waitress," said Janet Oestreich, twenty-four, who paid for college by working in restaurants and bars. She was in no position to say, "Get your crummy hands off me," because she needed the tips. Besides, she risked getting fired if she complained. Women were usually the ones who suffered any consequences, while the men who ogled or groped them often got away scot-free. The whole situation was "totally ridiculous," she said.[74]

Gender norms resisted change. Working women disproportionately faced the double burden of unpaid domestic labor. "It's the same old baloney," said Polly Ely, who worked as a counselor in a rape crisis center in Cedar Rapids, Iowa. "I come home so tired I can hardly see, and John flops down with the paper while I stumble into the kitchen."[75]

Many women found the pressure of doing it all—of bringing home the bacon, frying it up in a pan, and never, ever letting their significant other "forget he was a man," as a perfume ad later put it—to be crushing. HUD Secretary Carla Hills got up each morning at about 6 a.m. Before leaving for work at 7:15, she tried to spend time with her four children—making breakfast, braiding a daughter's hair, playing with another for a few minutes. She kept a bulletin board in the kitchen to keep track of family activities, from piano lessons and sports practices to business meetings and social engagements. But it was a lot to handle, she said. "I often feel like a piece of salami, with a slice here for one and a slice there for another, and there isn't enough to go around."[76]

Roe prompted a backlash. A 1976 Supreme Court ruling, *Planned Parenthood v. Danforth*, extending women's reproductive rights was "monumental," said the director of a reproductive rights group, as it buttressed the legal foundation the Court set in 1973. Coming amid the Bicentennial's fanfare, the announcement, *Philadelphia Tribune* editors wrote, represented a "heartwarming" confirmation of a woman's right to choose.[77]

But opponents vowed to restrict abortion to protect the right to life of the unborn. The 1976 extension of *Roe*, said New York Conservative Party Senator James L. Buckley, cast "a shadow on the festival of our independence. This year the rockets' red glare of our Bicentennial fireworks must remind us all of the mounting carnage all around us as the Supreme Court continues on its tragic course of outrage."[78]

ERA ratification stalled. Twenty-two states approved the amendment soon after receiving it from Congress in 1972. Eight more states joined in 1973. But only four approved between 1974 and 1976, and two states reversed course, leaving the ERA as many as six states short of the required thirty-eight as of July 4, 1976.

The amendment's straightforward language—"Equality of rights under the law shall not be denied or abridged . . . on account of sex"—concerned opponents. Conservative activist Phyllis Schlafly, a fifty-one-year-old suburban mother of six, headed the lobbying organization STOP ERA. Schlafly warned that the ERA would strip women of gender-specific privileges and protections, forcing them to surrender "dependent wife" Social Security benefits, to use unisex toilets, and to serve in the military, possibly as combat soldiers. In Schlafly's home state of Illinois, activists' lobbying tactics included delivering bread, jams, pies, and other homemade goods to (mostly male) legislators, accompanied by slogans such as "Preserve Us from a Congressional Jam; Vote Against the ERA Sham" and "I Am for Mom and Apple Pie."[79]

Boos greeted Betty Ford in June 1976 when she appeared in Plymouth, Massachusetts, to open a Bicentennial exhibition. Chanting "Go away, ERA," protestors carried signs reading, "Stop ERA" and "Equal Rights Amendment Stamps Out the Family." The First Lady was used to such displays. Her ERA support angered conservatives. But Ford, a breast cancer survivor who won plaudits for going public with her bout with alcoholism, knew how to fight back. Titled "Remember the Ladies," in honor of Abigail Adams's 1776 letter imploring her husband, John, to draft the Declaration in such a way as to "remember the ladies and be more generous and favorable to them than your ancestors," the Plymouth exhibition documented the lives of Revolutionary-era women. Ford used the opening to press for ERA ratification. To cheers of "ERA, all the way," she began, "We're here to honor the unsung women who helped to win our national revolution." Pausing, she continued, "and to focus attention on the unfinished business of our revolution for full freedom and justice for women."[80]

Days later, NOW's Karen DeCrow pressed ahead, as well, when she read Susan B. Anthony's "Declaration of Rights for Women" to the ERA supporters who marched in Philadelphia on July 4. DeCrow read the declaration in the same church where Anthony, Elizabeth Cady Stanton, and others had congregated in 1876 after forcibly introducing the declaration into the city's Centennial festivities. Anthony's generation had imagined a time 100 years hence when men and women would be fully equal. DeCrow's reading called for action by underscoring the limited progress women had made toward that goal. America's rights revolution remained incomplete.[81]

VIKING 1, AN UNMANNED SPACECRAFT, WAS ORBITING Mars in search of a landing site as Americans prepared to celebrate independence in 1976. Technology did not figure prominently in the Bicentennial, compared to previous jubilees. The president did not pull a lever unleashing the awesome power of a modern-day Corliss engine, as Ulysses Grant had done with the help of a foreign potentate in 1876. Nor did Philadelphia build an exposition to showcase America's industrial might, as the city had in 1926. Bicentennial planners concerned themselves mostly with spotlighting the nation's inner strength as opposed to outward "iron and steel" manifestations of its economic power, because America's economy was nothing to brag about in July 1976, with joblessness and inflation pushing the misery index to 13.57.[82]

But when the squat, three-legged Viking lander came to rest, upright and intact, on Mars's Chryse Planitia on July 20, the mission control room went into orbit. "Touchdown!" announced a flight controller once Viking's confirmation signals, traveling at light speed, reached the mainframe computer monitors in Pasadena, California's Jet Propulsion Laboratory, some 212 million miles away. "We have touchdown. We have several indications of touchdown." Digital images taken by the lander's cameras arrived moments later, giving humans their closest-ever look at the Red Planet.

Cheers echoed throughout the lab. It was an emotional time for the scientists and engineers of the $1 billion Viking project, many of whom had spent years preparing for this moment. "This has got to be the happiest time of my life," said James S. Martin Jr., the project manager. A National Aeronautics and Space Administration (NASA) official cried for the first time since his wedding day. "It's fantastic," he said.[83]

Viking 1, the world's first successful landing on Mars, a planet that had fascinated humankind for centuries, represented a major victory in the Cold War, the battle for global supremacy the United States and the Soviet Union had been waging since World War II. The Soviets had leapt to an early lead in the space race in 1957, when they placed Sputnik 1, the first artificial satellite, into Earth's orbit. Their lead widened four years later when the USSR put the first human, cosmonaut Yuri Gagarin, into outer space. But the United States quickly caught up, and the superpowers traded advances—launching satellites, probes, and other craft—until American astronauts Neil Armstrong and Edwin "Buzz" Aldrin landed on the moon on July 20, 1969. Viking's success, coming seven years to the day after the Apollo 11 lunar landing, confirmed the US lead.

There is no doubt that "megamachines," as critic Lewis Mumford called the superpowers' military-industrial complexes, increased civilization's capacity to destroy. The same rockets that sent satellites into orbit could drop nuclear warheads on Washington or Moscow in minutes, killing millions. Megamachines also misdirected national resources to military purposes, Mumford claimed, producing soulless technology that threatened individual freedom. "Do not fold, spindle or mutilate," student protestors demanded in the 1960s, inveighing against the punch cards that had come to reduce many human activities to manipulable numbers since IBM introduced the cards at the 1926 Sesquicentennial exposition.[84]

But megamachines also put the Viking lander on the leading edge of a technological transformation that promised an age of new possibilities. "During the 1970s," a decade known more for malaise, stagflation, and downsizing, writes historian Timothy Moy, technology "set the nation on a social and economic trajectory that would run through the end of the century." That transformation was far from complete. Viking 1, equipped with mechanical arms, antennae, sensors, and other devices, was just beginning a six-year search for signs of possible life on Mars. Another lander, Viking 2, was scheduled to arrive in September 1976. In 1977, NASA planned to launch a probe, Voyager 1, aimed at photographing Jupiter and Saturn. Something called a space shuttle, described in the press as a "reusable space 'airplane,'" was scheduled to become operational in the 1980s.[85]

To observers, though, Viking appeared to put the United States on the cusp of a third century of discovery. Charles Lindbergh had made history just fifty years earlier by flying solo from New York to Paris, a distance of some 3,600 miles. Now the frontier stood hundreds of millions of miles away. The Mars landing, wrote *Los Angeles Times* editors, paraphrasing Neil Armstrong's iconic words, took a small but "momentous step toward a better understanding of the unimaginably vast universe" and represented "a great leap forward in scientific progress" that promised to pay dividends down the road.[86]

Viking 1 demonstrated that the United States, despite all the trials and tribulations of the previous decade, still had the right stuff to lead—the ability to conquer new frontiers in the heavens, to go where others could not. In short, the Mars landing offered reassurance that the American century was still very much ongoing. According to *New York Times* editors, Viking provided "renewed vindication of the promise of space science and, with Bicentennial affirmations still loud in our ears, of the prowess of American scientists and the potential of American technology." Proud of the triumph on Mars as a demonstration of

American genius on the nation's 200th anniversary, syndicated columnist Marquis Childs "want[ed] to stand up and cheer."[87]

Other, arguably more important drivers of the technological revolution were happening out of the limelight. In July 1976, a hobbyist magazine, *Interface*, published the first review of the Apple I, a new personal computer system produced by the Apple Computer Company, a start-up cofounded earlier that year by two twenty-something Californians, Steve Jobs and Steve Wozniak. Jobs, twenty-one, Apple's marketing director, did not resemble the prototypical business executive. A vegetarian with shoulder-length hair, he regularly went barefoot, including to business meetings. "Steve was trying to be the embodiment of the counterculture," an associate recalled. "He had a wispy beard, was very thin, and looked like Ho Chi Minh."[88]

A practitioner of Zen Buddhism, Jobs saw the personal computer as much more than mere hardware. Like some other members of the counterculture, he saw the computer as a tool of personal liberation, a means of freeing individuals from the mainframe computers and other megamachines produced by large firms such as IBM. "Steve [was] right at the nexus of the counterculture and technology," said Stewart Brand, whose alternative magazine, *Whole Earth Catalog*, inspired Jobs. "He got the notion of tools for human use."[89]

"You know," Jobs told *Interface*, "most of the real creative and innovative ideas come about by communicating with [computer hobbyists]. If we can rap about their needs, feelings and motivations, we can respond appropriately giving them what they want."[90]

Wozniak, twenty-five, Apple's engineering director, didn't fit the image of a corporate executive either. A rumpled computer geek known, even among other computer geeks, as an electronics wizard, Wozniak developed the Apple I prototype in between TV dinners while moonlighting at Hewlett-Packard. "It's hard not to live, eat and sleep computer, when you're involved with such a responsive new market," he told

Interface. "But when you're growing as fast as we are, you just don't have time for anything else."[91]

Hewlett-Packard wasn't interested in Wozniak's design. So he sold his programmable calculator for $500 to self-finance production. Jobs sold his Volkswagen bus for $1,500, less repairs. With $1,300 in working capital, plus $5,000 borrowed from friends, they purchased parts on thirty-day credit and began assembly in the garage of Jobs's parents' house in Los Altos. By the Bicentennial summer of 1976, the Apple I was ready for sale. A base kit, the Apple I looked "as scruffy as its creators," wrote Jobs's biographer, Walter Isaacson. It consisted of a motherboard equipped with a central processing unit, random-access memory, and other features, but not a keyboard, monitor, power supply, or case. As such, the Apple I had limited appeal. "We're here for the hobbyist to give him the best performance system that makes sense economically," Jobs said.[92]

Wozniak set to work on the prototype for a new model, the Apple II. Though it wouldn't premiere until 1977, Jobs had already determined that the next Apple would have to be sleeker and more fully integrated, including a keyboard, monitor, power supply, and software, all contained in an attractive case. "My vision was to create the first fully packaged computer," he recalled. They were no longer aiming for the handful of hobbyists who liked to assemble their own computers, who knew how to buy transformers and keyboards. "For every one of them," Jobs said, "there were a thousand people who would want the machine to be ready to run."[93]

"Well, we made it, pardner," Chuck McClurg said as he and his fellow teamster pulled into Valley Forge on July 3, 1976. The two had come all the way from Blaine, Washington, and they felt proud to have made it. "I don't feel it's no big thing," McClurg, a fifty-seven-year-old

Boeing retiree, told reporters. "They call it courage and something like integrity to keep the thing going every day, but any one of a million people could have done it."[94]

Two hundred more wagons rolled into Valley Forge, led by the fifty state wagons, including California's piloted by Larry and Pauline Asmus all the way from Pasadena. The Asmuses had experienced some bumps along the way. A police officer in Albuquerque ticketed them for traveling fifteen miles per hour in a five-mph zone. Otherwise, the journey proved life changing, so much so that they sold their home in Azusa and relocated to a small logging community fifty miles north of Lake Tahoe. The wagon train, Larry told reporters, "was an opportunity to do something positive to celebrate the birthday of our nation and to do it in grand style."[95]

Idaho's Grace and Fred Ritchie also made it to Valley Forge. "We are really in the lime lights here in Pennsylvania," Grace wrote. "We know now what a goldfish feels like, sitting in his glass bowl for everyone to see." Pennsylvanians had waited a long time for the wagons to arrive, and many crowded around to welcome them with lemonade and cookies, flags and mementos, applause and even some tears. It was "a real honor" to be at the center of so much attention, Grace noted.[96]

The arrivals also included dozens of independent wagons that had joined the convoy along the way. While most were faithful reproductions of the Conestoga or schooner wagons of yore, the independents came in many forms, including a mule-drawn mobile home and a wheelchair helmed by a wounded World War II veteran, Norman Butler, of Orland, California. Pulled by a pony, Butler had ridden all the way from Pomona. "It was a great honor," he said of the trip, which had shown other persons with disabilities "that you can do anything, go anywhere, anyone else can."[97]

Remarkably, wagoners collected some twenty-two million signatures on rededication scrolls. The last signature belonged to President

President Ford salutes the Bicentennial Wagon Train. Valley Forge, Pennsylvania, July 3, 1976. (Credit: US Information Agency photo 306-PSE-1622c / Still Picture Branch, National Archives)

Gerald Ford, who signed when he greeted the wagon train on July 4. During his visit, Ford boarded Michigan's wagon to salute the crowd.

He also signed a law transferring custody of Valley Forge National Historical Park from the state of Pennsylvania to the US National Park Service. Intended to protect the area from private development, the move added the park to the list of historic sites preserved during the Bicentennial.

"Something happened at Valley Forge," said Ford in remarks directed more toward the present than the past. General George Washington's ragged army had suffered through the harsh 1777–1778 winter; however, Ford said, "they stayed. They stuck it out. When spring melted the snows and green returned to this beautiful countryside, a proud and disciplined fighting force marched out of this valley to victory." Americans were similarly poised for a rebound two centuries later.[98]

Chaos reigned in Valley Forge's historical park that July day in 1976. Some 75,000 revelers showed up to welcome the wagons, overwhelming the fourteen outdoor toilets that event planners had installed. "It was like Woodstock for history buffs," a reporter later remarked, referring to the 1969 music festival in upstate New York known almost as much for inadequate services as for peace and love. The rededication scrolls got lost in the maw, never to be found. The wagoners got pushed to the side, to a crowded mudhole of a campground with inadequate drinking water and negligible food options. Authorities should have provided better accommodations, they complained, especially after such a long journey.[99]

Nonetheless, Ron Scofield, forty-five, of Middletown, California, said the cross-country trip had restored his faith in America. "It showed me that the American people are pretty good-hearted people," said Scofield, who had sold his ranch and most of his belongings to make the trip with his wife, Sherry, and their children, Marie, twenty, and Tom, seven. Across the nation, well-wishers met them with homemade ice cream, baked goods, and other treats. In New Mexico, Good Samaritans brought beans to sustain them through a freak snowstorm. "These are the kind of things that make America hang together," he said.[100]

Other riders agreed. Said Harry Lee of Polk City, Florida, "The wagon trains proved to me and to all the thousands of people I talked with, that we are as strong and resourceful as we ever were." Merle Swineford, forty-seven, got a lump in his throat each time the wagons passed through a community and he saw people's eyes light up, children waving flags and adults shaking hands. "This is a great country with great people," said Swineford, who sold his radiator and glass company in Laverne, Oklahoma, to join the wagon train.[101]

"The Bicentennial Wagon Train seemed to pull people and communities together," concluded Walt Schaefer, a wagoner from South Dakota. "We found this all the way across the country. The Wagon Train was a wonderful experience."[102]

~

July Fourth weekend marked, *Time* said, "a culminating moment of raucous blowout compounded of Disneyland pageantry and kitsch, perfervid oratory, . . . dissent, 10,000 miles of bunting, phalanxes of politicians and majorettes in a din of John Philip Sousa brass."[103]

Events officially opened on Friday evening, July 2, with ceremonies at the National Archives in Washington, DC, honoring the Declaration of Independence and the other blueprints of American democracy: the US Constitution and the Bill of Rights. President Ford, House Speaker Carl Albert, and Chief Justice Warren Burger, representing the three branches of government, appeared together to symbolize the checks and balances that had guided the US government through two centuries. The documents remained on public display for the next seventy-six hours straight, during which time 25,000 visitors signed the official guest register.

Parades began Saturday morning, July 3. Celebrants from Wayne, New Jersey, to Mobile, Alabama, and beyond saw floats, marching bands, and kart-riding Shriners serpentine down Main Streets across the United States. In the nation's capital, more than 500,000 people lined Constitution Avenue for a parade very different from the one that had poured down Capitol Hill in September 1926. Then, thousands of robed members of the Ku Klux Klan had marched unmasked in support of "One Hundred Percent Americanism," their nativist creed that expressly excluded people of color, Catholics, Jews, and the foreign-born. Now, Americans of Italian, Greek, Polish, and Russian ancestry proudly walked side by side with citizens of Korean, Chinese, Filipino, and Bolivian descent in a multicultural show of force. The parade, said the ARBA, the federal Bicentennial administration, displayed "the flavor of America as a nation of nations"—a diverse country enriched by immigration.[104]

Children observe a Bicentennial parade in San Francisco's Golden Gate Park, July 4, 1976. (Credit: Dave Randolph / San Francisco Chronicle / Getty Images)

Dawn's early light struck the continental United States on Sunday, July 4, at Mars Hill, Maine, population 1,875. The northeastern Maine farming town began the nation's Independence Day festivities with a flag-raising ceremony, followed by speeches, songs, and a fifty-round cannon salute that continued the storied tradition of firing artillery on July Fourth. "That'll jolt 'em out of their beds," a spectator said.[105]

Though not at the center of attention, as in jubilees past, Philadelphians nevertheless marked the Fourth, an observer wrote, "with all the passion and dissension of their revolutionary ancestors." Crowds braved intermittent rain and heavy security to hear President Ford speak that morning outside Independence Hall. "Are the institutions under which we live working the way they should?" he asked. "Are the foundations laid in 1776 and 1789 still strong enough to resist the tremors of our times?" Afterward, some watched a five-hour-long parade that featured 40,000 marchers and floats representing each of the fifty states. Others toured Independence Hall or visited the Liberty

Bell, housed in a gleaming new stone-and-glass pavilion that drew a record 3.2 million visitors in 1976. "People have almost a religious experience when they visit Independence Hall," said a city official. "When they walk through the room where the Declaration of Independence was signed, they are reexamining their roots. We're all immigrants of some sort. But whether we're English-American or Italian-American or Irish-American, we're still Americans."[106]

The real action occurred outside Center City, in North Philadelphia, where thousands attended counterrallies. American politics may have shifted rightward, but the rallies, a reporter noted, carried "an echo of the protest days of the 1960s." One group, the July 4th Coalition, marched for women's, gay, Black, and Indigenous rights. Another, the leftist Rich Off Our Backs Coalition, marched for economic justice. As makeshift vendors hawked frozen treats, cold drinks, and hot dogs, speakers offered critical interpretations of America's past. Black Panther Party Chair Elaine Brown, a native Philadelphian, said that US history was marked by "murder and plunder." According to a display, the real victors of the American Revolution were the rich, elite White men who spoke of freedom even as they profited off the backs of enslaved people, small farmers, and laborers. A self-described "women's anti-imperialist singing group" indicted the 1 percent who continued to dominate:

> *Who is the guilty one?*
> *Ain't it the one who pulls the strings?*
> *Ain't it Rockefeller?*

They put the blame exactly where it ought to be, "on the rich of the society," said a young steelworker who attended.[107]

Despite official warnings, no incidents of violence were reported. According to an organizer, the peaceful gathering represented "a total victory for millions of people who [knew] they were not included in the government sham that took place downtown." Protestors had a right, *Philadelphia Inquirer* editors agreed, to call attention to America's failings and injustices as they saw them. Dissent was as fundamental to the Bicentennial as bunting and brass bands. Its existence confirmed "the strength and genius of American democracy."[108]

One of the day's most spectacular sights occurred in New York City, where 225 ships, including 16 tall ships, from around the world sailed into New York Harbor and up the Hudson River in homage to the nation's maritime history. An estimated six million spectators lining the shores saw the ships cruise past the Statue of Liberty and Manhattan's skyscrapers. President Ford helicoptered in from Philadelphia to ring a special Bicentennial bell thirteen times, once for each of the original colonies. At his signal, bells rang in places of worship and town halls across America, continuing a tradition that recalled the earliest July Fourth celebrations.

In Chicago, officials swore in 1,776 new US citizens, one of many Bicentennial activities honoring America's immigrant tradition. Though the Chicagoland area did not always provide such safe haven. In 1977, neo-Nazis announced plans to demonstrate in the suburb of Skokie, Illinois, home to thousands of Jews, including many Holocaust survivors. Generally, though, America was more welcoming than it had been in previous jubilee years, as signified by President Ford's participation in naturalization ceremonies held at Monticello, the Virginia home of Thomas Jefferson. Dedicated to the American people in 1926, Monticello had begun hosting naturalization ceremonies on July 4, 1963. Featuring an outdoor courtroom in which dozens of individuals took the oath of citizenship to become Americans, the ceremonies quickly became an annual July Fourth tradition. Ford, the first president to serve as the event's keynote speaker, said that America was founded on the principles of hard work, openness, and equal opportunity. "These beliefs," he concluded, "are the secrets of America's unity from diversity—in my judgment the most magnificent achievement of our 200 years as a nation."[109]

Festivals, fairs, and picnics filled the holiday calendar. New Orleans—never a city to miss an opportunity to party—celebrated with a jazz concert in the Louisiana Superdome, the city's sleek, new indoor stadium. A newly unveiled statue of jazz great Louis Armstrong memorialized the influence of Black Americans on the nation's musical heritage. Culinary, art, and film festivals honored New Orleans's rich multicultural traditions.

Residents of Clinton, Missouri, partied in their own way. Early arrivals applauded ceremonies dedicating the county museum while juggling platefuls of barbequed chicken lunch. Sounds of gospel and country music mixed in the afternoon humidity. Log-rolling contests, beard-growing contests, male beauty contests, watermelon-eating competitions, seed-spitting battles—those and more—jostled for attention. A local artist performed the "Battle Hymn of the Republic" on a saw. A couple of eleven-year-olds shared top honors in an egg-throwing contest. And two women defeated three men in a nail-driving contest, after which the firing of the town's Civil War–era cannon got the frog-jumping contests and turtle races underway.

Clinton's celebration, like many across the country, was "a homegrown event for hometown people." Jerry Osborn, the event's master of ceremonies, recognized 90 percent of the faces in the crowd: "We've been trying to promote the idea that you can stay in Clinton, and you don't really have to go anywhere else."[110]

Fireworks, maybe more than had ever been fired at once, illuminated nighttime skies across America. Instead of the customary two tons annually set off near the National Mall in Washington, handlers detonated some thirty-three tons at four locations strategically placed around the Washington Monument, the Jefferson Memorial, and the

Lincoln Memorial. President and First Lady Ford viewed the fireworks display from the White House's Truman Balcony, along with Vice President Nelson Rockefeller, Second Lady Margaretta "Happy" Rockefeller, and guests.

In Boston, site of so much Bicentennial-era rancor, more than 200,000 people gathered along the Charles River to hear the Boston Pops Orchestra. Conducted by Arthur Fiedler, the program climaxed with a rendition of Tchaikovsky's *1812 Overture*. As the piece reached its rousing finale, five 105-mm howitzers barked out forty blasts, launching synchronized bursts of red, white, and blue that sparkled for almost half an hour. The immigrant family of a local business leader picked up the show's $25,000 tab. "We are doing this to show our appreciation to this land of freedom for what it has given us," a spokesperson said.[111]

In between, Colorado mounted a historic car race up Pike's Peak, a vintage airshow in Colorado Springs, and a buffalo-chip-throwing contest in Salida. New Philadelphia, Ohio, hosted a hog-calling contest, while Cairo, Georgia, staged a marbles tournament. Antique tractors pulled in Calamus, Iowa. Hot air balloons rose over Seward, Nebraska. Indian rodeo contestants squared off in Flagstaff, Arizona. And 80,000 music fans gathered in Gonzales, Texas, for outlaw country singer Willie Nelson's fourth annual Fourth of July Picnic, where public intoxication and general rowdiness reigned in the pursuit of happiness, much as they had in Texas Guinan's Sesquicentennial-era nightclubs.[112]

That and much, much more was broadcast on television, a technology that hardly existed in 1926 yet was ubiquitous fifty years later. In 1970, more than 95 percent of American households owned at least one television set. The major networks—all three of them, ABC, CBS, and NBC—covered the Bicentennial from the first event on the East Coast to the last on the West. CBS News anchor Walter Cronkite, reputed to be the most trusted man in America at a time when public confidence in the news media was high, described the Bicentennial as "the greatest, most colossal birthday party in 200 years." TV did a bang-up job, according to the *Tulsa World*, which credited television for bringing July Fourth "into our homes—live and in color. It gave us a sense of drama and sweep, of the American Oneness out of diversity, and the remembrance of where we have been and what we have done."[113]

~

Backyard barbeques. Main street parades. Family picnics. What did it all mean? Lots of people were too sunburned or hungover (or both) the Monday morning after the long holiday weekend to care.

Many observers, though, sensed that America was headed in the right direction. Democrats and Republicans, in big cities and small towns from north to south, east to west, Americans all, waved flags in some form or fashion in 1976. South Carolina, Montana, Hawaii, and other states issued patriotic license plates. Indianapolis Motor Speedway wrecker trucks were painted red, white, and blue, as were Illinois state police cars, garbage trucks in Boston, and fire hydrants, buses, and subway cars in Chicago. A giant American flag, reportedly "the longest, widest, heaviest, starriest national banner ever lofted," was hoisted across a portion of the Verrazzano-Narrows Bridge spanning the entrance to New York Harbor. Though high winds tore the football-field-sized "superflag," its manufacturer, New Jersey's Annin Flagmakers, the nation's oldest and largest such concern, sold approximately 40,000 official Bicentennial flags, a welcome change for a company that had survived a decade of lean sales.[114]

The outpouring of patriotism was noteworthy, given recent events. "Only five years ago," *Time* noted, the American flag "was being burned, burlesqued and spat upon" by anti–Vietnam War protestors. "Today many of the self-same Americans who chose then to disown their flag are hoisting it high."[115]

Indeed, July 4, 1976, found the nation in better shape than it had been since at least November 23, 1963, *Newsweek*, *US News & World Report*, and other national publications reported. Watergate was in the rearview mirror. Recent presidential primaries had demonstrated the health of the political system. Even the economy was showing signs of life. "Above all," *Time* remarked, "after thirteen consecutive years of assassinations, race riots, youth rebellion, Vietnam, political scandal, presidential collapse, energy crisis, and recession, the nation's mood seems optimistic again."[116]

Local newspapers felt similarly. Alabama's *Birmingham News* believed that America had turned a corner, ending years of self-doubt in "a burst of national joy and celebration." Communities across the country rediscovered the spirit of '76, Oregon's *Reedsport Courier* agreed. "Americans, you're beautiful," enthused Ohio's *Akron Beacon Journal*. "For three glorious days, while blue skies prevailed over most of the nation and celebrations were held with hardly a hitch, you proved that the treasure of America is untarnished after 200 years."[117]

Opinion polls registered a shift too. Seventy percent of adults said the Bicentennial had met or exceeded their expectations. More importantly, 77 percent agreed that the United States, over its 200-year history, had made significant progress in achieving the country's foundational ideals.[118]

"The nation's wounds had healed," Ford would recall in his memoir, *A Time to Heal*. Americans had regained their pride and rediscovered their faith in the country. In so doing, he wrote, they laid the foundation for a hopeful future.[119]

In fact, flag-waving alone did not cure America's ills. The post-Bicentennial high was fleeting. Partisan politics would reemerge to divide Americans, and setbacks at home and abroad would test their faith in the country.

Gerald Ford, for example, went on to lose November 1976's presidential election, despite parading for most of the year atop the nation's birthday float, as it were. His Democratic opponent, Jimmy Carter, won a tight race—garnering 50.1 percent of the popular vote and 297 electoral votes to Ford's 240, the closest electoral margin since 1916—largely on the strength of his Washington outsider status. Despite President Carter's efforts, high prices, high unemployment, and poor economic conditions, generally, would continue to bedevil the country well beyond the Bicentennial year. In July 1979, he delivered a televised address warning Americans about a threat to the nation's future that was invisible yet ran deep—"deeper than gasoline lines or energy shortages, deeper even than inflation or recession." The problem, Carter said, was "a crisis of confidence," a crisis that struck "at the very heart and soul and spirit of our national will." And Carter would deliver his "malaise speech," as some dubbed it, months *before* Iranian militants overran the US embassy in Teheran, taking fifty-two Americans hostage and sparking an even deeper crisis that captivated America for the final 440-plus days of Carter's tenure.[120]

But Ford won bipartisan praise for lowering the temperature, for reducing the public anxiety that had risen in recent years. Massachusetts Democrat Tip O'Neill, Speaker of the US House of Representatives from 1977 to 1987, would give Ford high marks in his memoir, suggesting that Ford's presidential ascension owed something to divine guidance: "God has been good to America, especially during difficult times. At the time of the Civil War, he gave us Abraham Lincoln. And at the time of Watergate, he gave us Gerald Ford—the right man at the right time who was able to put the nation back together again."[121]

As Ford prepared to leave office, *Washington Post* columnist David Broder came to the realization that he "was the kind of president Americans wanted—and didn't know they had." What Americans wanted, after a decade of presidential excess, was "a man of modesty, good character, honesty, and openness. They wanted a president who was humane and prudent, peaceful but firm. Especially, they wanted one uncorrupted by the cynicism and lust for power that they had come to associate with Washington politicians." Ford, Broder wrote, was exactly this kind of leader.[122]

"If I'm remembered," Ford later told an interviewer, "it will probably be for healing the land." Not everyone agreed. But Americans returned to a common level of understanding to guide the country's direction. The United States, he said, "had weathered the storm."[123]

6

Semiquincentennial

> Democracy is a promise: a promise that every voice matters, that justice is not reserved for the "few" or the privileged, and that freedom is not a selective right.
>
> —JOHNNETTA BETSCH COLE (2025)[1]

JUST ONE YEAR BEFORE AMERICA WAS TO celebrate the Semiquincentennial, a CNN poll found that more than 80 percent of Americans believed democracy was either "under attack" or "being tested." The poll also revealed that nearly half of all respondents lacked confidence in the ability of either major political party to address the nation's challenges or provide strong leadership. Similarly, an April 2025 Marist University poll reported that 77 percent of Americans viewed the nation's divisions as a serious threat to the future of US democracy. Looking back to October 2024, a *New York Times* / Siena College survey of likely voters ahead of that year's presidential election found that half were skeptical about the effectiveness of American democracy, with 74 percent believing it is under threat.[2]

These numbers, while concerning in and of themselves, were especially worrisome because they represented a steep drop from years past. Whereas 35 percent of Americans trusted the government in 1976—not exactly a resounding vote of confidence, given that the percentage had exceeded three-fourths just a decade earlier—only about 22 percent trust Washington today. Trust in American institutions—in the presidency, in Congress, even in the Supreme Court—was down across the board as well. According to a Gallup Poll, only 28 percent of Americans expressed confidence in major institutions in 2024, down from 43 percent in 2004.[3]

Contributing to the growing malaise across the country was a marked escalation in political violence—a phenomenon with deep roots in American history but one that has accelerated sharply since the Bicentennial. In only the last few years, the FBI foiled a plot to kidnap the governor of Michigan; the governor of Pennsylvania's residence was firebombed; the husband of the Speaker of the US House of Representatives was bludgeoned with a hammer; the former speaker of the Minnesota House and her husband were shot and killed in their home; a political organizer was murdered on a Utah university campus; and there were two assassination attempts on Donald Trump during the 2024 presidential campaign. An April 2024 poll found that one in five Americans now think they "may have to resort to violence to get their country back on track."[4]

If the polls are to be believed, America's 250th anniversary finds democracy at a crossroads. Confronted by an array of challenges, both foreign and domestic, Americans are demoralized, uncertain about the state of the union, and deeply worried about where things are headed. While the headwinds to the American experiment appear overwhelming at times, historical precedent offers some reassurance. As Mark Twain reportedly said, "History doesn't repeat itself, but it often rhymes." Americans have weathered challenges to democracy before. The Civil War, of course, is the most serious example, but there have been other significant tests as well: Presidential elections have been called into question, most notably before the Jubilee in 1824, then again in 1876, and though not marked by a fifty-year celebration, the disputed 2000 election cast a shadow over the dawn of a new century. More recently, the violent attack by a mob of President Donald Trump's supporters on the Capitol on January 6, 2021, was intended to disrupt congressional certification of the 2020 presidential election.[5]

Even in the face of political division, America's democratic story continues to evolve—shaped not only by elections and politics but by social and technological change as well. Innovation has long served to connect Americans: The Erie Canal revolutionized transportation, and the telephone and the telegraph transformed communication. While modern innovations, such as social media, can bring people together, they can just as easily foster anxiety and isolation. And though Americans now, more than at any time in our 250-year history, enjoy the freedoms envisioned in the Declaration of Independence, these rights are neither universal nor equally applied in our society. In many ways, the American experiment in democracy remains a work in progress—unfinished and unproven, yet resilient and hopeful.

"If there is anyone out there who still wonders if the dream of our founders is alive in our time; who still questions the power of our democracy, tonight is your answer," declared Barack Obama on the November 2008 night he was elected the nation's forty-fourth president. In that year's presidential election, a then-record sixty-nine million voters cast ballots for a Black candidate because, he said, "they believed that this time must be different; that their voice could be that difference."[6]

Despite the historic milestone of electing a Black president, a little more than a decade later, the murder of George Floyd, a forty-six-year-old African American, by a White police officer in Minneapolis starkly revealed that Black Americans too often remain unequal before the law. At the time, Obama's successor, Donald Trump, expressed sympathy and said he felt "very, very badly" about Floyd's death. President Trump claimed to "understand the hurt" and "understand the pain." But when protests flared in a number of cities across the country, some of which turned violent, Trump tweeted that he would restore "law and order," using the military if necessary. He warned that "when the looting starts, the shooting starts." Twitter subsequently placed a warning label on his tweet as a violation of the company's rules against promoting violence.[7]

Three years after the murder of George Floyd, reacting to the shooting by police of another Black man, Jacob Blake, professional basketball coach Doc Rivers captured the enduring frustration, stating, "We keep loving this country, but it doesn't love us back." In short, injustice, inequality, and racial discrimination persist—often hidden beneath the surface, stubbornly resistant to change, yet clear, not only in the murders of Floyd and Blake but in the challenges faced in everyday life. For example, the median wealth of Black families is significantly lower than that of White families, a gap that has grown in recent years. Black Americans are about twice as likely as Whites to live below the poverty line, and their unemployment rate is about twice as high. They are less likely to own homes and more likely to be denied a mortgage than White Americans. School districts with a majority of Black students receive less funding compared to their White counterparts. These disparities are part of a broader pattern of inequity.[8]

Since the Bicentennial, Black Americans nevertheless have achieved remarkable progress across multiple fields. In 1976, there were just sixteen African American members of the US House of Representatives; by 2026, that number had grown to sixty-one. In 1976, not a single Black American led a Fortune 500 company. Nine Black CEOs headed Fortune 500 firms in 2025, a record high, though a level that still represented less than 2 percent of the total. The number of African Americans earning higher education degrees and entering professional careers has increased significantly, fueling the growth of the Black middle class. Meanwhile, Black Americans continue to shape American culture with significant contributions in the arts, music, sports, and media.[9]

Recent years, though, have also witnessed the rollback of the Civil Rights Act of 1964 and the Voting Rights Act of 1965, both hallmarks of the civil rights movement. These laws have been critical to dismantling legal barriers as well as supporting the social, political, and economic advancement of Black Americans.

In the spring of 2025, *The Washington Post* reported that President Trump, by executive order, directed his administration to stop using *disparate impact analysis*, a term first used and applied by the Supreme Court in a landmark decision, *Griggs v. Duke Power Co.*, and later codified by Congress. Disparate impact analysis addressed discrimination by holding that seemingly neutral practices disproportionately, even if unintentionally, potentially affected different races in a discriminatory manner. The test has been central to the enforcement of the 1964 Civil Rights Act for more than sixty years.[10]

The administration also built upon the Supreme Court's 2013 decision in *Shelby County v. Holder*, which struck down the requirement that states and localities with a history of discrimination obtain federal "preclearance" before changing election laws. By sharply curtailing its support for private rights of action in which individuals have brought suit to enforce protections against racial discrimination, the Trump administration further weakened enforcement mechanisms of the 1965 Voting Rights Act.[11]

In a widely discussed *New York Times Magazine* cover story essay from the spring of 2025, Nikole Hannah-Jones, a Pulitzer Prize–winning journalist and creator of the 1619 Project, argued that the first months of President Trump's second term in office "made it possible to imagine a future that looks eerily like the past."[12]

During the last fifty years America has experienced a demographic transformation that has profoundly changed American society. The population of the United States has grown in size, expanding from about 215 million in 1976 to some 344 million today. The population has also become significantly more diverse. While comparisons are complicated by the fact that Census Bureau definitions of race and ethnicity have changed over time, more than 86 percent of Americans identified as White in 1976, a share that has declined to around 58 percent today. African Americans, who made up about 11 percent of the population in 1976, are the one group that has remained largely static, with only a slight increase to roughly 12 percent.[13]

Asian Americans, who comprised just 1.3 percent of the population in 1976, now represent approximately 7 percent. Despite their relatively small percentage of the overall population, Asian Americans play an outsized role in business, politics, and the arts. Yo-Yo Ma, a world-renowned cellist, received the Presidential Medal of Freedom in 2001. Mazie Hirono became the first Asian American woman elected to the US Senate in 2013. And three of the four largest technology companies in the country were headed by CEOs of Asian descent.[14]

The Native American population has also grown, through both increased self-identification and immigration from Indigenous communities in Latin America. There are currently 574 federally recognized tribal nations within the United States. Since the Bicentennial, Indigenous tribes in America have made notable legal, cultural, and political advances. For instance, laws like the Tribal Self-Governance Act of 1994 and the Indian Self-Determination and Education Assistance Act of 1975 fundamentally shifted the relationship between the federal government and Native Americans, granting tribes greater authority to govern their own affairs and manage their resources.[15]

Yet Native Americans still confront persistent disparities in health, education, and economic opportunity. They have the lowest life expectancy of any racial or ethnic group in the United States, with an average life expectancy of sixty-eight years, compared to seventy-eight years for non-Hispanic Whites. They experience the highest rates of diabetes, suicide, and youth depression in the nation. Many Native communities still lack access to clean water, safe housing, and reliable transportation.[16]

The most significant demographic change in the last fifty years has been the rise in the Hispanic or Latino population, which has more than quadrupled from about 4 percent to nearly 19 percent, making it the largest minority group in the country. The Immigration and Nationality Act of 1965 ended the national-origins quota system put in place in the 1920s, opening the door for immigrants to the United States from a variety of countries. During the last decade, there has been a vast migration, both legal and illegal, from Mexico, Central America, the Caribbean, and elsewhere. Not surprisingly, the South and the West have seen the largest population gains, reflecting broader patterns of immigration, internal migration, and economic factors.[17]

Since the Bicentennial, Latino or Hispanic Americans have made notable contributions in virtually every facet of American life. In politics, Alexandria Ocasio-Cortez, though only in her mid-thirties, has emerged as a leading voice of the progressive wing of the Democratic Party. The arts have been enriched by Lin-Manuel Miranda, whose Broadway sensation *Hamilton* has captivated audiences for a decade and garnered sixteen Tony Awards, including for best musical. Humanitarian efforts have been advanced by José Andrés, whose nonprofit World Central Kitchen has provided critical aid to victims of war and natural disasters, earning him the Presidential Medal of Freedom and multiple Nobel Peace Prize nominations. Most recently, in religion, many in the Hispanic community point out that Pope Leo XIV, the 267th pontiff, is of Spanish heritage and a dual citizen of the United States and Peru, further exemplifying the growing impact of Latino or Hispanic Americans on our nation and the world.

Latinos helped propel Trump to the White House in 2024 despite the inflammatory rhetoric he'd used to describe undocumented immigrants and his promises of mass deportations. According to an investigation by NBC News in the summer of 2025, US Immigration and Customs Enforcement (ICE) agents arrested roughly 30,000 immigrants during the first months of Trump's second term in office, the most since monthly data was made publicly available in November 2020. Though ICE enforcement did not always match his heated rhetoric, the number of immigrants deported in June 2025—more than 18,000—amounted to roughly half the number of arrests. Polls conducted during the second half of 2025 showed that Trump's support among Hispanics and Latinos had dropped sharply.[18]

In addition to shifting demographics, the United States has experienced profound societal transformations, particularly in the evolving role of women. In 1976, more than half of all employed women worked in twenty traditional occupations, such as in clerical roles and as nurses and teachers. Over the past several decades, women have moved into a much wider array of industries and professions. Today, they are the majority in fields such as education and health services and represent more than half of the workforce in sectors such as leisure and hospitality and financial services. Despite these gains, disparities in pay between men and women persist in nearly every professional category.[19]

The quest for women's rights, like that of civil rights, has been a long and arduous struggle. Voters in the United States have yet to send a woman to the White House, though other nations have chosen women as leaders: Britain, Germany, Israel, India, Canada, Mexico, Ireland, New Zealand, and Argentina, to name but a few. Hillary Clinton became the first woman to win a major party's presidential nomination in 2016. But she lost to Donald Trump, who in 2024 defeated another woman, Kamala Harris, despite Harris's attempts to mobilize women voters behind abortion rights following the US Supreme Court's 2022 *Dobbs v. Jackson Women's Health Organization* decision that overturned *Roe v. Wade*. Their defeats at the hands of a candidate such as Trump—who once bragged about grabbing women by the genitals and had been held liable by a jury of his peers for sexual abuse—led some to wonder if a woman would ever break through the "highest, hardest glass ceiling," as Hillary Clinton once called the presidency.[20]

Nevertheless, women have broken through other glass ceilings: Half of President Joe Biden's cabinet members were women, including Treasury Secretary Janet Yellen, the first woman to hold that post; Secretary of the Interior Debra Haaland, the first Native American cabinet secretary; and Katherine Tai, the first Asian American to serve as US trade representative. And in 2022 Ketanji Brown Jackson became the first Black woman to serve on the Supreme Court, joining three other women—Amy Coney Barrett, Elena Kagan, and Sonia Sotomayor, who in 2009 became the first woman of color to serve on the Court—for a record total of four female justices.

The Semiquincentennial arrives as women make concrete progress on another front. Three cities on the East Coast—Washington, Boston, and Philadelphia—are playing outsized roles in the festivities, as they have throughout much of the nation's history. All are governed by mayors who are women of color, further evidence that women in the United States have advanced substantially since 1976—not to mention since 1776, when the "founding fathers," all White men, gathered in the Pennsylvania State House to adopt the Declaration of Independence.

Another recent societal milestone is that Americans are now permitted to marry the person they love, regardless of gender or sexual orientation. During the Bicentennial era, the gay and lesbian movement had begun to organize but faced significant political, legal, and social barriers, with widespread public acceptance still decades away. In the 1976 case *Doe v. Commonwealth's Attorney of Richmond*, the US Supreme Court summarily affirmed a lower-court decision that upheld the constitutionality of a Virginia law banning homosexual acts, even in the privacy of one's home. Yet, juxtaposed with that legal decision—during the same year—an energetic, charismatic gay activist named Harvey Milk was appointed by San Francisco's mayor, George Moscone, to the Permit Board of Appeals, making him the first openly gay city commissioner in the United States. Months later, Milk won election to the city's Board of Supervisors, San Francisco's legislative branch—the equivalent of a city council. Milk's election as the first openly gay man to public office in California was considered a breakthrough moment for the gay community. But on November 27, 1978, both Milk and Moscone were assassinated by a former member of the Board of Supervisors.[21]

Milk's assassination was followed by other setbacks for the LGBTQ community. Thirty years ago, Congress passed the Defense of Marriage Act, barring federal recognition of same-sex marriages and permitting states to refuse recognition of gay marriages performed elsewhere. However, in 2015, the Supreme Court ruled in a landmark decision, *Obergefell v. Hodges*, that the Constitution guarantees the fundamental right to marry to same-sex couples. And in 2020 the Court determined in *Bostock v. Clayton County* that firing an employee for being gay or transgender is a violation of Title VII of the Civil Rights Act of 1964, which prohibits discrimination on the basis of sex. These decisions helped lead to a change in societal attitudes, nowhere more obvious than when the 119th Congress opened in 2025 with a record-tying number of members—thirteen—who openly identified as lesbian, gay, bisexual, transgender, or queer. This total included Congress's first openly trans member.[22]

Inequality and discrimination undoubtedly persist in the United States, but over the past fifty years, government, business, and even the military have become far more representative of the nation, drawing on a broader spectrum of experiences, identities, and skills—at least until recently.

On January 20, 2025, biting cold temperatures in Washington, DC, forced the presidential inauguration indoors, where Donald Trump took the oath of office once again, this time in the Capitol Rotunda. Raising his right hand to be sworn in as the nation's forty-seventh president, Trump became only the second president in American history to lose a reelection bid—as he did in 2020—only to return to office four years later. Even more notably, he made history as the only president ever to reclaim the presidency after being impeached twice.

Although he refused to acknowledge defeat in 2020, Trump lost the presidential election to Democrat Joseph Biden by more than 4 percent of the popular vote and seventy-four electoral votes. On January 6, 2021, thousands of Trump's supporters, many claiming to be 1776-style patriots, ransacked the US Capitol and injured more than 140 police officers. According to the House of Representatives' article of impeachment issued against him on January 13, 2021, President Trump "incited an insurrection against the government of the United States," and his actions on that day "threatened the integrity of the democratic system." The US Senate, however, acquitted Trump along mostly partisan lines on February 13, 2021. The day after being sworn in as president in 2025, President Trump signed a proclamation pardoning or commuting the sentences of more than 1,200 people convicted of crimes in the January 6 riot at the Capitol, as well as dismissing more than 450 pending cases.[23]

Trump is also the first president to have been convicted of a felony. After leaving office in 2021, he was convicted of fraudulent business practices in the state of New York. In the years between his terms in office, he was charged with a total of more than eighty felonies in four different criminal cases, though only one case made it to trial before the election due to delays and prosecutorial setbacks.

Yet the then seventy-eight-year-old Trump made a startling and impressive comeback in 2024, easily winning the nomination of the Republican Party and then decisively defeating Vice President Kamala Harris, who had become the Democratic nominee after the incumbent, Joe Biden, gave an enfeebled debate performance and then bowed out of the race only months before the election. For roughly half the country, according to *The New York Times*, Trump's convincing victory portended "a dark turn for American democracy," the future of which depended on a man who openly talked about undermining the rule of law and who spoke during his 2024 campaign of using military force against his political opponents. Trump's victory, a *Times* political reporter wrote, put America "on the precipice of an authoritarian style of governance never before seen in its 248-year history."[24]

Upon returning to the presidency, Trump and his team swiftly set about reversing decades of progressive reforms. In circumventing long-standing governmental practices and dismantling established institutions, he dramatically reshaped American democracy. On one hand, President Trump insisted he was "making America great again" by confronting those who he claimed had undermined "the timeless principles and other pillars of our liberty." On the other hand, Trump seemed intent, as author and journalist Peter Baker wrote in 2025, on "repealing much of the 20th century."[25]

Nine days after his 2025 inauguration, sitting at a desk piled high with leather-bound folders, President Trump invoked "the Constitution and the laws of the United States of America" and issued an executive order—one of dozens that poured forth from the White House in the early days of his second administration—declaring that in anticipation of the Semiquincentennial, it was "the policy of the United States . . . to provide a grand celebration worthy of the momentous occasion of the 250th anniversary of American Independence on July 4, 2026."[26]

The order reinstated plans made during his first term to build a "National Garden of American Heroes" in the Black Hills region of South Dakota and announced a new "Task Force 250"—which he would chair—to determine an agenda for the Semiquincentennial. In fact, event planning had been going on for nearly a decade: In 2016, Congress authorized the US Semiquincentennial Commission to begin work as a nonpartisan enterprise in planning and orchestrating the 250th anniversary of the signing of the Declaration of Independence.

Minutes after issuing his order related to the 250th anniversary, President Trump signed another executive order, "Ending Radical Indoctrination in K–12 Schooling," with the goal of instilling "a patriotic admiration for our incredible nation." This order essentially revived the work of the 1776 Commission, an advisory group composed of conservative activists, politicians, and intellectuals—but no professional historians—that President Trump had created before leaving office in 2021.[27]

The 1776 Commission released *The 1776 Report* on January 18, 2021, just two days before the end of President Trump's first term in office. The report drew immediate and intense criticism from historians. "It's a hack job. It's not a work of history," American Historical Association executive director James R. Grossman told *The Washington Post*. "It's very hard to find anything in here that stands as a historical claim, or as the work of a historian," said Eric Rauchway, history professor at the University of California, Davis. "Almost everything in it is wrong, just as a matter of fact." Kali Nicole Gross, professor of history at Emory University, said the report was "dusty, dated" and offered "the usual dodge on the long-lasting, harmful impacts of settler-colonialism, enslavement, Jim Crow, the oppression of women, the plight of queer people . . . as the true threat to democracy." President Biden terminated the commission by executive order on his first day in office in January 2021.[28]

Four years later, in 2025, with Trump back in office, the nation's approaching Semiquincentennial suddenly became more contested and partisan than any jubilee has been in recent memory. As he did at the end of his first term, President Trump worked once again to shape the narrative of America's 250-year history. He accused the Smithsonian, the world's largest institution of twenty-one separate museums and fourteen research and educational centers, as "OUT OF CONTROL." He specifically complained that the Smithsonian placed too much emphasis on "how horrible our Country is, how bad Slavery was, and how unaccomplished the downtrodden have been." As *The New York Times* reported,

> The administration has worked to scrub or minimize government references to the contributions of Black heroes, from the Tuskegee Airmen, who fought in World War II, to Harriet Tubman, who guided enslaved people along the Underground Railroad. Mr. Trump commemorated Juneteenth, the celebration of the end of slavery in the United States that became a federal holiday in 2021, by complaining that there were too many non-working holidays in America. He has called for

the return of Confederate insignia and statues honoring those who fought to preserve slavery.[29]

Trump's executive order with respect to the 250th anniversary specified only that the task force would "coordinate" with the US Semiquincentennial Commission. It became clear, though, that celebrating the nation's 250th anniversary had rapidly become another battleground in America's culture wars.[30]

The very first skirmish over the Semiquincentennial broke out only weeks after Trump's 2025 inauguration and concerned the approval of a fireworks display at Mount Rushmore in South Dakota's Black Hills. Originally, fireworks displays at Mount Rushmore ran from 1990 until 2010 when the US Forestry Service cautioned President Obama that due to ongoing drought conditions and an infiltration of pine beetles that had decimated local ponderosa pine forests, setting off fireworks risked igniting wildfires. President Obama decided to pause the fireworks indefinitely.[31]

After Trump became president in 2016, however, he ignored the warnings and revived the fireworks display. He also ignored opposition from local Indigenous peoples who consider the Black Hills to be sacred land, a region promised to the Lakota by the Fort Laramie Treaty of 1868. When he arrived at Mount Rushmore on July 3, 2020, for that year's Independence Day celebration, more than 100 American Indians, calling themselves "treaty defenders," briefly blocked a road leading to the national monument. After the Secret Service cleared away the protestors and the president stepped up to the podium at the monument's site, Trump declared he was "waging battle against a new far-left fascism" that imperiled "American values and [sought] to erase history."[32]

Four years later, with Trump ensconced in the White House for a second term, newly installed Secretary of the Interior Doug Burgum approved the display of fireworks at Mount Rushmore for the 250th celebration. His decision followed on legislation introduced in early 2025 by Congresswoman Anna Paulina Luna of Florida to add the profile of President Trump to Mount Rushmore, joining the sculpted likenesses of George Washington, Thomas Jefferson, Theodore Roosevelt, and Abraham Lincoln.[33]

Reacting to the news that Mount Rushmore would once again be used as a backdrop for the Semiquincentennial, Nick Tilsen, director of the NDN Collective, an Indigenous people's advocacy organization, said, "We've been resisting for hundreds of years—expect that resistance to continue."[34]

Though some traditions have changed, Americans in the 2020s ring in independence much the same as they have since 1776, with toasts and fireworks and flags and public readings of the Declaration of Independence.

While President Trump occasionally makes reference to the Declaration, his relationship with one of America's founding documents is complicated. On the one hand, Trump enjoys comparing himself to a king, the very thing from which American patriots broke in 1776, motivated by a long list of King George III's "abuses and usurpations" to institute a new, republican form of government that derived its "just powers from the consent of the governed." Journalist and author Rick Atkinson has observed, "The fact that we're looking for a monarch to draw parallels to [Trump] is telling in and of itself, because that's not what we do. That's what the whole shooting match was about in the 1770s."[35]

President Trump has added gold ornamentation to the Oval Office, but his home in Florida, the Mar-a-Lago Club, with its 126 rooms, gilded chandeliers, and white marble floors, situated on seventeen acres, is the only residence of a sitting US president that can be compared

Official White House X account post, February 2025.
(Credit: @WhiteHouse)

to a palace. When he is not in Washington, DC, the president often holds press conferences at the club, where he knows the members—twenty-first-century courtiers who reportedly pay up to $1 million in membership fees—will warmly receive whatever message he chooses to deliver. But Trump's infatuation with royalty goes beyond the trappings of wealth. In a post on his social media platform Truth Social in early 2025, the president explicitly compared himself to a king: "LONG

LIVE THE KING!" he wrote. The official White House account on social media platform X amplified the message with an illustration of Trump wearing a crown.[36]

Reacting to President Trump's use of executive power, and in particular his deployment of the military in response to protests against his immigration policy, millions of Americans took part in the nationwide "No Kings" protests on June 14, 2025. These demonstrations took place on the same day as an elaborate military parade in Washington, DC, marking the 250th anniversary of the US Army, which happened to also fall on the president's seventy-ninth birthday.

The parade featured tanks, armored vehicles, and 6,000 active service members who marched up Constitution Avenue past a reviewing stand where President Trump sat for more than three hours. The parade fulfilled a long-standing ambition of the president, who had previously sought such a display during his first term but was denied due to cost concerns. The 2025 parade ultimately went forward, attended by a crowd estimated in the tens of thousands.

Organizers of the "No Kings" protests estimated that more than five million people gathered in over 2,000 cities and towns across the United States, making it the largest coordinated demonstration in our nation's history. (Some seven million people reportedly participated in "No Kings" protests in October 2025.) "A lot of times it can feel very doom and gloom," said twenty-one-year-old Carlie Woods, who protested in Springfield, Massachusetts, with her father and sister, "but this makes you feel like you're not alone, to be around so many people fighting for our future." The "No Kings" movement emphasized nonviolent resistance, and while there were isolated confrontations between demonstrators and law enforcement in some locales, the vast majority of protests were peaceful.[37]

Protesters voiced their opposition to Trump's military parade, which they viewed as an excessive display of power and a waste of public

"No Kings" protestors, Los Angeles, June 14, 2025. (Credit: Jay L. Clendenin / Getty Images)

funds, especially at a time when many Americans faced cuts to social programs. "It's outrageous. We're not in Russia or North Korea . . . or China. That's what they do. . . . It's also costing a lot of money and people's resources," declared a seventy-six-year-old retired economist, who said he supported the US Army but opposed the parade. Another man, a nineteen year-old who attended the parade and hoped one day to join the Marines, had a different viewpoint, arguing that Trump was "acting completely within the law" and that "we have to have a powerful president who's willing to push some boundaries."[38]

There is no shortage of irony that 250 years ago Americans threw off the yoke of British royalty, only to have a billionaire president compare himself to a king. And yet Trump has also successfully cast himself as a "disruptor" representing working Americans who feel disserved by and alienated from the political establishment. Moreover, some of his supporters claim that he is only exercising presidential power under the unitary executive theory, which holds that a president has sole and total command of the executive branch and that the American people willingly augmented that power by giving the Republican Party control over both houses of Congress.

Another phenomenon predates the Trump presidency but is also emblematic of the 250th anniversary of the United States: the rise of an American oligarchy. The top 1 percent of wealthy Americans, which includes Trump, now controls nearly one-third of all wealth in the country, while the lowest 50 percent of wage earners control only 2.5 percent of all wealth. Even more shocking, the richest 400 Americans have more wealth than the bottom half of all Americans combined.[39]

A number of reasons underlie the massive redistribution of wealth, including the boom in technology, intergenerational transfer of wealth, and tax policies that favor the richest Americans. Although privileged elites have long wielded significant economic, social, and political influence in America, a new cohort of libertarian tech magnates has extended their reach well beyond wealth. This small group now shapes everything from the way Americans access news to the structure and scope of the federal civil service.

Paradoxically, as the wealth of the top 1 percent surged, initiatives aimed at supporting underserved communities—particularly through diversity, equity, and inclusion (DEI) programs—had been gaining traction in both government and the corporate sector. On his inauguration day, however, President Trump sharply condemned the Biden administration's DEI initiatives, asserting that they had introduced "illegal and immoral discrimination programs . . . into virtually all aspects of the federal government, from airline safety to the military." He signed executive orders to dismantle DEI programs across federal agencies, arguing for a return to what he called a "colorblind and merit-based" system.

Many corporations, especially those that had federal contracts, reduced or eliminated their DEI programs in concert with the government.[40]

On Tuesday, September 17, 2024, an unusually warm, late-summer day in Boston, a Paul Revere reenactor rode a horse up Beacon Street, past the nineteenth-century brownstone and brick mansions on one side of the road and the Boston Common on the other, to the gold-domed Massachusetts State House at the top of Beacon Hill. There, he was joined by Governor Maura Healey, Boston Mayor Michele Wu, other public officials, and a gaggle of print and television reporters, who had gathered to unveil the state's campaign to celebrate the nation's 250-year history.

In her prepared remarks, Governor Healey highlighted the historical importance of the upcoming celebration, but she also touted the economic benefits that the Bay State might expect as tens of thousands of tourists flocked to Massachusetts in 2026. Healey claimed the Semiquincentennial would provide an opportunity for the state to showcase its modern economy, noting that Massachusetts ranked as a top state in the country for innovation. As the governor spoke, Spot, a doglike robot manufactured by robotics company Boston Dynamics, moved in fits and starts next to the lectern and, after an acknowledgment from the governor, bowed its metal head. Spot is the first commercially available robot capable of navigating, sensing, and manipulating objects. The robot, with its futuristic yellow frame and mechanical legs that loosely resemble a four-legged canine, "can perform site inspections, search and rescue missions, and data collection." According to engineers at Boston Dynamics, the robot can climb and descend stairs, walk and trot, and pick up and carry a payload of more than thirty pounds. It can even skip rope.[41]

Boston Dynamics has sold thousands of Spot units globally, describing them as "dependable" coworkers "delivering consistent results," and claims, "Spot is changing how organizations monitor and operate their sites, ensure the safety of their teams, and make data-driven decisions." On the 250th anniversary of the Declaration of Independence, Spot, powered by artificial intelligence (AI), is emblematic of America's modern-day technological revolution—innovation that has been central to the American experience since 1776.[42]

Just as the Corliss steam engine captivated audiences at the 1876 Centennial Exhibition by signaling the advent of a new industrial age, today's rapid advances in technology are reshaping the landscape of work, the economy, and society at large. As Americans face a combination of political uncertainty and transformative social challenges, perhaps nothing is more pressing than adapting to the seismic impact of AI, which has swiftly become a cornerstone of the modern economy. "We're at the beginning of a new industrial revolution," declared Jensen Huang, CEO of Nvidia, a leading technology company that designs and builds the graphic processing chips and other software and hardware used in AI.[43]

Nvidia is the largest company in the United States with a market capitalization of $4 trillion. Huang, born in the United States to immigrant parents from Taiwan, was only a teenager during the Bicentennial. He grew up in a middle-class neighborhood in the small town of Oneida, Kentucky, later moving to the Portland, Oregon, area where he graduated from high school and earned extra money by washing dishes in a fast-food restaurant. Now he is worth an estimated $125 billion. He predicts that AI will usher in a new era of computing that will transform industries worldwide, signaling a new industrial revolution. AI also will most certainly impact America's democracy.[44]

Thomas Jefferson could never have imagined the advent of social media, artificial intelligence, or quantum computing when he opined on the challenges of self-government, famously noting, "A choice by the people themselves is generally not distinguished for its wisdom." Yet Jefferson, who founded the University of Virginia in 1819, was a steadfast believer in education as a cornerstone of American democracy. As he wrote to Massachusetts public official William Charles Jarvis in 1820, "I know no safe depository of the ultimate powers of the society, but the people themselves: and if we think them not enlightened enough to exercise their controul with a wholsome discretion, the remedy is, not to take it from them, but to inform their discretion by education. This is the true corrective of abuses of constitutional power."[45]

As a transformative force, AI will not only drive innovation but also serve as a powerful tool for sharing practical information and providing access to education and knowledge. If developed responsibly, with appropriate safeguards, it can help lower barriers to civic participation and foster a more transparent, responsive, and inclusive democracy.[46]

Yet AI also comes with potential significant risks. AI can be weaponized by malicious actors to undermine democracy, enabling the creation of verisimilitudinous content, including "deep fake" texts and images, as well as the spreading of disinformation about political candidates or electoral processes. Once uploaded on social media, these false narratives can easily outpace both governmental oversight and society's capacity to respond. As a nineteenth-century Englishman keenly observed, "A lie will go round the world while truth is pulling its boots on."[47]

Ultimately, while AI has the capacity to strengthen democracy, it could just as easily sow confusion and exacerbate division among an uncritical and overwhelmed electorate, deepening distrust in government and threatening the very foundations of self-rule that Thomas Jefferson so valued.[48]

MONTICELLO, THOMAS JEFFERSON'S VIRGINIA ESTATE, WILL MARK July Fourth in 2026 much as it has July Fourths since trustees dedicated the architectural masterpiece to the American people on Independence Day 1926. But with at least one major difference: Visitors can now tour the quarters where enslaved persons like Sally Hemings once lived.

Rumors swirled for centuries that Hemings was the mother of six or more of Jefferson's children. In 1802, a pugnacious newspaperman claimed, "[Jefferson] keeps and for many years has kept, as his concubine, one of his slaves. Her name is Sally. The name of her eldest son is Tom."[49]

But Jefferson's powerful defenders long denied these stories as legends told and retold by Hemings's descendants. That is, until 1998, when Annette Gordon-Reed, a thirty-nine-year-old law professor who grew up in Jim Crow–era Texas, reopened the case with *Thomas Jefferson and Sally Hemings: An American Controversy*. Based on the evidence, the book, Gordon-Reed's first, concluded that the two probably had a sexual relationship. A DNA study subsequently confirmed that Jefferson was the biological father of Hemings's youngest son.[50]

In 2018, after decades of controversy, Monticello finally affirmed that Jefferson had fathered children with Hemings. Websites, exhibitions, and other displays detailing the experiences of enslaved persons are now regular features of Monticello's outward-facing programs. "Symbolically," Gordon-Reed said, such inclusion is tremendously important, for it serves as "a way of establishing black people's birthright to America."[51]

The story of Jefferson and Hemings made headlines because it challenged the prevailing image of Jefferson as the "Apostle of Freedom," the founder whose "original Rough draught" of the Declaration of Independence condemned the slave trade as a "cruel war against human nature itself," a violation of the "most sacred rights of life & liberty." Though deleted from the final draft, these words showed that Jefferson was philosophically opposed to slavery, admirers had long insisted. "All of Jefferson's values and goals dictated the extermination of slavery," the historian Merrill Peterson wrote in 1970. "This was as self-evident as the principles of 1776 themselves."[52]

Yet the Hemings case showed a Jefferson who said one thing and did another: a slaveholder who held 600 persons in bondage during his lifetime; a Virginia planter who bought, sold, bred, and flogged slaves and hunted down fugitives much like his fellow Virginia planters did; a founder who, unlike George Washington, did not free all his slaves, with the notable exceptions of Hemings's children; a writer who expressed "great aversion" to sexual relations between Whites and Blacks, yet impregnated a teenage Hemings when he was in his forties. In short, Jefferson was a hypocrite.[53]

And if Jefferson was hypocritical, so, too, was America, for at some level his shortcomings were America's, since he had authored the nation's founding creed. Throughout US history, Jefferson's reputation has served as a barometer of America's image, an indicator of citizens' faith in the American experiment, a measure of the nation's standing in the eyes of the world. "If Jefferson was wrong," wrote a biographer in 1874, "America is wrong. If America is right, Jefferson was right."[54]

Americans in 2026 are certainly struggling over what is right and what is wrong with their country. And they are struggling in part because Jefferson's words, despite his personal failings, as well as our own as a nation, are still worth fighting for. They remain "pregnant with our own, and the fate of the world" centuries after he wrote of their legacy just days before his death in 1826, at the age of eighty-three. The Declaration of Independence's pronouncement that all are created equal provided a central argument for ending slavery, for bringing African Americans into citizenship, for establishing women's rights, and for doing much else besides. Over the centuries all, from working Americans and Native Americans to Asian Americans, Muslim Americans, and Hispanic and Latino Americans, have drawn on the Declaration's principles to complete the unfinished work of the American Revolution. As such, as Annette Gordon-Reed herself wrote in 2004, they still offer the last "best hope" for conquering not only the doctrine of White supremacy but also the lure of authoritarianism.[55]

Epilogue

> Whether they have the freedoms that we have known up until now will depend on what we do here.
>
> —RONALD REAGAN (1976)[1]

"WE WANT REAGAN!" A CHORUS OF SUPPORTERS cheered—looking skyward to a box in the upper reaches of Kansas City's Kemper Arena, where former California Governor Ronald Reagan and his wife, Nancy, watched President Gerald Ford accept the Republican Party's 1976 presidential nomination. After a bruising Bicentennial-year fight that went all the way to the Republican National Convention, President Ford, the establishment's choice, had won an arm-twisting, narrow roll call victory over Reagan, the insurgent conservative. Now it was time for reconciliation, to end the convention with a show of party unity heading into November's general election contest against the Democratic nominee, Jimmy Carter. As the applause for Reagan grew louder, Ford invited his former opponent down to the stage to make some remarks. "And bring Nancy," he added.[2]

Though sources differ on whether the moment was staged, Reagan, the former Hollywood actor, gave every appearance of being taken by surprise. Smiling shyly, he waved Ford off, shaking his head no. Again and again, he lowered his palms as a signal for his supporters to sit down or raised a finger to his lips to quiet the crowd. But the cheers grew louder: "Speech! Speech!" the floor-stomping delegates yelled. His son Michael Reagan said the din "seemed to last an hour. The pianist must have played 'California, Here I Come' a dozen times."[3]

At last the Reagans were coaxed down, and as they made their way to the stage, the commotion continued. Horns blew. Cowboy hats waved to and fro. Placards bounced up and down, including a hand-lettered one that read, "Gov. Reagan We Almost Made That Long Hard Climb Didn't We?"[4]

Taking the microphone, Reagan began by praising the party's conservative platform—"a banner of bold, unmistakable colors with no pastel shades"—that his allies had succeeded in pushing through over opposition from the more moderate wing of the party. He spoke of the realistic aspirations of all Americans, and borrowing a phrase from John Winthrop, the first governor of the Massachusetts Bay Colony, Reagan declared America should be a "shining city on a hill." As the crowd cheered, Reagan paused and appeared to search for his next words. Stammering, he said that someone had asked him to write a letter for a time capsule that would be opened in Los Angeles in 2076, on the occasion of America's Tricentennial. Considering the assignment while riding down the California coast—the blue Pacific on his right, the Santa Ynez Mountains to the left—he wondered, would it be "that beautiful a hundred years from now as it was on that summer day?" Then it dawned on him, he said, as TV cameras cut to shots of a hushed crowd now raptly listening. "Those who would read this letter a hundred years from now will know whether . . . we met our challenge," the challenge of protecting America's future. For their ability to enjoy "the freedoms that we have known up until now will depend on what we do here. Will they look back with appreciation and say, 'Thank God for those people in 1976 who headed off that loss of freedom?'" Or would they curse them for squandering it? As he concluded, applause erupted. Horns again blew. Hands clapped to the house band's rousing rendition of "The Victors," the fight song of the University of Michigan, President Ford's alma mater. But Reagan had stolen the show.[5]

Reagan, of course, was neither the first nor the last presidential candidate to talk about freedom as the cornerstone of the American way of life, and he was not elected president in 1976—he would have to wait four years. During his time in public life, including as president, his record on civil rights for all Americans was decidedly mixed. For instance, campaigning for the presidency in 1980, Reagan gave a speech before a crowd estimated at 15,000 at the Neshoba County Fair in Mississippi. The fairgrounds were not far from the site where three civil rights workers were murdered and buried in shallow graves by members of the Ku Klux Klan in 1964. Echoing Stephen Douglas's campaign in 1858, Reagan asserted, "I believe in states' rights." Reagan had seldom used the term before, but he was well aware that "states' rights" had long been invoked by Southern secessionists to defend slavery and, later, by segregationists to oppose federal efforts to dismantle Jim Crow laws and advance civil rights for Black Americans. As Reagan biographer Max Boot has written, "This was the dark side of his pragmatism: He was willing to tap into dangerous and disreputable prejudices to win the presidency while insisting to everyone, even himself, that his intentions were pure." Showing greater empathy for Black Americans three years later, Reagan, now president, signed legislation making the third Monday in each January a national holiday: Martin Luther King Jr. Day.[6]

The America of 2026 bears little resemblance to that of 1776—or to that of 1858, when Lincoln made reference to "the electric cord" of the Declaration that linked generations of Americans together in a common quest for liberty—and it is easy, in these difficult times, to lose sight of the big picture. But the long view shows that the American experiment has faced challenges before, many of them severe. Each fifty-year marker on America's 250-year journey since 1776 has found our country at a crossroads of some sort. Yet the American experiment has proved resilient, strengthened at key junctures by jubilees that encouraged Americans to rediscover their common heritage. In 1826, memories were still fresh of the corrupt bargain that, Jacksonians said, had stolen the presidential election of 1824. With the passing of both Thomas Jefferson and John Adams on July 4, 1826, the country lost its last physical links with the Revolutionary generation. The radical potential of the American Revolution to level distinctions of race, class, and gender was all but forgotten.[7]

Abolitionists, women's rights advocates, laborers, and other groups soon called for the nation to live up to its founding principles, and the Centennial year of 1876 found America in a more optimistic mood. With slavery eradicated and the Civil War over, the United States was eager to showcase its economic prowess to the world. However, the year ended with another disputed election settled by a political deal, the Compromise of 1877, that supporters of the losing candidate alleged was corrupt. And while the Centennial celebration in Philadelphia was by all accounts a great success, the decades that followed—the post-Reconstruction era—were among the darkest in our nation's history, especially for African and Native Americans.

Notwithstanding White nationalists who marched unmasked in the streets of the nation's capital in 1926, the Sesquicentennial was relatively placid from a political point of view. Only a few years earlier, President Calvin Coolidge had taken decisive action in response to Teapot Dome, arguably exposing and ultimately addressing the then-biggest scandal in US political history. By 1926, Teapot Dome was yesterday's news, and, more importantly, the economy was humming. During the Great War in Europe, the United States had proved itself a world economic and military power. Yet the deadly war and an even deadlier pandemic caused the country to turn inward, arrayed against foreign immigrants and other outside influences that seemed injurious to the national interest. "America must be kept American," President Coolidge said while signing an immigration-quota act, expressing a viewpoint that rhymes with the America First rhetoric of today.[8]

The Bicentennial year of 1976 also rhymes with many of the concerns of today. It found the country still reeling from Watergate, the gravest constitutional crisis since the Civil War, whose final chapter—the pardoning of Richard Nixon by President Gerald Ford, an accidental president like Coolidge—led to claims of yet another corrupt bargain, namely, that Ford, Nixon's former vice president, had traded the presidency for a pardon. Ford at times stumbled his way through office, but during the Bicentennial year he helped heal the nation following Watergate. Indeed, in July 1976 *The Washington Post* noted that the American flag—the same flag that had been politicized during the Vietnam War, worn on hard hats in support of US soldiers fighting overseas, stitched on the backsides of blue jeans in protest—was "common property again." The *Post* found the Stars and Stripes "stapled onto parade floats, stuck in hats, and hung from porches." It was also an election year, and for the first time in decades, a son of the South assumed the presidency.[9]

"For ourselves," Thomas Jefferson wrote in 1826, "let the annual return of this day, forever refresh our recollections of these rights and an undiminished devotion to them." The Declaration of Independence's statement of those rights served, he said, as the "Signal of arousing men to burst the chains" in search of liberty. As such, the historical memory of its noble principles provided an endless wellspring "of hope for others." Yet America now appears headed in the wrong direction 250 years after the Declaration of Independence was "submitted to a candid world," to judge by the document's declining influence today.[10]

Jefferson's words are not as vital as they once were. Granted, the Declaration gained a new lease on life after the Cold War, when more than thirty states in the Baltics, the Balkans, Eastern Europe, and Central Asia issued declarations of independence from the Soviet Union or its client states between 1990 and 1993. Many of these post–Cold War declarations drew from the American blueprint, insofar as they asserted a right to self-determination based on international norms and grievances against the former ruling power. Some also vowed to protect human rights.[11]

Today, though, the international community draws less often on not only the Declaration of Independence but also the US Constitution and the Bill of Rights, in part because the United States is not currently seen as a model democracy. According to the Pew Research Center, a median of four in ten people surveyed across thirty-four nations believe democracy in the United States used to be a good example for other countries to follow but is not anymore.[12]

America, of course, has never fully lived up to the Declaration's aspirational language. Indeed, the founders themselves did not, and for 250 years Americans have been striving to make the United States a beacon for the world where "life, liberty, and the pursuit of happiness" are truly "unalienable rights" for all citizens. While the journey at times has been dark, difficult, and too often inhumane, America has made incontrovertible progress—no matter how it is defined. But the grand vision expressed in the Declaration of Independence remains nothing more than words on paper, as Jefferson himself made clear, unless and until it is secured by a government that represents the "consent of the governed"—free from the tyranny of "absolute Despotism." And even then, as the Declaration acknowledges, governments are fallible.

Ronald Reagan's speech at the convention in 1976 and his story about the Tricentennial were testament to the fact that the ideals adumbrated in 1776 continue to resonate centuries later. The promise of the benefits that flow from freedom, from unalienable rights, and from liberty is why every year Americans continue to celebrate Independence Day and why every fifty years, as articulated by the America 250 Commission, we take the "opportunity to pause and reflect on our nation's past, honor the contributions of all Americans, and look ahead toward the future we want to create for the next generation and beyond."[13]

The Semiquincentennial will undoubtedly showcase America's incredible spirit of innovation and economic achievement. There will be many celebrations across the country, and they will be filled with energy, excitement, and optimism for the future. But July 4, 2026, also should remind us that democracy cannot, and should not, be taken for granted: Flag waving, patriotic songs, and fireworks alone won't save it when it is threatened by those who care little for its enriching diversity, its democratic processes, and its historical traditions. Only citizen participation, respect for one another, and adherence to the rule of law can preserve our democracy and move our nation forward. When that time capsule is opened in 2076, will the Americans of tomorrow thank us for securing the freedoms we have known up until now? Or will they curse us for squandering them?

ACKNOWLEDGMENTS

I AM DEEPLY GRATEFUL TO CLIVE PRIDDLE, former publisher of PublicAffairs, for his help in shaping the book proposal and his willingness to bring *The Flag Was Still There* into print. I also owe thanks to Lara Heimert and Brian Distelberg at Basic Books, whose support sustained the project from the start.

Professor Mike Schroeder at American University was extremely helpful at the beginning of the project.

Several friends offered wise counsel on early drafts, and I am particularly indebted to Douglas Frantz, David Gerken, Joe Bower, Patrick Granfield, and Jonathan Winer for their careful readings and encouragement. At later stages, Cliff Sloan and Larry Gurwin provided detailed comments and incisive edits that proved invaluable.

At Basic Books, Brandon Proia guided the manuscript with steady encouragement and discerning advice. During Brandon's brief paternity leave, Roger Labrie stepped in, bringing a set of fresh eyes that strengthened the work even further.

Most of all, I want to thank my coauthor, Todd Bennett. I did not know him before beginning our collaboration; over time I discovered not only a superb historian and gifted writer but also the ideal partner for this book. I could not have asked for better.

Finally, my deepest gratitude goes to my wife, Kathleen Kaye. For each of the seven books I have written, she has been both the first and the last reader of every draft. Her patience, keen eye, and unwavering support have been indispensable.

—*David McKean*

THOUGH TWO NAMES MAY APPEAR ON THE cover, this book represents a collective effort, starting with that of the librarians and archivists who fielded my research requests and pointed me toward key holdings, files, and collections. Thanks to the dedicated staffs at the Library of Congress, the US National Archives, and especially the Gerald R. Ford Presidential Library, including Donna Lehman, Helmi Raaska, Stacy Davis, Mark Fisher, William McNitt, and Geir Gundersen.

I have had the good fortune of working with many wonderful colleagues over the years, including Kristin Ahlberg, a friend from my State Department days, who kindly shared her expertise on the presidency of Jimmy Carter. Faculty members of East Carolina University's Department of History read and commented on drafts of this book. Thanks to Gerald Prokopowicz, Karin Zipf, Jarvis Hargrove, Christopher Oakley, and department chair Tim Jenks for their time and insight.

Dr. Allison Danell, dean of ECU's Thomas Harriot College of Arts and Sciences, generously supported this project with a college research fellowship, which provided me with the precious gift of time to research and write. A research grant from the Gerald R. Ford Presidential Foundation yielded a wealth of documentation on the 1976 Bicentennial, only a fraction of which is reflected in this book.

I owe an enormous debt to my coauthor, David McKean, for bringing me onto the project. Though I had a couple of books under my belt by the time we met, Ambassador McKean taught me a great deal about not only writing but the publication process. David is a superb writer, always in command of the prose, and he deserves full credit for originating the book's insightful conceit of taking a longitudinal approach to the study of American history at fifty-year intervals since 1776. I would also like to acknowledge Clive Priddle, former publisher of PublicAffairs, for his early encouragement of the book.

At Basic Books, Executive Editor Brandon Proia had the unenviable task of turning a manuscript drafted by two authors into a finished book. Yet he always handled that job with good cheer and even better advice, with assistance from Roger Labrie, Alex Cullina, Shena Redmond, and Jennifer Kelland. I am deeply grateful to Basic's leadership, including associate publisher Brian Distelberg and publisher Lara Heimert, for supporting *The Flag Was Still There* and bringing it into print.

Thanks, especially, to my spouse, Kathy, and our daughter, Zoë. They tolerate my frequent absences, both physical and mental, and give me a home. Appreciate you.

That said, all errors, omissions, and mistakes are mine and David's alone.

—M. Todd Bennett

NOTES

Prologue

1. “Great Republican Demonstration on Saturday Evening,” *Chicago Daily Tribune*, July 12, 1858, 1.

2. Abraham Lincoln, “A House Divided Speech at Springfield, Illinois,” June 16, 1858, in *The Collected Works of Abraham Lincoln*, ed. Roy P. Basler (Rutgers University Press, 1953), 2:461.

3. James M. McPherson, *Battle Cry of Freedom: The Civil War Era* (Oxford University Press, 1988), 182.

4. “Great Republican Demonstration.” For the tension in American history between racial nationalism and civic nationalism, see Gary Gerstle, *American Crucible: Race and Nation in the Twentieth Century* (Princeton University Press, 2017).

5. Abraham Lincoln, “Speech at Chicago, Illinois,” July 10, 1858, in Basler, *Collected Works*, 484–502.

6. Lincoln, “Speech at Chicago, Illinois,” 499–500.

7. “Thomas Jefferson to Roger Chew Weightman, June 24, 1826,” Founders Online, https://founders.archives.gov; “President McKinley’s Last Public Utterance to the People in Buffalo,” September 5, 1901, American Presidency Project, www.presidency.ucsb.edu. McKinley was shot on the grounds of Buffalo’s Pan-American Exposition the day after making these remarks. He died from his wounds a little over a week later.

Leviticus 25, as translated in English around 1382, speaks of an institution “to be kept every fifty years, and to be proclaimed by the blast of trumpets throughout the land; during [which] the fields were to be left uncultivated, Hebrew slaves were to be set free, and lands and houses . . . that had been sold were to revert to their former owners or their heirs.” “Jubilee (n.), sense 1.a,” *Oxford English Dictionary*, December 2024.

8. John Quincy Adams quoted in Andrew Burstein's study of 1826, *America's Jubilee* (Knopf, 2001), 4–5.

9. The persistent gap between the promise of American ideals and the reality of American institutions drives US political history, argued political scientist Samuel P. Huntington in *American Politics: The Promise of Disharmony* (Belknap Press of Harvard University Press, 1981).

10. Celebratory accounts of American history include William J. Bennett, *America: The Last Best Hope*, 3 vols. (Thomas Nelson, 2006–2011); Daniel J. Boorstin, *The Americans*, 3 vols. (Random House, 1958–1973); Samuel Eliot Morison and Henry Steele Commager, *The Growth of the American Republic* (Oxford University Press, 1930); George Bancroft, *A History of the United States of America, from the Discovery of the American Continent*, 10 vols. (Little, Brown, and Company, 1855–1875). "Stopping history cold at any particular point . . . negates the historical flow and stifles the voices and activities of actual people attempting to define the operations of government," cautioned Sean Wilentz in *The Rise of American Democracy: Jefferson to Lincoln* (Norton, 2005), xviii.

Chapter 1. First Fourths

1. "John Adams to Abigail Adams, 3 July 1776," Founders Online, https://founders.archives.gov.

2. "Abigail Adams to John Adams, 31 March 1776," Founders Online. Another Adams child, Susanna, had died in 1770 at the age of thirteen months.

3. Woody Holton, *Abigail Adams* (Atria, 2009), xvii.

4. Holton, *Abigail Adams*, xix–xxiii; Mary Beth Norton, *Liberty's Daughters: The Revolutionary Experience of American Women, 1750–1800* (Little, Brown, 1980), xv. The American Revolution was about not only "home rule" but also "who should rule at home," Carl Becker wrote in "The History of Political Parties in the Province of New York, 1760–1776" (PhD diss., University of Wisconsin, 1907), 22.

5. "Abigail Adams to John Adams, 31 March 1776"; L. H. Butterfield, Marc Friedlaender, and Mary-Jo Kline, introduction to *The Book of Abigail and John: Selected Letters of the Adams Family, 1762–1784*, ed. L. H. Butterfield, Marc Friedlaender, and Mary-Jo Kline (Harvard University Press, 1975), 8.

6. "Abigail Adams to John Adams, 31 March 1776"; Holton, *Abigail Adams*, 99.

7. "John Adams to Abigail Adams, 14 April 1776," Founders Online; Linda K. Kerber, *No Constitutional Right to Be Ladies: Women and the Obligations of Citizenship* (Hill and Wang, 1998).

8. "John Adams to Mary Palmer, 5 July 1776," Founders Online.

9. Edwin G. Burrows and Mike Wallace, *Gotham: A History of New York City to 1898* (Oxford University Press, 1999), 193.

10. Pauline Maier, *American Scripture: Making the Declaration of Independence* (Random House, 1997), 159.

11. Maier, *American Scripture*, 156.

12. Ron Chernow, *Washington: A Life* (Penguin Press, 2010), 237.

13. Thomas Paine, *Common Sense* (W. & T. Bradford, 1776), 40, 107, Project Gutenberg, www.gutenberg.org.

14. Publication claims may well have been exaggerated, given the limitations of eighteenth-century printing and distribution. Isaac Kramnick, introduction to Thomas Paine, *Common Sense*, ed. Isaac Kramnick (1776; Penguin Books, 1986), 8–9.

15. *Dunlap's Maryland Gazette*, July 30, 1776, quoted in John H. Hazelton, *The Declaration of Independence: Its History* (Dodd, Mead and Co., 1906), 575. For repurposed traditions, see David Waldstreicher, *In the Midst of Perpetual Fetes: The Making of American Nationalism, 1776–1820* (University of North Carolina Press, 1997), 30–31.

16. "John Adams to Samuel Chase, 9 July 1776," Founders Online.

17. Hazelton, *Declaration*, 243–244, 258–262, 273; Waldstreicher, *In the Midst*, 33–35.

18. David Armitage, *The Declaration of Independence: A Global History* (Harvard University Press, 2007), 17–22.

19. Peter de Bolla, *The Fourth of July and the Founding of America* (Overlook Press, 2007), 169.

20. Richard B. Morris, "Europe, the Press and the Declaration of Independence," *Journalism History* 2 (summer 1975): 48.

21. Morris, "Europe," 48.

22. Morris, "Europe," 49.

23. Morris, "Europe," 49; Richard B. Sheridan, *Sugar and Slavery: An Economic History of the British West Indies*, 1623–1775 (Johns Hopkins University Press, 1974).

24. Armitage, *Declaration of Independence*, 74.

25. Armitage, *Declaration of Independence*, 76.

26. Armitage, *Declaration of Independence*, 80.

27. Armitage, *Declaration of Independence*, 80–82.

28. Morris, "Europe," 49.

29. Nikole Hannah-Jones, "Our Democracy's Founding Ideals Were False When They Were Written; Black Americans Have Fought to Make Them True," *New York Times Magazine*, August 14, 2019; Annette Gordon-Reed, *The Hemingses of Monticello: An American Family* (W. W. Norton, 2008), 23, 125.

30. Hannah-Jones, "Our Democracy's Founding Ideals"; Alan Taylor, *American Revolutions: A Continental History, 1750–1804* (W. W. Norton, 2016). White freedom's very existence depended on Black enslavement, according to Edmund

S. Morgan in *American Slavery, American Freedom: The Ordeal of Colonial Virginia* (Norton, 1975).

31. Danielle Allen, "A Forgotten Black Founding Father," *Atlantic*, March 2021, 44. Hall's freemasonry is a main subject of historian Charles H. Wesley's *Prince Hall: Life and Legacy* (United Supreme Council, Southern Jurisdiction, Prince Hall Affiliation, 1977).

32. "Petition for Freedom to the Massachusetts Council and the House of Representatives," January [13,] 1777, Jeremy Belknap Papers, Massachusetts Historical Society, Boston, www.masshist.org.

33. Allen, "Forgotten Black Founding Father," 44.

34. George Washington Williams, *History of the Negro Race in America from 1619 to 1800* (G. P. Putnam's Sons, 1885), 115–116.

35. Jake Silverstein, "The 1619 Project and the Long Battle over US History," *New York Times Magazine*, November 9, 2021; Martha S. Jones, *Birthright Citizens: A History of Race and Rights in Antebellum America* (Cambridge University Press, 2018), 4, 11.

36. Robert Middlekauff, *The Glorious Cause: The American Revolution, 1763–1789* (Oxford University Press, 2005), 370–384.

37. John Ferling, *A Leap in The Dark: The Struggle to Create the American Republic* (Oxford University Press, 2003), 192.

38. Ferling, *A Leap in The Dark*, 193–194.

39. Kit Hinrichs and Delphine Hirasuna, *Long May She Wave: A Graphic History of the American Flag* (Ten Speed Press, 2001), 8, 11.

40. "John Adams to Abigail Adams 2d, 5 July 1777," Founders Online.

41. "John Adams to Abigail Adams, 3 July 1776."

42. "John Adams to Abigail Adams 2d, 5 July 1777."

43. *Virginia Gazette*, July 18, 1777; "John Adams to Abigail Adams 2d, 5 July 1777"; Len Travers, *Celebrating the Fourth: Independence Day and the Rites of Nationalism in the Early Republic* (University of Massachusetts Press, 1997), 18–19. In 1777, fireworks were limited to one color: orange. "There were no elaborate sparkles, no red, white and blue stars—nothing more than a few glorified (although uplifting) explosions in the sky." Alexis Stempien, "The Evolution of Fireworks," Smithsonian Science Education Center, July 1, 2015, https://ssec.si.edu.

44. "John Adams to Abigail Adams 2d, 5 July 1777."

45. "John Adams to Abigail Adams 2d, 5 July 1777."

46. Travers, *Celebrating the Fourth*, 18; Diana Karter Appelbaum, *The Glorious Fourth: An American Holiday, an American History* (Facts on File, 1989), 17.

47. Appelbaum, *Glorious Fourth*, 17–18.

48. Travers, *Celebrating the Fourth*, 24; Waldstreicher, *In the Midst*, 40.

49. *Pennsylvania Evening Post*, July 5, 1777, quoted in Travers, *Celebrating the Fourth*, 24.

50. Isabel Thompson Kelsay, *Joseph Brant, 1743–1807: Man of Two Worlds* (Syracuse University Press, 1984), 175–176.

51. Ned Blackhawk, introduction to *The Rediscovery of America: Native Peoples and the Unmaking of US History* (Yale University Press, 2023), Kindle.

52. Nicole Eustace, "An Expanding Vision of America," *New York Review of Books*, March 27, 2025; Blackhawk, *Rediscovery*, intro. Some of America's founders were complicit—directly or indirectly—in the dispossession of Native American lands. George Washington, for example, personally accumulated thousands of acres of Indigenous land in the Ohio Valley and elsewhere. As president, he pursued policies that divested Indians of millions more acres. Colin G. Calloway, *The Indian World of George Washington: The First President, the First Americans, and the Birth of the Nation* (Oxford University Press, 2018), 7.

53. Blackhawk, *Rediscovery*, intro. and chap. 6; Colin G. Calloway, *The American Revolution in Indian Country: Crisis and Diversity in Native American Communities* (Cambridge University Press, 1995); Alan Taylor, *The Divided Ground: Indians, Settlers, and the Northern Borderland of the American Revolution* (Knopf, 2006).

54. Taylor, *Divided Ground*, 4, 88. The British superintendent, Sir William Johnson, was married to Brant's sister, Molly.

55. Taylor, *Divided Ground*, 89; Kelsay, *Joseph Brant*, 165–166; "Joseph Brant," in *Oxford Dictionary of Quotations*, ed. Elizabeth Knowles, 8th ed. (Oxford University Press, 2014).

56. Taylor, *Divided Ground*, 89. Not all Indigenous nations aligned with the British; Oneida and Tuscarora, for example, sided with the patriots.

57. Blackhawk, *Rediscovery*, intro.

58. William Gordon, the clergyman who spoke in Boston in 1777, is credited with giving the first July Fourth oration. James R. Heintze, ed., *The Fourth of July Encyclopedia* (McFarland & Co., 2007), 125.

59. David Ramsay, "An Oration on the Advantages of American Independence," July 4, 1778, in "David Ramsay, 1749–1815: Selections from His Writings," ed. Robert L. Brunhouse. *Transactions of the American Philosophical Society* 55, no. 4 (1965): 183, 185. For the rise of republicanism, see Gary Nash, *The Urban Crucible: The Northern Seaports and the Origins of the American Revolution* (Harvard University Press, 1986), 222; Gordon S. Wood, *The Radicalism of the American Revolution* (Vintage, 1993).

60. Interpretations emphasizing the limited nature of the American Revolution include Charles A. Beard, *An Economic Interpretation of the Constitution of the United States* (Macmillan, 1913); Howard Zinn, "A Kind of Revolution," in *A People's History of the United States, 1492–Present* (Harper, 2017), e-book.

61. Ramsay, "Oration," 183–184; Ramsay, *The History of the American Revolution*, 2 vols. (R. Aitken & Son, 1789).

62. Ramsay, "Oration," 183, 185.

63. *South Carolina and American Gazette*, July 9, 1778, quoted in Brunhouse, "David Ramsay: Selections," 182.

64. Appelbaum, *Glorious Fourth*, 36; Willard Keyes, "A Journal of Life in Wisconsin One Hundred Years Ago," *Wisconsin Magazine of History* 3 (June 1920): 444.

65. "John Adams to Abigail Adams, 3 July 1776."

Chapter 2. Jubilee

1. "Thomas Jefferson to Roger Chew Weightman, 24 June 1826," Founders Online, https://founders.archives.gov.

2. John Quincy Adams to Charles Carroll, July 4, 1826, in *The Writings of John Quincy Adams*, ed. Worthington Chauncey Ford (Macmillan, 1917), 7:542–543.

3. Estimates of early-nineteenth-century Native American populations vary widely, due to incomplete census coverage and inconsistent record keeping. See Russell Thornton, *American Indian Holocaust and Survival: A Population History Since 1492* (University of Oklahoma Press, 1987); Marlita A. Reddy, ed., *Statistical Record of Native North Americans* (Gale Research, 1993).

4. "The Constitution of the United States," National Archives, www.archive.gov.

5. Jill Lepore, *These Truths: A History of the United State*s (Norton, 2018), 182.

6. Andrew Burstein, *America's Jubilee* (Knopf, 2001), 22.

7. Sean Wilentz, *Andrew Jackson* (Times Books, 2005), 39.

8. John Quincy Adams, *Memoirs of John Quincy Adams, Comprising Portions of His Diary from 1795 to 1848*, ed. Charles Francis Adams (J. B. Lippincott & Co., 1876), 7:110.

9. Edward G. Lengel, "Adams v. Jackson: The Election of 1824," Gilder Lehrman Institute of American History, www.gilderlehrman.org.

10. Joseph Cummins, *Anything for a Vote: Dirty Tricks, Cheap Shots, and October Surprises in US Presidential Campaigns* (Quirk Books, 2015), 44; Wilentz, *Andrew Jackson*, 47.

11. Burstein, *America's Jubilee*, 182–185.

12. William J. Bennett, *America: The Last Best Hope* (Thomas Nelson, 2006), 1:222.

13. Robert V. Remini, "Election of 1828," in *The Coming to Power: Critical Presidential Elections in American History*, ed. Arthur M. Schlesinger Jr. (McGraw Hill, 1971), 67–90.

14. Cummins, *Anything for a Vote*, 46.

15. George C. Herring, *From Colony to Superpower: US Foreign Relations Since 1776* (Oxford University Press, 2008), 161–163.

16. "John Adams to Thomas Jefferson, 17 April 1826," Founders Online. In 1828, four times as many White men cast a ballot as had in 1824. And in a rematch between Adams and Jackson, Jackson won an overwhelming 56 percent of the popular vote. Twenty thousand Americans attended Jackson's inaugural, and in his address, the first delivered to the American people from the steps of the Capitol, Jackson proclaimed, "The first principle of our system is that the majority is to govern." Some who remembered the events of 1776—"an aging political elite," as characterized by Jill Lepore—feared the Republic "could not survive the rule of the people." John Randolph of Virginia wrote, "The country is ruined past redemption." Lepore, *These Truths*, 186.

17. US Census Bureau, *Historical Statistics of the United States, Colonial Times to 1970* (US Government Printing Office, 1975), 8; L. H. Butterfield, "July 4 in 1826," *American Heritage* 6 (June 1955).

18. Census Bureau, *Historical Statistics*, 8.

19. "Celebration of the Fourth of July 1825 in Easton," *Easton Gazette*, July 9, 1825; Butterfield, "July 4 in 1826"; Robert V. Remini, *John Quincy Adam*s (Times Books, 2002), 89, 112.

20. Blackhawk, *Rediscovery*, 235, 241–242; Lisa Ford, *Settler Sovereignty: Jurisdiction and Indigenous People in America and Australia, 1788–1836* (Harvard University Press, 2010), 141.

21. Heike Paul, *The Myths That Made America: An Introduction to American Studies* (transcript Verlag, 2014), 335; Remini, *John Quincy Adams*, 97.

22. Roxanne Dunbar-Ortiz, *An Indigenous Peoples' History of the United States* (Beacon Press, 2014), 142–143.

23. Burstein, *America's Jubilee*, 267.

24. Tom Wheeler, *Mr. Lincoln's T-Mails: How Abraham Lincoln Used the Telegraph to Win the Civil War* (Collins, 2006); James M. McPherson, *Battle Cry of Freedom: The Civil War Era* (Oxford University Press, 1988), 474–475.

25. Jeanne Boydston, *Home and Work: Housework, Wages, and the Ideology of Labor in the Early Republic* (Oxford University Press, 1990); Thomas Dublin, *Women at Work: The Transformation of Work and Community in Lowell, Massachusetts, 1826–1860* (Columbia University Press, 1979).

26. Eric Foner, *Free Soil, Free Labor, Free Men: The Ideology of the Republican Party Before the Civil War* (Oxford University Press, 1970).

27. "Notice to House Carpenters in the Country," *Columbian Centinel*, April 23, 1825; Philip S. Foner, *We, the Other People: Alternative Declarations of Independence by Labor Groups, Farmers, Woman's Rights Advocates, Socialists, and Blacks, 1829–1975* (University of Illinois Press, 1976), 3, 7–8. George Washington referred to these soldiers as "the exceeding dirty & nasty people" in an August 20, 1775, letter to Lund Washington, Founders Online.

28. Foner, *We, the Other People*, 6–7.

29. "Unlettered Mechanic," "An Address, Delivered Before the Mechanics and Working Classes Generally, of the City and County of Philadelphia" (*Mechanics' Gazette*, 1827), 5–6.

30. George Henry Evans, "The Working Men's Declaration of Independence," December 1829, in Foner, *We, the Other People*, 48–50.

31. Foner, *We, the Other People*, 32; Staughton Lynd, *Intellectual Origins of American Radicalism* (Pantheon Books, 1968), 4.

32. Eric T. Hilt, "Wall Street's First Corporate Governance Crisis: The Panic of 1826" (Working Paper 14892, National Bureau of Economic Research, 2009), 3, 22.

33. John Hope Franklin, "The Two Worlds of Race: A Historical View," *Daedalus* 94 (fall 1965): 903.

34. Thomas Jefferson to Frances Wright, August 7, 1825, in *The Papers of Thomas Jefferson: Retirement Series*, vol. 10: *1 May 1825 to 31 August 1825*, ed. J. Jefferson Looney (Princeton University Press, 2013), 551–552.

35. Helen Elliott, "Frances Wright's Experiment with Negro Emancipation," *Indiana Magazine of History* 35, no. 2 (1939): 154; John M. Keating, *History of the City of Memphis Tennessee* (D. Mason and Co., 1888), 124–126.

36. Frances Wright, "Address Delivered in the New Harmony Hall, on the Fourth of July 1828," in *Course of Popular Lectures* (Published by the author, 1829), 275.

37. David Walker, *Appeal, in Four Articles, Together with a Preamble, to the Colored Citizens of the World* (Boston, 1829), 27–28; William Lloyd Garrison, "Walker's Appeal," *Liberator*, January 8, 1831.

38. Walker, *Appeal*, 73–74.

39. Ibram X. Kendi, *Stamped from the Beginning: The Definitive History of Racist Ideas in America* (Bold Type Books, 2016), 167; Howard Zinn, *A People's History of the United States: 1492 to the Presen*t (HarperCollins, 2003), 180; Lepore, *These Truths*, 204.

40. Jefferson to Weightman, June 24, 1826.

41. Burstein, *America's Jubilee*, 233–234.

42. Burstein, *America's Jubilee*, 234.

43. Kit Hinrichs and Delphine Hirasuna, *Long May She Wave: A Graphic History of the American Flag* (Ten Speed Press, 2001), 12; Gillian Brockell, "The Ugly Reason 'The Star-Spangled Banner' Didn't Become Our National Anthem for a Century," *Washington Post*, October 18, 2020.

44. *Alexandria Gazette*, July 7, 1821, quoted in James R. Heintze, ed., *The Fourth of July Encyclopedia* (McFarland & Co., 2007), 144–145.

45. Burstein, *America's Jubilee*, 242; *The First Jubilee of American Independence and Tribute of Gratitude to the Illustrious Adams and Jefferson* (M. Lyon and Co., 1826), 9.

46. Burstein, *America's Jubilee*, 235.

47. Burstein, *America's Jubilee*, 243.

48. Burstein, *America's Jubilee*, 246.

49. William Maynadier, *An Oration Prepared for Delivery Before the Corps of Cadets at West Point on the Fiftieth Anniversary of American Independence* (Parmenter and Spalding, 1826), 14–16.

50. Lepore, *These Truths*, 186.

51. Lepore, *These Truths*, 185.

52. Burstein, *America's Jubilee*, 262.

53. There are varying accounts of Jefferson's last words, which were "apparently unrecorded." Indeed, even the time of his death is in dispute. Nonetheless, those who witnessed Jefferson's final hours described "the scene . . . with similar facts and similar emotion" (Burstein, *America's Jubilee*, 263).

54. Burstein, *America's Jubilee*, 266.

55. Lepore, *These Truths*, 186.

56. Butterfield, "July 4 in 1826"; Remini, *John Quincy Adams*, 90.

57. Burstein, *America's Jubilee*, 265.

58. Alfred F. Young, *The Shoemaker and the Tea Party: Memory and the American Revolution* (Beacon Press, 1999), 140; Daniel Webster, "A Discourse in Commemoration of the Lives and Services of John Adams and Thomas Jefferson, Delivered in Faneuil Hall, Boston, August 2, 1826" (Cummings, Hilliard and Co., 1826), 6–8; Hugh A. Garland, ed., *The Life of John Randolph of Roanoke* (D. Appleton and Co., 1850), 2:273.

59. David Armitage, "The Declaration of Independence in World History," in *Declaring Independence: The Origins and Influence of America's Founding Document*, ed. Christian Y. Dupont and Peter S. Onuf (University of Virginia Library, 2008), 31; "Acta de la independencia de las Provincias Unidas en Sud-América," July 9, 1816.

60. Shira Lurie, "The Early Republic: What's in an Era?," Organization of American Historians, spring 2024, www.oah.org.

Chapter 3. Centennial

1. National Woman Suffrage Association, "Declaration of Rights for Women," July 4, 1876, in *History of Woman Suffrage*, ed. Elizabeth Cady Stanton, Susan B. Anthony, and Matilda Joslyn Gage (Charles Mann, 1887), 3:31.

2. Frederick Douglass, "Oration Delivered on the Occasion of the Unveiling of the Freedmen's Monument in Memory of Abraham Lincoln in Lincoln Park, Washington, DC," April 14, 1876 (Gibson Brothers Printers, 1876).

3. Frederick Douglass, *Life and Times of Frederick Douglass* (De Wolfe & Fiske, 1892), 358–359.

4. Frederick Douglass, "What to the Slave Is the Fourth of July?," in *My Bondage and My Freedom* (Miller, Orton & Mulligan, 1855), 441–445.

5. Douglass, "Oration."

6. US Census Bureau, *Historical Statistics of the United States, Colonial Times to 1970* (US Government Printing Office, 1975), 8, 224; Herbert S. Klein, *A Population History of the United States* (Cambridge University Press, 2004), 62; William Cronon, *Nature's Metropolis: Chicago and the Great West* (W. W. Norton, 1991), 297; Richard R. John, *Network Nation: Inventing American Telecommunications* (Harvard University Press, 2010), 156. See also James D. Reid, *The Telegraph in America: Its Founders, Promoters, and Noted Men* (Derby Brothers, 1879), 572.

7. Eric Foner, *Reconstruction: America's Unfinished Revolution, 1863–1877* (HarperPerennial, 2014), 718.

8. President Lincoln had not only led the Union in the Civil War and emancipated enslaved people but also greatly enlarged the federal government and augmented its influence. As historian Jeremi Suri has written, "Freeing slaves meant removing the claimed property of slaveholders, taking away their forced labor, and creating new citizens in their communities with new rights. Lincoln also promoted homesteading, railroad construction, and higher education as no president had before. He empowered thousands of immigrants and poor whites, as well as former slaves. Lincoln turned George Washington's distant and dispassionate presidency into a commanding office that transformed cities, towns, and rural areas." Jeremi Suri, *Civil War by Other Means: America's Long and Unfinished Fight for Democracy* (PublicAffairs, 2022), 16.

9. Abraham Lincoln, "Proclamation of Amnesty and Reconstruction," December 8, 1863, in *The Collected Works of Abraham Lincoln*, ed. Roy P. Basler (Rutgers University Press, 1953), 7:53.

10. Allen C. Guelzo, *Our Ancient Faith: Lincoln, Democracy, and the American Experiment* (Knopf, 2024), 121.

11. Nathaniel Philbrick, *The Last Stand: Custer, Sitting Bull, and the Battle of the Little Bighorn* (Penguin Books, 2011), 49, 50. For first-person accounts of the 7th Cavalry's mission, see Fergus M. Bordewich, *Klan War: Ulysses S. Grant and the Battle to Save Reconstruction* (Alfred A. Knopf, 2023), 233–238.

12. Timothy Egan, *A Fever in the Heartland: The Ku Klux Klan's Plot to Take Over America, and the Woman Who Stopped Them* (Viking, 2023), 10.

13. Stephen Kantrowitz, *Ben Tillman and the Reconstruction of White Supremacy* (University of North Carolina Press, 2000), 38.

14. Robert W. Rydell, *All the World's a Fair: Visions of Empire at American International Expositions, 1876–1916* (University of Chicago Press, 1984), 17.

15. Rydell, *All the World's a Fair*, 17.

16. Rydell, *All the World's a Fair*, 10.

17. Robert C. Post, *1876: A Centennial Exhibition* (Smithsonian Institution Press, 1976), 6.

18. Elizabeth Cady Stanton, Susan B. Anthony, and Matilda Joslyn Gage, *History of Woman Suffrage* (Charles Mann, 1887), 1:70.

19. Ibram X. Kendi, *Stamped from the Beginning: The Definitive History of Racist Ideas in America* (Bold Type Books, 2016), 242–243.

20. Robert K. Krick, *Stonewall Jackson at Cedar Mountain* (University of North Carolina Press, 1990), 1.

21. Ulysses S. Grant, letter to the mayor and council of Birmingham, England, October 16, 1877, in *The Papers of Ulysses S. Grant*, ed. John Y. Simon (Southern Illinois University Press, 1979), 28:232.

22. "A Crusty Old Baseball Field in Brewerytown," Society for American Baseball Research, November 11, 2022, https://sabr.org.

23. Neil W. Macdonald, *The League That Lasted: 1876 and the Founding of the National League of Professional Baseball Clubs* (McFarland, 2004), 28–29; Chris Wimmer, *The Summer of 1876: Outlaws, Lawmen, and Legends in the Season That Defined the American West* (St. Martin's Press, 2023), 50.

24. Rydell, *All the World's a Fair*, 11.

25. Linda P. Gross and Theresa R. Snyder, *Philadelphia's 1876 Centennial Exhibition* (Arcadia Publishing, 2005), 9–11, 21.

26. Rydell, *All the World's a Fair*, 11.

27. *Official Catalogue of the US International Exhibition of 1876* (Centennial Catalogue Co., 1876).

28. Philbrick, *Last Stand*, 134–135; Wimmer, *Summer of 1876*, 54; Ron Chernow, *Grant* (Penguin, 2017), 828.

29. Keila Grinberg, "The Emperor and the Abolitionist: A Brazilian Royal Visits the US," *Americas Quarterly*, January 13, 2020.

30. "Brazil and the Centennial Exposition," Brazilian Centennial Commission pamphlet (1876), as quoted in Jeffrey D. Needell, *The Party of Order: The Conservatives, the State, and Slavery in the Brazilian Monarchy, 1831–1871* (Stanford University Press, 2006), 271.

31. Rydell, *All the World's a Fair*, 28.

32. Gross and Snyder, *Philadelphia's 1876 Centennial Exhibition*, 16.

33. Philbrick, *Last Stand*, 34.

34. Gross and Snyder, *Philadelphia's 1876 Centennial Exhibition*, 29.

35. William Dean Howells, "A Sennight of the Centennial," *Atlantic* (July 1876): 92–107.

36. Julia Dent Grant, *The Personal Memoirs of Julia Dent Grant* (Mrs. Ulysses S. Grant), ed. John Y. Simon (G. P. Putnam's Sons, 1975), 188.

37. Grant, *Personal Memoirs*, 188.

38. George Eastman, letter to his mother, 1876, in Elizabeth Brayer, *George Eastman: A Biography* (Johns Hopkins University Press, 2006), 33.

39. Wimmer, *Summer of 1876*, 61.

40. Elizabeth Mitchell, *Liberty's Torch: The Great Adventure to Build the Statue of Liberty* (Atlantic Monthly Press, 2014), 47.

41. Judy Braun Zegas, "North American Indian Exhibit at the Centennial Exhibition," *Curator* 19, no. 2 (1976): 169; Rydell, *All the World's a Fair*, 26.

42. Gary B. Nash, *First City: Philadelphia and the Forging of Historical Memory* (University of Pennsylvania Press, 2006), 272; Ellen Fitzpatrick, *Endless Crusade: Women Social Scientists and Progressive Reform* (Oxford University Press, 1990).

43. Russell F. Weigley et al., *Philadelphia: A 300-Year History* (W. W. Norton, 1982), 466.

44. Chernow, *Grant*, 110.

45. Rutherford B. Hayes, "Inaugural Address." March 5, 1877, American Presidency Project, www.presidency.ucsb.edu.

46. Chernow, *Grant*, 827.

47. Philbrick, *Last Stand*, 211. The term *Sioux* refers broadly to a confederation of Indigenous peoples known as the Oceti Sakowin, which includes three main groups: Lakota, Nakota, and Dakota.

48. Philbrick, *Last Stand*, 96.

49. Wimmer, *Summer of 1876*, 104.

50. Philbrick, *Last Stand*, 91, 92, 226.

51. Philbrick, *Last Stand*, 278.

52. Philbrick, *Last Stand*, 505.

53. Philbrick, *Last Stand*, 505.

54. Wimmer, *Summer of 1876*, 188, 189.

55. James D. McCabe, *The Illustrated History of the Centennial Exhibition, Held in Commemoration of the One Hundredth Anniversary of American Independence* (National Publishing Company, 1876), 661.

56. Robert J. Havlik, "Centennial Fourth of July Celebrations: 1876 and 1976," *American Quarterly* 28, no. 4 (1976): 430–431.

57. "No Celebration in Washington," *New York Times,* July 4, 1876, 5.

58. "Opening of the American Centennial Exhibition," *Illustrated London News*, July 22, 1876, 4.

59. "President Grant and the 1876 Centennial Exposition in Philadelphia," US National Park Service, www.nps.gov. Congress established July 4 as a legal national holiday ninety-four years after the signing of the Declaration of Independence, forty-four years after America's Jubilee in 1826, and six years before the 1876 American Centennial.

60. Elizabeth Cady Stanton, *Eighty Years and More: Reminiscences, 1815–1897* (European Publishing Company, 1898), 329–330; Stanton, Anthony, and Gage, *History of Woman Suffrage*, 27.

61. "Declaration of Rights for Women," in Stanton, Anthony, and Gage, *History of Woman Suffrage*, 27–34.

62. Advertisement in *The Enterprise and Mountaineer* (Greenville, SC), July 4, 1876.

63. Kantrowitz, *Ben Tillman*, 64.

64. Kantrowitz, *Ben Tillman*, 65.

65. Kantrowitz, *Ben Tillman*, 67.

66. Kantrowitz, *Ben Tillman*, 67.

67. Kantrowitz, *Ben Tillman*, 67.

68. Kantrowitz, *Ben Tillman*, 67.

69. Kantrowitz, *Ben Tillman*, 67.

70. Wimmer, *Summer of 1876*, 206.

71. Custer's wife's full name was Elizabeth Bacon Custer.

72. Ari Hoogenboom, *Outlawing the Spoils: A History of the Civil Service Reform Movement, 1865–1883* (University of Illinois Press, 1961), 179.

73. "Mark Twain in Politics," *New York Times*, October 2, 1876, 1.

74. Paul F. Boller Jr., *Presidential Campaigns* (Oxford University Press, 2004), 133–135.

75. Boller, *Presidential Campaigns*, 133–135.

76. Roy Morris Jr., *Fraud of the Century: Rutherford B. Hayes, Samuel Tilden, and the Stolen Election of 1876* (Simon & Schuster, 2003), 221.

77. Chernow, *Grant*, 848.

Chapter 4. Sesquicentennial

1. Calvin Coolidge, "First Annual Message," December 6, 1923, American Presidency Project, www.presidency.ucsb.edu.

2. "Ku Klan Thousands in Colorful Review as Conclave Opens," *Washington Post*, September 14, 1926, 1; Kevin Boyle, "The Not-So-Invisible Empire," *New York Times*, November 25, 2011. In November 1925, a jury found D. C. Stephenson, the Indiana state Klan leader, guilty of the murder of Madge Oberholtzer, a twenty-eight-year-old state employee whom he had abducted, raped, and tortured. See Timothy Egan, *A Fever in the Heartland: The Ku Klux Klan's Plot to Take Over America, and the Woman Who Stopped Them* (Viking, 2023).

3. Hiram Wesley Evans, "The Klan's Fight for Americanism," *North American Review* 223 (March 1926): 52; Thomas R. Pegram, *One Hundred Percent American: The Rebirth and Decline of the Ku Klux Klan in the 1920s* (Ivan R. Dee, 2011).

4. "Ku Klan Thousands."

5. Charles H. Wesley and Thelma D. Perry, introduction to Carter G. Woodson, *The Mis-education of the Negro* (1933; Associated Publishers Inc., 1969), 4–5; Woodson, "Negro History Week: The Fifth Year," *Journal of Negro History* 16 (April 1931): 127.

6. Woodson, "Negro History Week," *Journal of Negro History* 11 (April 1926): 240; Woodson, *The Negro in Our History* (Associated Publishers Inc., 1922), vii.

7. "Woodbury Man First at Sesqui," *Philadelphia Evening Bulletin*, May 31, 1926, 15.

8. E. L. Austin and Odell Hauser, *The Sesqui-centennial International Exposition: A Record Based on Official Data and Departmental Records* (Current Publications, 1929), 309–311; US Census Bureau, *Historical Statistics of the United States, Colonial Times to 1970* (US Government Printing Office, 1975), 224, 783.

9. "Huge Sesqui Light Nears Completion," *Philadelphia Bulletin*, July 19, 1926, quoted in Thomas H. Keels, *Sesqui! Greed, Graft, and the Forgotten World's Fair of 1926* (Temple University Press, 2017), 144; Census Bureau, *Historical Statistics*, 820.

10. Austin and Hauser, *Sesqui-centennial*, 321, 336–337; Census Bureau, *Historical Statistics*, 827.

11. Ruth Schwartz Cohen, *More Work for Mother: Women and Household Technology* (Oxford University Press, 1977), 163.

12. William E. Leuchtenburg, *The Perils of Prosperity, 1914–1932* (University of Chicago Press, 1958), 9, 178, 193–194.

13. Austin and Hauser, *Sesqui-centennial*, 341.

14. Austin and Hauser, *Sesqui-centennial*, 345–346; "Red Circle and Gold Leaf," *Time*, November 13, 1950, 89.

15. Warren G. Harding, "Readjustment," transcript, May 14, 1920, Presidential Speeches, Miller Center, https://millercenter.org.

16. Austin and Hauser, *Sesqui-centennial*, 81–82, 95–96.

17. "Sesquicentennial Opens as Sun Shines; 100,000 Pass Gates," *New York Times*, June 1, 1926, 1, 8.

18. Census Bureau, *Historical Statistics*, 1102.

19. Austin and Hauser, *Sesqui-centennial*, 114, 119, 357–360; Census Bureau, *Historical Statistics*, 8.

20. "Hustling to Finish High St. for Sesqui," *Philadelphia Bulletin*, April 6, 1926, quoted in Keels, *Sesqui!*, 99.

21. "Philadelphia's Fair Appears Assured," *New York Times*, December 9, 1925, 14; Keels, *Sesqui!*, xi, 66–68.

22. Keels, *Sesqui!*, 119–121.

23. "Sesqui Buildings Have Few Exhibits," *Philadelphia Bulletin*, June 4, 1926, 2; Austin and Hauser, *Sesqui-centennial*, 49.

24. R. B. Bernstein, *Thomas Jefferson: The Revolution of Ideas* (Oxford University Press, 2004), 228; Francis D. Cogliano, *Thomas Jefferson: Reputation and Legacy* (Edinburgh University Press, 2006), 4–5, 116. See also Merrill D. Peterson, *The Jefferson Image in the American Mind* (Oxford University Press, 1960).

25. "Jefferson's Home Is Given to Nation as People's Shrine," July 6, 1926, *Washington Post*, 1; Cogliano, *Jefferson*, 131 n 12.

26. David Armitage, *The Declaration of Independence: A Global History* (Harvard University Press, 2007), 109, 132–133.

27. Philp S. Foner, ed., *We, the Other People: Alternative Declarations of Independence by Labor Groups, Farmers, Woman's Rights Advocates, Socialists, and Blacks, 1829–1975* (University of Illinois Press, 1976), 32–33.

28. Ned Blackhawk, *The Rediscovery of America: Native Peoples and the Unmaking of US History* (Yale University Press, 2023), 3–4.

29. Zitkala-Ša, "The School Days of an Indian Girl," *Atlantic* 85 (February 1900): 185–194.

30. Gertrude Bonnin, "Editorial Comment," *American Indian Magazine* 6 (winter 1919): 162; Tadeusz Lewandowski, *Red Bird, Red Power: The Life and Legacy of Zitkala-Ša* (University of Oklahoma Press, 2016), 16.

31. Lewandowski, *Red Bird, Red Power*, 171–172; Helen L. Peterson, "American Indian Political Participation," *Annals of the American Academy* 311 (May 1957): 121–122.

32. Gertrude Bonnin, "Petition of the National Council of American Indians to the Senate of the United States of America Assembled, Under Amendment I of the Constitution," 1926, in *Zitkala-Ša: Letters, Speeches and Unpublished Writings, 1898–1929*, ed. Tadeusz Lewandowski (Brill, 2018), 237.

33. Bonnin, "Petition," 219.

34. Stephen Graham, *New York Nights* (George H. Doran Company, 1927), 92–93.

35. Angela J. Latham, *Posing a Threat: Flappers, Chorus Girls, and Other Brazen Performers of the American 1920s* (Wesleyan University Press, 2000), 5; Martha H. Patterson, ed., *The American New Woman Revisited: A Reader, 1894–1930* (Rutgers University Press, 2008) 1–2, 15; Lynn Yaeger, "Celebrating Texas Guinan, the Original 'Nasty Woman,'" *Vogue*, January 12, 2017, www.vogue.com.

36. *Variety* quoted in James Fisher, "Texas Guinan," *American National Biography*, February 2000, https://doi.org/10.1093/anb/9780198606697.article.1801833.

37. "Texas Guinan Dies in the West After Operation," *New York Herald Tribune*, November 6, 1933, 17. Guinan quoted in Fisher, "Texas Guinan."

38. Louise Berliner, *Texas Guinan: Queen of the Nightclubs* (University of Texas Press, 1993), Kindle.

39. Lipstick [Lois Long], "Tables for Two," *New Yorker*, October 9, 1926, 65–66; Graham, *New York Nights*, 87.

40. "Two Senators See Guinan Club Raided," *New York Times*, July 4, 1926, 3.

41. Michael A. Lerner, *Dry Manhattan: Prohibition in New York City* (Harvard University Press, 2007), 148–149.

42. Lerner, *Dry Manhattan*, 185–188.

43. "Texas Guinan Jailed in Dry Raid on Club," *New York Times*, February 17, 1927, 1–2.

44. "Tex Guinan, Out of Prison, Goes Back to Club," *New York Herald Tribune*, February 18, 1927, 19.

45. "Texas Guinan Arraigned Wearing All Her Diamonds," *New York Herald Tribune*, February 22, 1927, 15; "Texas Guinan Freed on Liquor Charge," *New York Times*, March 31, 1927, 25.

46. Lerner, *Dry Manhattan*, 157–158; Tom Pettey, "Texas Guinan Goes on Trial with a Laugh," *Chicago Tribune*, April 10, 1929, 4.

47. Graham, *New York Nights*, 105, 107.

48. Calvin Coolidge, *The Autobiography of Calvin Coolidge* (Cosmopolitan Book Corporation, 1929), 189–190.

49. Coolidge, *Autobiography*, 190; Robert E. Gilbert, *The Tormented President: Calvin Coolidge, Death, and Clinical Depression* (Praeger, 2003), 2–3.

50. Keels, *Sesqui!*, x, 126, 133, 158–160. See also Bruce J. Evensen, "'Saving the City's Reputation: Philadelphia's Struggle over Self-Identity, Sabbath-Breaking and Boxing in America's Sesquicentennial Year," *Pennsylvania History* 60 (January 1993): 6–34.

51. Quoted in Robert H. Ferrell, *The Presidency of Calvin Coolidge* (University Press of Kansas, 1998), 46.

52. Wilson Brown, "Aide to Four Presidents," *American Heritage*, February 1955, www.americanheritage.com.

53. Brown, "Aide to Four Presidents."

54. Brown, "Aide to Four Presidents."

55. Brown, "Aide to Four Presidents"; William Allen White, *A Puritan in Babylon: The Story of Calvin Coolidge* (Macmillan, 1940).

56. Ferrell, *Presidency*, 40–41; Arthur F. Fleser, "Coolidge's Delivery: Everybody Liked It," *Vermont History* 38 (autumn 1970): 322.

57. Fleser, "Coolidge's Delivery," 322–325.

58. "President's Unseen Audience Equal to Population in 1865," *New York Times*, September 4, 1927, 11; William Allen White, *Calvin Coolidge, the Man Who Is President* (Macmillan, 1925), 139.

59. David Pietrusza, ed., *Calvin Coolidge on the Founders: Reflections on the American Revolution and the Founding Fathers* (Church & Reid Books, 2012), Kindle.

60. Calvin Coolidge, "The Inspiration of the Declaration," July 5, 1926, in *Foundations of the Republic: Speeches and Addresses* (1926; Books for Libraries Press, 1968), 441–454. Coolidge's thin hands often "trembled when turning the manuscript," especially at the beginning of a speech, according to Ferrell, *Presidency*, 40–41.

61. Coolidge, "Inspiration of the Declaration"; Donald R. McCoy, "Calvin Coolidge," *American National Biography*, 1999, https://doi.org/10.1093/anb/9780198606697.article.0600109.

62. Coolidge, "Inspiration of the Declaration."

63. Coolidge, "Inspiration of the Declaration." For sacred readings of early-American texts, see Pauline Maier, *American Scripture: Making the Declaration of Independence* (Knopf, 1997); Catherine Drinker Bowen, *Miracle at Philadelphia: The Story of the Constitutional Convention* (Little, Brown and Co., 1966).

64. "Coolidge Invokes Founders' Ideals as Guide to Nation," *New York Times*, July 6, 1926, 1. Coolidge's speech resonated with conservative thinkers almost a century later. Political philosopher Harry Jaffa called it "the greatest speech I have read on the Declaration since Abraham Lincoln." More recently, columnist Jonah Goldberg said it was the "best thing ever written about Independence Day other than the Declaration itself—and even so, it's pretty close." Jaffa and Goldberg quoted in Pietrusza, *Calvin Coolidge on the Founders*.

65. Coolidge quoted in James E. Watson, *As I Knew Them: Memoirs of James E. Watson, Former United States Senator from Indiana* (Bobbs-Merrill, 1936), 239.

66. Watson, *As I Knew Them*, 239; Frederick Lewis Allen, *Only Yesterday: An Informal History of the 1920s* (1931; Harper & Row, 1957), 186–225.

67. Woodson, "Negro History Week," 238, 241; Alain Locke, "Enter the New Negro," 1925, in *Milestone Documents in American History: Exploring the Primary Sources That Shaped America*, ed. Kelli McCoy. 2nd ed. (Schlager Group, 2020); Daryl Michael Scott, "The Origins of Black History Month," Association for the Study of African American Life and History, https://asalh.org.

68. Woodson, "Negro History Week: The Fifth Year," 125; Jarvis R. Givens, *Fugitive Pedagogy: Carter G. Woodson and the Art of Black Teaching* (Harvard University Press, 2023), 171–172.

69. Boyle, "Not-So-Invisible Empire."

70. Preston William Slosson, *The Great Crusade and After, 1914–1928* (Macmillan, 1930), 301.

71. R. A. Patton, "A Ku Klux Klan Reign of Terror," *Current History*, April 1, 1928, 53.

72. "Sidelights on Klan Parade," *Washington Post*, September 14, 1926, 5.

73. "Member of Original Klan Is Chief Flag-Bearer's Aid," *Washington Post*, September 14, 1926, 5.

74. "Kleveland Konvention," *Time*, June 23, 1924, 5–6; Boyle, "Not-So-Invisible Empire."

75. "Evans, Saying Klan Is Perfect, Calls Forces to Battle," *Washington Post*, September 15, 1926, 1; Boyle, "Not-So-Invisible Empire."

76. "Dr. Woodson's Negro History Confiscated in Oklahoma," *Baltimore Afro-American*, August 1, 1925, A1; Givens, *Fugitive Pedagogy*, 167–168; Pegram, *One Hundred Percent Americanism*, 174.

77. Woodson, "Negro History Week," 240.

78. Givens, *Fugitive Pedagogy*, 168.

79. "Acres of Notables in Ringside Seats," *Philadelphia Inquirer*, September 24, 1926, 16; Bruce J. Evensen, *When Dempsey Fought Tunney: Heroes, Hokum, and Storytelling in the Jazz Age* (University of Tennessee Press, 1996), 90; Randy Roberts, *Jack Dempsey, the Manassa Mauler* (Louisiana State University Press, 1979), 228–229. Tex Rickard quoted in Mel Heimer, *The Long Count* (Atheneum, 1969), 15.

80. Heimer, *Long Count*, 3; Katharine Brush, *Young Man of Manhattan* (Farrar & Rinehart,1930), 4.

81. John L. Sullivan quoted in Roberts, *Jack Dempsey*, 20.

82. "Dempsey, Sporting Monocle, Back Home," *New York Times*, May 20, 1922, 17.

83. "Jack Dempsey, New Heavyweight Champion, Announces He Will Draw the Color Line," *New York Times*, July 6, 1919.

84. "On the Decline," *Chicago Defender*, September 18, 1926, 14; "Black, White and Yellow," *Opportunity*, January 1924, 4. See also "The Fight Game Degraded," *New Journal and Guide* (Norfolk, VA), September 11, 1926, 12. Artist George Bellows immortalized Firpo's blow in the 1924 painting *Dempsey and Firpo*.

85. John B. Kennedy, "If Dempsey's Afraid Let Him Say So," *Collier's*, March 20, 1926, 11, 43.

86. "Dempsey Ordered to Sign Wills Bout," *New York Times*, June 2, 1926, 19; "Final Ban Placed on Dempsey-Tunney," *New York Times*, June 23, 1926, 21.

87. Roberts, *Jack Dempsey*, 143–144. Wills would end 1926 by losing convincingly to Jack Sharkey, an up-and-coming White heavyweight whom Dempsey had knocked out months later.

88. "Rickard Inspects Philadelphia Bowl," *New York Times*, August 20, 1926, 12.

89. John Howe, "Tunney and Dempsey Will Fight Here as Mayor and Clergy Play Turn About," *Philadelphia Tribune*, August 21, 1926, 1.

90. "Philadelphia Jubilant over Dempsey Bout," *New York Herald Tribune*, August 20, 1926, 1; "America's Greatest Flop," *Variety*, August 25, 1926, 1; Keels, *Sesqui!*, x, 163.

91. Gene Tunney, "My Fights with Jack Dempsey," in *The Aspirin Age, 1919–1941*, ed. Isabel Leighton (Simon & Schuster, 1949), 155–156.

92. Tunney, "My Fights with Jack Dempsey," 162; Heimer, *Long Count*, 19.

93. Nat Fleischer, *Jack Dempsey: The Idol of Fistiana* (The Ring, 1929), 219; Heimer, *Long Count*, 20.

94. Tunney, "My Fights with Jack Dempsey," 162.

95. Grantland Rice, "World's Title Changes Hands as Heavy Rain Pelts Multitude," *New York Herald Tribune*, September 24, 1926, 1; Fleischer, *Jack Dempsey*, 217.

96. "How Radio Carried News of Big Bout," *New York Times*, September 24, 1926, 4.

97. "Philadelphia Sees Bout as Great Boon," *New York Times*, September 25, 1926, 14; "Big Fight Crowd Stampedes Trains," *Philadelphia Inquirer*, September 25, 1926, 2.

98. Eugene V. Debs, *Canton Speech* (Socialist Party of the United States, n.d.), 18.

99. David M. Kennedy, *Over Here: The First World War and American Society*. 25th anniv. ed. (Oxford University Press, 2004), 80; Adam Hochschild, *American Midnight: The Great War, a Violent Peace, and Democracy's Forgotten Crisis* (Mariner Books, 2022). Although the 1918 amendments were repealed by Congress in 1920, many provisions of the Espionage Act remain in effect today.

100. *Debs v. United States*, 249 U.S. 211 (1919) at 214.

101. David Karsner, *Debs: His Authorized Life and Letters* (Boni and Liveright, 1919), 15.

102. Karsner, *Debs*, 27, 126; Nick Salvatore, *Eugene V. Debs: Citizen and Socialist* (University of Illinois Press, 1982), xii, 343.

103. Karsner, *Debs*, 29–30; Salvatore, *Debs*, 295.

104. Salvatore, *Debs*, xii.

105. "Eugene V. Debs, Dies After Long Illness," *New York Times*, October 21, 1926.

106. "Eugene V. Debs, Dies."

107. "Gene Debs, Socialists' Chief, Dies," *Omaha Morning Bee*, October 21, 1926, 1; "Debs Is Mourned by Socialists Here," *New York Times*, October 22, 1926, 11.

108. "15,000 Honor Debs at Garden Meeting," *New York Times*, October 25, 1926, 8; "Pay Tribute to Debs," *New York Times*, October 21, 1926, 25.

109. "Men of All Ranks Meet to Pay Last Tributes to Debs," *Washington Post*, October 26, 1926, M6.

110. Arthur Brisbane quoted in "Eugene V. Debs," *Time*, November 1, 1926; see also Salvatore, *Debs*, xii, 343–344.

111. Givens, *Fugitive Pedagogy*, 1–2.

112. Givens, *Fugitive Pedagogy*, 221.

113. "The Other Rosa Parks: Now 73, Claudette Colvin Was First to Refuse Giving Up Seat on Montgomery Bus," Democracy Now, March 29, 2013, www.democracynow.org.

114. Givens, *Fugitive Pedagogy*, 207; Jacquelyn Dowd Hall, "The Long Civil Rights Movement and the Political Uses of the Past," *Journal of American History* 91, no. 4 (2005): 1233–1263.

115. Givens, *Fugitive Pedagogy*, 207.

Chapter 5. Bicentennial

1. Gerald R. Ford, "Address Before a Joint Session of the Congress Reporting on the State of the Union," January 15, 1975, American Presidency Project, www.presidency.ucsb.edu.

2. Andrew R. Malcolm, "Wagon Train Gets Underway on Year's Trip to Valley Forge," *New York Times*, June 16, 1975.

3. "Wagon Train," n.d., Clippings—Before the Trip, Box 3, Larry and Pauline Asmus Papers, Gerald R. Ford Presidential Library and Museum, Ann Arbor, Michigan.

4. Thelma Gray, "The Idea Is Born," in *Bicentennial Wagon Train Pilgrimage*, ed. Bill Sherman (Jem Publishers, 1977), 4.

5. "Bicentennial Wagon Train Departs," *Pasadena Star-News*, January 3, 1976.

6. Encyclopedia Britannica Inc., "Pledge of Rededication," n.d., Scrolls, Certificates, Public Notices, Box 3, Asmus Papers. Ellipses in the original.

7. American Revolution Bicentennial Administration (ARBA), *A Final Report to the People* (US Government Printing Office, 1977), 1:130.

8. Malcolm, "Wagon Train Gets Underway."

9. Gerald Ford, "Remarks on Taking the Oath of Office," August 9, 1974, American Presidency Project; David Farber, "The Torch Had Fallen," in *America in the Seventies*, ed. Beth Bailey and David Farber (University Press of Kansas, 2004), 12.

10. Gerald Ford, "Remarks on Signing a Proclamation Granting Pardon to Richard Nixon," September 8, 1974, American Presidency Project.

11. Philip Shabecoff, "President Booed," *New York Times*, September 10, 1974.

12. "The Fallout from Ford's Rush to Pardon," *Time*, September 23, 1974, 11; Yanek Mieczkowski, *Gerald Ford and the Challenges of the 1970s* (University Press of Kentucky, 2005), 32, 52–53. For a skeptical account of Ford's actions, see Seymour Hersh, "The Pardon: Nixon, Ford, Haig, and the Transfer of Power," *Atlantic* 252 (August 1983): 55–78.

13. Seymour Hersh, "Huge CIA Operation Reported in US Against Antiwar Forces, Other Dissidents in Nixon Years," *New York Times*, December 22, 1974, 1; Daniel Schorr, *Clearing the Air* (Houghton Mifflin, 1977), 130–152. *New York Times* columnist Tom Wicker attended the January 1975 meeting. For his firsthand account, see Tom Wicker, *On Press* (Viking, 1978), 190. Historian Kathryn S. Olmsted explores opposition to the deep state in *Challenging the Secret Government:*

The Post-Watergate Investigations of the CIA and FBI (University of North Carolina Press, 1996).

14. Olmsted, *Challenging the Secret Government*, 99.

15. Farber, "Torch Had Fallen," 13. News coverage "opened up," according to Katherine Fink and Michael Schudson, "The Rise of Contextual Journalism, 1950s–2000s," *Journalism* 15 (2014): 3–6.

16. Mieczkowski, *Gerald Ford*, 54, 67–68, 70.

17. Mieczkowski, *Gerald Ford*, 71.

18. Michael Schneider, interview with author, December 16, 2013, Washington, DC.

19. "Declaration of Independence of the Democratic Republic of Vietnam," September 2, 1945, in Ho Chi Minh, *Selected Writings, 1920–1969* (Foreign Languages Publishing House, 1977), 53.

20. Lynn Hunt, *Inventing Human Rights: A History* (Norton, 2007), 15, 21; David Armitage, *The Declaration of Independence: A Global History* (Harvard University Press, 2007), 100, 104, 111. "There would have been no concept of human rights in the West" without the vocabulary first voiced in the American and French declarations, according to Lynn Hunt in "Paradoxical Origins of Human Rights," in *Human Rights and Revolutions*, ed. Jeffrey N. Wasserstrom, Greg Grandin, and Marilyn B. Young, 2d ed. (Rowman & Littlefield, 2007), 4.

21. Eugene L. Meyer, "The Big Birthday Bungle," *Washington Post*, July 2, 1972, C1.

22. Meyer, "Big Birthday Bungle"; Eugene L. Meyer, "Bicentennial Commission: Deeply Involved in Politics," *Washington Post*, August 14, 1972, A1.

23. Eugene L. Meyer, "Red, White, Blue—and Green," *Washington Post*, August 15, 1972; "Ringing in the Buycentennial," *Economist*, December 21, 1974, 49.

24. "Bucks from the Bicentennial," *Time*, September 29, 1975, 73.

25. Ted Howard, *The PBC: A History* (1976), 5, People's Bicentennial Commission, Pamphlet Collection, Wisconsin State Historical Society Library, Madison. "The two words most muted during the 200th year of American independence have been 'people' and 'revolution,'" observed historian Richard B. Morris in "'We Are the People of the United States': The Bicentennial of a People's Revolution," *American Historical Review* 82 (February 1977): 1.

26. Stephen Isaacs, "Boston Tea Party Restaged," *Washington Post*, December 17, 1973; Jill Lepore, *The Whites of Their Eyes: The Tea Party's Revolution and the Battle over American History* (Princeton University Press, 2010), 83.

27. ARBA, *Final Report*, 1:9, 57; Christopher Capozzola, "It Makes You Want to Believe in the Country," in Bailey and Farber, *America in the Seventies*, 32.

28. J. Anthony Lukas, "Who Owns 1776? The Battle in Boston for Control of the American Past," *New York Times Magazine*, May 18, 1975, 39.

29. Lukas, "Who Owns 1776?," 50, 54; Lukas, *Common Ground: A Turbulent Decade in the Lives of Three American Families* (Alfred A. Knopf, 1985). See also Ronald P. Formisano, *Boston Against Busing: Race, Class, and Ethnicity in the 1960s and 1970s* (University of North Carolina Press, 1991).

30. Lukas, "Who Owns 1776?," 38.

31. Lukas, "Who Owns 1776?," 38, 40. Bruce J. Schulman discusses grassroots conservatism in *The Seventies: The Great Shift in American Culture, Society, and Politics* (Free Press, 2001).

32. Lukas, "Who Owns 1776?," 40.

33. Lukas, "Who Owns 1776?," 39; Lukas, *Common Ground*, 316.

34. Lukas, "Who Owns 1776?," 39–40.

35. Lukas, *Common Ground*, 316.

36. Louis P. Masur, *The Soiling of Old Glory: The Story of a Photograph That Shocked America* (Bloomsbury, 2008), 4, 17–18.

37. Joseph Driscoll, "Youths Beat Black Lawyer at City Hall," *Boston Herald American*, April 6, 1976, 1; Masur, *Soiling of Old Glory*, 60, 121. Stanley Forman's photograph won the 1977 Pulitzer Prize for Spot Photography.

38. "The Bicentennial Blues," *Ebony*, June 1976, 152; Masur, *Soiling of Old Glory*, 122.

39. Quoted in Masur, *Soiling of Old Glory*, 69.

40. "Bicentennial Blues."

41. "Bicentennial Blues."

42. Edward D. Berkowitz, *Something Happened: A Political and Cultural Overview of the Seventies* (Columbia University Press, 2006), 105–107; Jonathan Alter, *His Very Best: Jimmy Carter, a Life* (Simon & Schuster, 2020), 217, 221.

43. Alter, *His Very Best*, 198, 216, 226.

44. R. W. Apple Jr., "Reagan Tops Ford in N. Carolina for First Triumph in a Primary; Carter Easily Defeats Wallace," *New York Times*, March 24, 1976; Alter, *His Very Best*, 217; Schulman, *Seventies*, 121.

45. Alter, *His Very Best*, 206, 209, 226–227, 243.

46. Julia M. Klein, "Jimmy Carter Tells Law School Forum He'll Restore Faith," *Harvard Crimson*, September 27, 1975; Alter, *His Very Best*, 262; Zachary J. Lechner, "'Fuzzy as a Georgia Peach': The Ford Campaign and the Challenge of Jimmy Carter's Southernness," *Southern Cultures* 23 (winter 2017): 62–81.

47. Alter, *His Very Best*, 257.

48. Ronald Reagan, "A Time for Choosing," speech, October 27, 1964, American Presidency Project.

49. Rick Perlstein, *The Invisible Bridge: The Fall of Nixon and the Rise of Reagan* (Simon & Schuster, 2014), 799.

50. "Wagon: A Nugget of the Past or Fool's Gold, Circa 1975?," [November 25, 1975], *Bicentennial Scrapbook*, Asmus Papers.

51. "Eastward Ho! The Wagons," *Time*, July 5, 1976, 15.

52. Pauline Asmus, "The Spirit Lives On," in Sherman, *Bicentennial Wagon Train Pilgrimage*, 274.

53. Malcolm, "Wagon Train Gets Underway"; "Wagoneers Are Tiring," *Reading Eagle*, July 1, 1976.

54. Grace Ritchie, diary, April 7, 8, and 16, 1976, Personal Writings, Box 3, Asmus Papers.

55. Doug Brown, "Wagons Complete Bicentennial Trek to Valley Forge," *Washington Post*, July 4, 1976.

56. Ritchie diary, April 7, 1976; "Trail of Self-Determination Caravan Heads Toward US Capital in Serious Effort to Bring Changes," *Akwesasne Notes*, June 30, 1976, 28; "The Trail of Self-Determination, 1976," US National Park Service, www.nps.gov.

57. "Indians Divided on Bicentennial," *New York Times*, December 8, 1975, 10.

58. Capozzola, "It Makes You Want to Believe," 35.

59. Ritchie diary, May 13, 1976.

60. Ritchie diary, April 8, 1976.

61. Alex Haley, *Roots: The Saga of an American Family*, 30th anniv. ed. (Vanguard, 2007), 856–860, 867; James Baldwin, "How One Black Man Came to Be an American," *New York Times*, September 26, 1976, BR1.

62. Frank Rich, "A Super Sequel to Haley's Comet," *Time*, February 19, 1979.

63. Edgar T. Rouzeau, "Black America Wars on Double Front for High Stakes," *Pittsburgh Courier*, February 7, 1942, 5.

64. Martin Luther King Jr., "Love, Law, and Civil Disobedience (1961)," in *A Testament of Hope: The Essential Writings of Martin Luther King Jr.*, ed. James Melvin Washington (Harper & Row, 1986), 50. The US Coast Guard formally desegregated in 1948.

65. Gary Gerstle, *American Crucible: Race and Nation in the Twentieth Century* (Princeton University Press, 2017), 295–296.

66. Malcolm X, with Alex Haley, *The Autobiography of Malcolm X* (1964; Ballantine Books, 1999), 205; Malcolm X, "The Ballot or the Bullet," April 8, 1964, in *Malcolm X Speaks: Selected Speeches and Statements*, ed. George Breitman (New York, 1965), 26. Though copyrighted in 1964, Malcolm X's autobiography was not published until October 1965, months after his February 1965 assassination. For details, see David Remnick, "This American Life: The Making and Remaking of Malcolm X," *New Yorker*, April 25, 2011, 74–78.

67. Maya Angelou, "Haley Shows Us the Truth of Our Conjoined Histories," *New York Times*, January 23, 1977, 81. Haley quoted in Henry Louis Gates Jr., "The

Lasting Impact of Alex Haley's *Roots*," *Reader's Digest*, January 7, 2022. Gates named his PBS series *Finding Your Roots* in homage to Haley's book.

68. Michael Eric Dyson, "Haley's Comet," in Haley, *Roots*, ix–x. Haley was sued for plagiarism. See Arnold H. Lubasch, "'Roots' Plagiarism Suit Is Settled," *New York Times*, December 15, 1978.

69. ARBA, *Final Report*, 1:229; Nick Tabor, "There Were Few Black Historic Landmarks. Two Brothers Changed That," *Washington Post*, February 11, 2023.

70. Elizabeth Duff, "Women's March Jubilant," *Philadelphia Inquirer*, July 5, 1976, B1.

71. "Women of the Year: Great Changes, New Chances, Tough Choices," *Time*, January 5, 1976, 6. Frances Perkins, Franklin Roosevelt's labor secretary, and Oveta Culp Hobby, Dwight Eisenhower's health, education, and welfare secretary, preceded Hills.

72. "Women of the Year," 8; "Number and Real Median Earnings of Total Workers and Full-Time, Year-Round Workers by Sex and Female-to-Male Earnings Ratio: 1960 to 2018," Table A-7, in Jessica Semega et al., *Income and Poverty in the United States: 2018*, US Census Bureau, September 2019 (rev. September 2021), www.census.gov.

73. Enid Nemy, "Women Begin to Speak Out Against Sexual Harassment at Work," *New York Times*, August 19, 1975.

74. Nemy, "Women Begin to Speak Out."

75. "Women of the Year," 15.

76. "Women of the Year," 15.

77. "The Decision on Abortion," *Philadelphia Tribune*, August 3, 1976.

78. Janis Johnson, "Abortion Foes Vow Intensified Fight," *Washington Post*, July 2, 1976.

79. Judy Klemesrud, "Opponent of ERA Confident of Its Defeat," *New York Times*, December 15, 1975, 53; Rosalind Rosenberg, *Divided Lives: American Women in the Twentieth Century*, rev. ed. (Hill and Wang, 2008), 225.

80. Judy Klemesrud, "Mrs. Ford Helps 'Remember the Ladies' of Revolutionary Era," *New York Times*, June 30, 1976.

81. Margot Hornblower, "Philadelphia: Everything Raucous, Noble, and Corny," *Washington Post*, July 4, 1976, 13; John Kifner, "2 Counterrallies in Philadelphia," *New York Times*, July 5, 1976, 14.

82. "The Iron Within," *Time*, July 12, 1976, 8.

83. John Noble Wilford, "Viking Robot Sets Down Safely on Mars and Sends Back Pictures of Rocky Plain," *New York Times*, July 21, 1976, 1.

84. Lewis Mumford, *The Pentagon of Power* (Harcourt Brace Jovanovich, 1970), 257; Walter Isaacson, *Steve Jobs* (Simon & Schuster, 2021), 57.

85. "The World Grows Larger: A Robot Is on Mars, Reporting What It Finds," *New York Times*, July 25, 1976, 111; Timothy Moy, "Culture, Technology, and the Cult of Tech in the 1970s," in Bailey and Farber, *America in the Seventies*, 208.

86. "A Response to Wonder," *Los Angeles Times*, July 21, 1976. See also "The Age of Discovery," *New York Times*, July 27, 1976.

87. "The Viking Spirit," *New York Times*, August 1, 1976, 132; Marquis Childs, "The Triumph of Mars," *Washington Post*, August 3, 1976.

88. R. S. Jones, "Comparing Apples and Oranges," *Interface*, July 1976, 91; Isaacson, *Steve Jobs*, 75.

89. Isaacson, *Steve Jobs*, 59.

90. Jones, "Comparing Apples and Oranges."

91. Jones, "Comparing Apples and Oranges"; Steve Wozniak, with Gina Smith, *iWoz: Computer Geek to Cult Icon: How I Invented the Personal Computer, Co-founded Apple, and Had Fun Doing It* (W. W. Norton, 2006).

92. Jones, "Comparing Apples and Oranges"; Isaacson, *Steve Jobs*, 70.

93. Isaacson, *Steve Jobs*, 71.

94. "200-Member Wagon Train Ends Journey," July 1976, Clippings—July, Box 2, Asmus Papers.

95. Brown, "Wagons Complete Bicentennial Trek."

96. Ritchie diary, June 28 and July 4, 1976.

97. Brown, "Wagons Complete Bicentennial Trek."

98. Gerald Ford, "Remarks in Valley Forge, Pennsylvania," July 4, 1976, American Presidency Project.

99. Jonathan Neumann, "Valley Forge a Letdown, Wagon Train Riders Claim," *Philadelphia Inquirer*, July 5, 1976, B3; Monica Hesse, "Bicentennial Wagon Train Signatures Are Lost Pieces of American Past," *Washington Post*, July 3, 2011.

100. Joseph D. McCaffrey, "Wagon Train Rider: 'We Made It, Pard,'" [July 4, 1976], Clippings—July, Box 2, Asmus Papers.

101. Brown, "Wagons Complete Bicentennial Trek."

102. ARBA, *Final Report*, 1:61.

103. "The Big 200th Bash," *Time*, July 5, 1976, 8.

104. ARBA, *Final Report*, 1:16, 20.

105. Susan Stranahan, "First Light at Mars Hill—America's Celebration Begins," *Philadelphia Inquirer*, July 5, 1976.

106. Hornblower, "Philadelphia."

107. Kifner, "2 Counterrallies."

108. Harry Amana, "40,000 Take Part in Peaceful J4C People's March in N. Phila.," *Philadelphia Tribune*, July 6, 1976; "It Was a Glorious Fourth, an Ennobling Confirmation," *Philadelphia Inquirer*, July 7, 1976.

109. Scheduling conflicts pushed Ford's Monticello appearance to July 5. Gerald Ford, "Remarks at Naturalization Ceremonies at Monticello, Virginia," July 5, 1976, American Presidency Project. See Philippa Strum, *When the Nazis Came to Skokie: Freedom for Speech We Hate* (University Press of Kansas, 1999).

110. ARBA, *Final Report*, 1:23, 26.

111. "Big 200th Bash," 8, 13.

112. ARBA, *Final Report*, 1:26.

113. ARBA, *Final Report*, 1:17, 31.

114. "Hooray for the Old RWB," *Time*, July 5, 1976, 66; Annin Flagmakers, company history brochure, 2014, https://annin.com.

115. "Hooray for the Old RWB."

116. "Big 200th Bash," 8.

117. ARBA, *Final Report*, 1:51.

118. Roper Report 76-7, July 1976, and Gallup Organization, State of the Nation, June 1976, Roper Center for Public Opinion Research, https://ropercenter.cornell.edu.

119. Gerald Ford, *A Time to Heal* (Harper & Row, 1979), 393.

120. Jimmy Carter, "Address to the Nation on Energy and National Goals," July 15, 1979, American Presidency Project.

121. Tip O'Neill, with William Novak, *Man of the House: The Life and Political Memoirs of Speaker Tip O'Neill* (Random House, 1987), 271.

122. David S. Broder, "The President the Country Needed," *Washington Post*, January 16, 1977.

123. Alan M. Webber, "Gerald R. Ford: The Statesman as CEO," *Harvard Business Review* 65 (September–October 1987): 77. Historians credit Ford with stabilizing the United States after Watergate. "The nation was stronger in 1976 than it had been in 1974," writes John Robert Greene in *The Presidency of Gerald R. Ford* (University Press of Kansas, 1995), 92–93. "Ford provided a personal and institutional stability that allayed national cynicism," adds Mieczkowski in *Gerald Ford and the Challenges of the 1970s*, 65. Though Ford may not have healed the country, he succeeded in "resetting the course of domestic and foreign policy," concludes Richard Norton Smith in *An Ordinary Man: The Surprising Life and Historic Presidency of Gerald R. Ford* (Harper, 2023), audiobook.

Chapter 6. Semiquincentennial

1. Johnnetta Betsch Cole, "Understanding the 2024 Election: A Call to Action for Inclusive Democracy," Charles F. Kettering Foundation, February 13, 2025, https://kettering.org.

2. James Powell, "Americans Pessimistic About Both Parties, Democracy Being Tested, New Poll Finds," *USA Today*, June 1, 2025; "Democracy in the United States," Marist Poll, April 30, 2025, https://maristpoll.marist.edu; Nick Corasaniti,

Ruth Igielnik, and Camille Baker, "Voters Are Deeply Skeptical About the Health of American Democracy," *New York Times*, October 27, 2024.

3. "Public Trust in Government: 1958–2024," Pew Research Center, June 24, 2024, www.pewresearch.org; Megan Brenan, "US Confidence in Institutions Mostly Flat, but Police Up," Gallup News, July 15, 2024, https://news.gallup.com.

4. "2024 Presidential Election," Marist Poll, April 3, 2024.

5. Mark Twain, attributed, quoted in Fred R. Shapiro, *The Yale Book of Quotations* (Yale University Press, 2006), 502. Though Twain did not write these words exactly, he wrote a close approximation in an 1873 novel cowritten with his neighbor, Charles Dudley Warner: "History never repeats itself, but the Kaleidoscopic combinations of the pictured present often seem to be constructed out of the broken fragments of antique legends." Mark Twain and Charles Dudley Warner, *The Gilded Age: A Tale of Today* (1873), chap. 47, Project Gutenberg, www.gutenberg.org.

6. Barack Obama, "Address in Chicago Accepting Election as the 44th President of the United States," November 4, 2008, American Presidency Project, www.presidency.ucsb.edu.

7. Maggie Astor, "What Trump, Biden, and Obama Said About the Death of George Floyd," *New York Times*, May 29, 2020; Maggie Haberman and Alexander Burns, "Trump's Looting and 'Shooting' Remarks Escalate Crisis in Minneapolis," *New York Times*, June 1, 2020; Davey Alba, Katie Conger, and Raymond Zhong, "Twitter Adds Warnings to White House Tweets, Fueling Tensions," *New York Times*, May 29, 2020.

8. Ben Golliver, "Clippers Coach Doc Rivers Delivers Emotional Response to Shooting of Jacob Blake: 'We Keep Loving This Country, and This Country Does Not Love Us Back,'" *Washington Post*, August 26, 2020; Patrick Sharkey, Keeanga-Yamahtta Taylor, and Yaryna Serkez, "The Gaps Between White and Black America, in Charts," *New York Times*, June 19, 2020. See also Michelle Alexander, *The New Jim Crow: Mass Incarceration in the Age of Colorblindness* (New Press, 2020).

9. Lily Mae Lazarus, "The Top Black CEO in the Fortune 500 Is Steering $83 Billion in Investment," *Fortune*, June 2, 2025.

10. Erica L. Green, "Trump Seeks to Strip Away Legal Tool Key to Civil Rights Enforcement," *New York Times*, May 9, 2025; Kim Bellware, "What Trump's Order on 'Disparate Impact' Means for Civil Rights," *Washington Post*, April 25, 2025.

11. Hansi Lo Wang, "Sixty Years Later, Voting Rights Protections for Minority Voters Face New Threats," National Public Radio, August 6, 2025, www.npr.org. See also Kareen Crayton, "The Voting Rights Act Explained," Brennan Center for Justice, July 17, 2023.

12. Nikole Hannah-Jones, "How Trump Upended 60 Years of Civil Rights in Two Months," *New York Times Magazine*, June 27, 2025.

13. US Census Bureau, US and World Population Clock, www.census.gov/pop clock;US Census Bureau, *Statistical Abstract of the United States, 1977*, September 1977, xiii, www.census.gov.

14. Stephanie Mehta, "Three of the Four Most Valuable Companies Are Run by Asian Americans," *Inc.*, May 6, 2024.

15. See US Census Bureau, "National Native American Heritage Month: November 2024," October 25, 2024.

16. "Official US Records Underestimate Native American Deaths and Life Expectancy," Boston University School of Public Health, June 16, 2025, www.bu.edu/sph.

17. US Census Bureau, "Quick Facts: United States," 2024; "Modern Immigration Wave Brings 59 Million to US, Driving Population Growth and Change Through 2065," Pew Research Center, September 28, 2015; Muzaffar Chishti, Faye Hipsman, and Isabel Ball, "Fifty Years On, the 1965 Immigration and Nationality Act Continues to Reshape the United States," Migration Policy Institute, October 15, 2015, www.migrationpolicy.org.

18. Julia Ainsley and Laura Strickler, "Trump's Immigration Enforcement Record So Far: High Arrest, Low Deportations," NBC News, July 10, 2025, www.nbcnews.com; Fareed Zakaria, "Trump Is Deporting Fewer People Than Obama: He's Just Louder and Meaner," *Washington Post*, July 18, 2025.

19. Rashmi Chimmalgi and Meghan Kissell, "The Not So Simple Truth About the Gender Pay Gap," American Association of University Women, February 2025, www.aauw.org.

20. Katie Rogers, "Will a Woman Ever Be President?," *New York Times*, November 7, 2024.

21. *Doe v. Commonwealth's Attorney of Richmond*, 403 F. Supp. 1199 (E.D. Va. 1975).

22. David Kent, "119th Congress' LGBTQ Members Include First Trans Representative," Pew Research Center, January 30, 2025.

23. H. Res. 24, "Impeaching Donald John Trump, President of the United States, for High Crimes and Misdemeanors," January 13, 2021, 117th Cong., 1st sess., www.congress.gov.

24. Shane Goldmacher and Lisa Lerer, "Donald Trump Returns to Power, Ushering in New Era of Uncertainty," *New York Times*, November 6, 2024; Lisa Lerer, "America Hires a Strongman," *New York Times*, November 6, 2024.

25. Peter Baker, "Trump's Way Forward Is to Go in Reverse, by About a Century," *New York Times*, July 13, 2025, 1.

26. Donald J. Trump, Executive Order (EO) 14189, "Celebrating America's 250th Birthday," January 29, 2025, *Federal Register*, www.federalregister.gov.

27. Donald Trump, EO 14190, "Ending Radical Indoctrination in K–12 Schooling," January 29, 2025, *Federal Register*.

28. Gillian Brockell, "Trump Commission's '1776 Report' Outrages Historians," *Washington Post*, January 19, 2021; Michael Crowley and Jennifer Schuessler, "Trump's 1776 Commission Critiques Liberalism in Report Derided by Historians," *New York Times*, January 20, 2021.

29. Zolan Kanno-Youngs, "Trump Says Smithsonian Focuses Too Much on 'How Bad Slavery Was,'" *New York Times*, August 19, 2025.

30. Trump, EO 14189, "Celebrating America's 250th Birthday."

31. Bill Gabbert, "Mount Rushmore July 4th Fireworks Canceled Due to Fire Danger," *Wildfire Today*, January 14, 2010, https://wildfiretoday.com.

32. Kevin Abourezk, "Nonprofit Condemns South Dakota Governor's Invitation to Trump," *ICT News*, February 7, 2025, https://ictnews.org; Annie Karni, "Trump Uses Mount Rushmore Speech to Deliver Divisive Culture War Message," *New York Times*, July 3, 2020.

33. Adeola Adeosun, "GOP Leaders Announce Return of Mount Rushmore Fireworks Show," *Newsweek*, February 15, 2025.

34. Nick Tilsen quoted in "Mount Rushmore to Be Backdrop for US Semiquincentennial Despite Indigenous Opposition," *Guardian*, June 10, 2025, www.theguardian.com.

35. Rick Atkinson quoted in Maureen Dowd, "Who's the Mad King Now?," *New York Times*, June 21, 2025.

36. Naomi Feinstein, "'We Are Not Desperate': Trump's Mar-a-Lago Membership Fee Blasts Off to $1 Million Ahead of Election," *Miami New Times*, July 23, 2024; Benjamin Oreskes, "'Long Live the King': Trump Likens Himself to Royalty on Truth Social," *New York Times*, February 19, 2025. The White House has 132 rooms. However, the West Wing of the White House is primarily offices for the president and his staff.

37. Jenna Russell et al., "No Kings Protesters Nationwide Share Why They Took to the Streets," *New York Times*, June 14, 2025; David E. Sanger, "As Trump Celebrates Army's Founding, His Critics Take to the Streets," *New York Times*, June 14, 2025; Richard Hall and Rebecca Schneid, "Millions Attend 'No Kings' Protests Against Trump in Towns and Cities Across the US," *Time*, October 18, 2025.

38. Frank Langfitt, "Military Parade and No Kings Protests: A Split Screen of a Divided America," National Public Radio, June 16, 2025, www.npr.org.

39. Emmanuel Saez and Gabriel Zucman, "Wealth Inequality in the United States Since 1913: Evidence from Capitalized Income Tax Data," *Quarterly Journal of Economics* 131, no. 2 (2016): 519–578. See also Chuck Collins and Josh Hoxie, "Billionaire Bonanza: The Forbes 400 and the Rest of Us," Institute for Policy Studies, December 2015, https://ips-dc.org.

40. Donald Trump, EO 14151, "Ending Radical and Wasteful Government DEI Programs and Preferencing," January 20, 2025, *Federal Register*, www.federalregister

.gov; Emma Goldberg, Aaron Krolik, and Lily Boyce, "How Corporate America Is Retreating from DEI," *New York Times*, March 13, 2025.

41. Sam Doran, "Mass. Is Pulling Out All the Stops for America's 250th Birthday," *State House News Service*, September 18, 2024, www.masslive.com. In 2025, WalletHub ranked Massachusetts number one in innovation potential. See Adam McCann, "Best & Worst State Economies (2025)," WalletHub, June 2, 2025, https://wallethub.com.

42. "Spot: The Mobile Robot That Makes Work Safer, Smarter and More Efficient," Boston Dynamics, https://bostondynamics.com (accessed June 6, 2025).

43. Hayden Field, "Nvidia, OpenAI, Anthropic and Google Execs Meet with White House to Talk AI Energy and Data Centers," CNBC, September 12, 2024, www.cnbc.com.

44. Tripp Mickle, "Nvidia Doubles Profit as AI Chip Sales Soar," *New York Times*, November 20, 2024.

45. "Thomas Jefferson to William Charles Jarvis, 28 September 1820," Founders Online, https://founders.archives.gov.

46. Hélène Landemore, "Fostering More Inclusive Democracy with AI," *F&D*, December 2023, 12–14.

47. Raluca Csernatoni, "Can Democracy Survive the Disruptive Power of AI?," Carnegie Endowment for International Peace, December 18, 2024, https://carnegieendowment.org; Charles Haddon Spurgeon, "Joseph Attacked by the Archers," sermon, April 1, 1855, Spurgeon Gems, www.spurgeongems.org.

48. Landemore, "Fostering."

49. Quoted in Fawn Brodie, *Thomas Jefferson: An Intimate History* (1974; Bantam Books, 1979), 464. Historians savaged Brodie's biography, the first modern work to seriously address the Jefferson-Hemings relationship. See Garry Wills, "Uncle Thomas's Cabin," *New York Review of Books*, April 18, 1974, 26.

50. Annette Gordon-Reed, *Thomas Jefferson and Sally Hemings: An American Controversy* (University of Virginia Press, 1998); Eugene A. Foster et al., "Jefferson Fathered Slave's Last Child," *Nature* 396 (November 5, 1998): 27–28.

51. Thomas Jefferson Foundation, "Monticello Affirms Thomas Jefferson Fathered Children with Sally Hemings," statement, Monticello, June 6, 2018, www.monticello.org; interview with Annette Gordon-Reed, *Frontline*, 2000, www.pbs.org/wgbh/frontline.

52. "III. Jefferson's 'Original Rough Draught' of the Declaration of Independence, 11 June–4 July 1776," Founders Online; Merrill D. Peterson, *Thomas Jefferson and the New Nation: A Biography* (Oxford University Press, 1970), 998; Francis D. Cogliano, "Merrill D. Peterson and the Apostle of Freedom: Thomas Jefferson and the New Nation," in *Thomas Jefferson's Lives: Biographers and the Battle for History*, ed. Robert M. S. McDonald (University of Virginia Press, 2019), 244–264.

53. Gordon S. Wood, "The Trials and Tribulations of Thomas Jefferson," in *Jeffersonian Legacies*, ed. Peter S. Onuf (University of Virginia Press, 1993), 396–397.

54. Quoted in Wood, "Trials and Tribulations," 395.

55. "Jefferson to Roger Weightman, 24 June 1826," Founders Online; Annette Gordon-Reed, "Was the Sage a Hypocrite?," *Time*, July 5, 2004.

Epilogue

1. Ronald Reagan, "Remarks at the Republican National Convention," August 19, 1976, Presidential Speeches, Miller Center, https://millercenter.org.

2. Rick Perlstein, *The Invisible Bridge: The Fall of Nixon and the Rise of Reagan* (Simon & Schuster, 2014), 799.

3. Perlstein, *Invisible Bridge*, 799; Craig Shirley, *Reagan's Revolution: The Untold Story of the Campaign That Started It All* (Nelson Current, 2005), xxi.

4. Reagan, "Remarks at the Republican National Convention."

5. Reagan, "Remarks at the Republican National Convention."

6. Howell Raines, "Reagan Campaigns at Mississippi Fair: Stresses 'States' Rights,'" *New York Times*, August 4, 1980; Max Boot, *Reagan: His Life and Legend* (W. W. Norton, 2024), 402; Robert Pear, "President, Signing Bill, Praises Dr. King," *New York Times*, November 3, 1983.

7. Alfred F. Young, *The Shoemaker and the Tea Party: Memory and the American Revolution* (Beacon Press, 1999), 133–134.

8. Dan Barry, "Divided and Undecided, 2024's America Rhymes with 1924's," *New York Times*, July 5, 2024.

9. "The Great Celebration," *Washington Post*, July 7, 1976.

10. "Thomas Jefferson to Roger Chew Weightman, 24 June 1826," Founders Online, https://founders.archives.gov.

11. David Armitage, *The Declaration of Independence: A Global History* (Harvard University Press, 2007), Kindle, 103, 112. Latvia's instrument, for example, enacted in 1990, protected social, economic, and cultural rights, as well as political freedoms, in accordance with international human rights standards.

12. Richard Wike et al., "Is US Democracy a Good Example to Follow?," Pew Research Center, June 11, 2024, www.pewresearch.org.

13. "About America 250," US Semiquincentennial Commission, https://america250.org (accessed July 12, 2025).

INDEX

Photo credit: Meghan Rogers

David McKean is a former US ambassador to Luxembourg and director of policy planning in the US Department of State. The author or coauthor of six previous books, he divides his time between Washington, DC, New Hampshire, and North Carolina.

Photo credit: Tim Devine

M. Todd Bennett is professor of history at East Carolina University. He was formerly a historian at the US Department of State. The author of two previous books, he lives in Washington, DC.